Wellington's Campaigns in India

Wellington's Campaigns in India

Division of the Chief of the Staff
Intelligence Branch

The Naval & Military Press Ltd

Published by
The Naval & Military Press Ltd

PREFACE

THIS complete and connected account of the campaigns of the Duke of Wellington, when in India, has been written by Major R. G. Burton, 94th Russell's Infantry, and is now published in the hope that it may prove to be a useful addition to Indian Military History.

It is requested that any errors or omissions that may be found in this book may be brought to the notice of the Division of the Chief of the Staff, Intelligence Branch.

W. MALLESON, *Lieut.-Colonel,*
Assistant Quarter Master General, Intelligence Branch, Division of the Chief of the Staff.

SIMLA :
The 6th June 1908.

INTRODUCTION.

THE various works on the life of the greatest of British soldiers do not deal in detail with that portion of his career which was passed in India. No doubt his later deeds in the great struggle in the Iberian Peninsula, where he was fighting for the liberties of a Continent, and finally on the field of Waterloo, the culminating point of his military glory, overshadowed all that he had previously accomplished in the East. Yet that early portion of his life is the more interesting from the fact that in its records can be discerned the beginnings of the development of that great genius, both for war and for the administration of affairs, which led him triumphant to the crowning glory of his career. He learnt his lessons and proved his worth on the battlefields of Southern India, and the foundations of the victories of Badajos, Vittoria, and Waterloo were laid at Gawilgarh, Assaye, and Argaum.

Précis of the Commissions, services, official commands and public honours of the Duke of Wellington up to the time of his departure from India.

Born	1st May 1769.
Ensign	7th March 1787.
Lieutenant	25th December 1787.
Captain	30th June 1791.
Major	30th April 1793.
Lieutenant-Colonel	30th September 1793.
Colonel	3rd May 1796.
Major-General	29th April 1802.

1796.

Joined the 33rd Regiment at the Cape of Good Hope, September.

1797.

Arrived in Bengal	February.
Proceeded with Manila Expedition, but recalled from Penang . . .	August
Returned to Calcutta	November.

1798.

Proceeded on a visit to Madras . .	January.
Returned to Calcutta . . .	March.
33rd Regiment placed on the Madras Establishment	September.

1799.

Appointed to command the Hyderabad Subsidiary Force	February.
Advance on Seringapatam . . .	March.
Battle of Malavelly	27th March.
Arrival before Seringapatam . .	3rd April.
Attack on the Sultanpettah . .	5th April.
Second attack on the Sultanpettah .	6th April.
Siege of Seringapatam until assault and capture on	4th May.
Colonel Wellesley appointed Governor of Seringapatam	9th July.

1800.

Takes the field against the freebooter Dhoondiah Waugh	July.
Defeat and death of Dhoondiah Waugh	10th September.
Sent to command a force at Trincomalee	October.
Appointed to command this force for service to Mauritius or the Red Sea .	15th November.

1801.

The expedition ordered to proceed to the Red Sea under command of General Baird	11th February.
Colonel Wellesley sailed for Bombay .	15th February.
Resumed his Government of Mysore .	28th April.

1803.

Appointed to command a force assembled at Hurryhur to march into Mahratta territory	27th February.
Advance from Hurryhur . . .	9th March.
Arrival at Poona	20th April.
Empowered to control political and military affairs in the Deccan . .	26th June.
Mahratta War commenced . . .	6th August.
Siege and capture of Ahmadnagar .	11th August.
Battle of Assaye	23rd September.
Battle of Argaum	29th November.
Siege and capture of Gawilgarh . .	15th December.
Treaty of peace with the Raja of Berar .	17th December.
Treaty of peace with Daulat Rao Sindhia	30th December.

1804.

Destruction of a body of freebooters at Munkaisir	6th February.
A sword to the value of £1,000 voted to General Wellesley by the British inhabitants of Calcutta	21st February.
At Bombay	4th March to 16th May.

(Fêtes and Address by Garrison and Inhabitants.)

A service of plate presented by the officers of his Division	26th February.
Returned to the Army near Poona .	25th May.
Called to Calcutta to assist in military deliberations	24th June.

Resigned the political and military powers vested in him by the Governor General	24th June.
Left the army for Seringapatam . .	28th June.
Received by the Governor General .	12th August.
Appointed Knight Companion of the Bath	1st September.
His civil and military powers renewed .	9th November.
Returned to Seringapatam by Madras .	30th November.

1805.

Resigned political and military powers in the Deccan	24th February.
Addresses on quitting India from Officers of his Division, Officers of the 33rd Regiment, Native Inhabitants of Seringapatam.	
Grand entertainment in his honour at the Madras Pantheon	5th March.
Thanks of King and Parliament for his services published in G. O. . .	8th March.
Embarked on H. M. S. *Trident* for England	March.
Landed at Deal. . . .	11th September.

CONTENTS.

PRÉCIS OF THE SERVICES OF THE DUKE OF WELLINGTON IN INDIA.

CHAPTER I.

THE MYSORE WAR.

CHAPTER II.

THE FALL OF TIPU SULTAN.

CHAPTER III

THE SETTLEMENT OF MYSORE.

CHAPTER IV.

THE MAHRATTA WAR.

MAPS AND PLANS IN POCKETS OF COVER.

Map of Southern India.
Plan of Seringapatam.
Map showing Wellesley's Route in the Deccan.
Field of Assaye.
Field of Argaum.
Gawilgarh.

Wellington's Campaigns in India

CHAPTER I.

THE MYSORE WAR.

Wellington's Career in India.

THE career of the Duke of Wellington in India may be properly divided into two periods. The years he spent in that country were passed—the first five in Mysore, where he took part in the campaign which resulted in the capture of Seringapatam and the death of Tipu Sultan, and subsequently commanded the forces; while the remaining portion of his time was mainly concerned with his campaign against the Mahrattas.

To the student of the history of the British conquest of India the career of the illustrious soldier whose military genius, first revealed in the East, attained its culminating point on the field of Waterloo, must ever be of transcendent interest. Nor is it as a soldier only, but as a great administrator that his genius illuminates the records of his life and the pages of his despatches. In these documents, remarkable alike for their literary quality and their perfect lucidity, can be traced the development of the great character of the man, his attention to all details that contributed to success, and his clearness of insight into the matters he was engaged upon, whether the administration of affairs, arrangements for the well-being of his troops, or dispositions for attacking the enemy to whom he was opposed.

After taking part in a somewhat inglorious campaign in the Netherlands, Colonel the Honourable Arthur Wellesley,* as he then was, welcomed the opportunity of proceeding to the East, where the prospects of gaining distinction in the field appeared to be brighter than in Europe. Having been detained at home by illness on the

* The family name was then Wesley, but was changed to the archaic form of Wellesley in 1798.

B

departure of the regiment he commanded, the 33rd* Foot, he joined at the Cape, and arrived at Calcutta early in February 1797. In August 1797 the 33rd formed part of an expedition intended for the conquest of Manila, but the force was recalled from Penang, and Wellesley and his regiment returned to Calcutta. In January 1798 he proceeded on a two months' visit to Lord Hobart at Madras, and in September of the same year his regiment was placed on the Madras establishment. The voyage to Madras occupied three weeks and was not uneventful, as may be seen from the following extract written by Wellesley to his brother Henry: "The ship struck this morning at about five upon what is called Sangor Reef, and remained fast until about one, when she was got off, I may almost say, by the bodily strength of the soldiers of the 33rd . . . . If the weather had not been more moderate than it is usually we must all have been lost."

Policy of the Marquis Wellesley.

In May 1798 Colonel Wellesley's brother, Lord Mornington, better known as the Marquis Wellesley, with his brother Henry† as Private Secretary, reached Calcutta as Governor-General, and set about that active policy which was to be productive of so much glory to the British arms, and of such great influence on the destinies of the British Empire in India. His efforts were mainly directed towards the suppression of French influence which threatened our supremacy throughout India.

State of India.

The effects of the great revolutionary disturbance which convulsed France and swept over the whole of Europe at the close of the eighteenth century were not confined to the Western Continent, but were experienced throughout the civilised world; and although British territories in India were not shaken by the tramp of revolutionary or Napoleonic armies, the English power in that country was affected by concurrent or consequent events. The struggle for

The French in India.

supremacy between the French and English during the eighteenth century

* Now the Duke of Wellington's West Riding Regiment. Lord Cornwallis, who had conducted the campaign against Tipu Sultan in 1792, was Colonel of the Regiment and on his death in 1806 was succeeded by Wellesley.

† Afterwards Lord Cowley.

had terminated in the complete triumph of the latter, thanks to the efforts of Stringer Lawrence, Clive, and Eyre Coote, but some vestiges of gallic influence still remained.

The Nizam of Hyderabad had in his employment a force officered by 124 Frenchmen, amounting to 14,000 men, who bore the Colours of the French Republic and had the Cap of Liberty engraved upon their buttons.

In Mysore there were some French officers in the service of Tipu Sultan, while many adventurers* of the same restless and enterprising nation held commands in the armies of the Mahratta Chieftains whose regular forces they had organised and trained.

The Mahratta Confederacy.

There were, moreover, bitter enemies of British power in all the Native States from the banks of the Ganges to the southern point of the Peninsula. Over a large portion of this area the Chiefs of the Mahratta Confederacy, which had risen on the ashes of the Moghal Empire, held sway, and only awaited a favourable opportunity to oppose the aliens by intrigue or by force of arms. They, too, had eventually to be dealt with, and were not crushed until the conclusion of two great wars.

The Sultan of Mysore.

Tipu Sultan of Mysore, though stripped of much territory and humbled by Cornwallis, was full of animosity and eager to measure swords again with the army of the East India Company. The peace concluded with him by Cornwallis could not be lasting; the Tiger of Mysore still nourished in his heart black hatred against the British, and it would have been better had the siege of Seringapatam in 1792 been carried to the bitter end, and the walls of that stronghold razed to the ground. Shortly after the arrival of Lord Mornington in India it came to his knowledge that Tipu Sultan had despatched an embassy to the French Governor of Mauritius, asking for aid against the English, and consequent on a proclamation issued by General Malartic, Governor of Mauritius, calling for volunteers to

* A full account of the European military adventurers of Hindustan will be found in Mr. Herbert Compton's book. Among the most famous were De Boigne, George Thomas and Perron, whose adventures are among the most remarkable episodes recorded in history.

serve with the Mysore Army, a small body of adventurers* disembarked at Mangalore from the French frigate *La Preneuse* on April 26th, 1798, and proceeded to Seringapatam. Being then at war with France this could only be regarded by the British Government as a hostile act.

Napoleon and Oriental Conquest.

It is interesting to note also that the mightiest figure of those times was concerned to some extent in the events about to be narrated. It was the apprehension of French influence and French aggression that formed the main motive of the Governor-General's policy. In 1798 Napoleon Bonaparte stood in the shadow of the Pyramids on the threshold of Oriental Empire, his eyes directed towards the East, where he dreamt of following in the footsteps of Alexander of Macedon. He said at this time—"My glory is already at an end; there is not enough of it in this little Europe. I must go to the East. All great glory comes from there."† Later on his visions took more definite shape. On August 30th, 1798, he wrote to the Directory—"Mistress of Egypt, France will by and by be mistress of India," and in January 1799 he wrote a letter to Tipu Sultan asking him to "send to Suez some able man in your confidence with whom I could confer." It is interesting to conjecture what would have happened to Napoleon had he attempted to march on India and found himself opposed to that Sepoy General whom he subsequently affected to despise, but who contributed to his downfall scarcely less in the Iberian Peninsula than on the field of Waterloo.

The French at Hyderabad.

Meanwhile the French at Hyderabad were in communication with their compatriots in Mysore, and were prepared to place their very considerable military power, as well as their political influence with the Nizam, at the disposal of the Sultan. It will be seen therefore that the fears of the Governor-General were by no means groundless;

* This force consisted of Citizen Chapuy, General of the land service; Dubuc, General of the marine; Desmoulins, Commandant of the Europeans; 2 officers of artillery; 6 marine officers; 4 ship-builders and others; 26 officers, captains, sergeants, and linguist; 36 European soldiers, and 22 half-castes; together with M. De Bay, the watchmaker, who accompanied the deputation from Tipu and returned with it. On the fall of Seringapatam the French, to the number of 300, took refuge in the Sultan's palace, where they surrendered and were sent prisoners to the Carnatic.

† Appendix I "Napoleon and Oriental Conquest."

especially as the French had considerable naval strength in the East, and it was not until more than a dozen years had elapsed that the British were in a position to undertake oversea expeditions against the French Colonies in that part of the world.

War with Mysore being imminent, it was feared that the French at Hyderabad might attempt to seize the Nizam's Dominions and secure them to the domination of France ; or that, if the Corps raised by the celebrated adventurer Raymond were brought into the field against Tipu, it would endanger the cause of the British, with whom the Mahrattas and the Nizam were allied against that potentate. Accordingly a treaty, providing for the disbandment of the French Corps and the increase of the British Subsidiary Force at Hyderabad, was concluded with the Nizam's Government. In pursuance of this agreement, and by the advice of Colonel Wellesley, a British force under Colonel Roberts was marched to Hyderabad to awe the French Corps into submission. On the 20th October 1798 a portion of the British troops took up a position in rear of the French, while the remainder were disposed ready to march against their front. The French battalions, clamouring for their arrears of pay, now broke into open mutiny, and seized and confined their officers. Next morning Colonel Roberts drew up his force opposite the French lines, and summoned the men to unconditional surrender.* Eventually after some delay they were induced by Captain Malcolm, the Political Officer, to lay down their arms. The French officers were delivered up and deported to their own country, while many of the men remained in the Nizam's service, and were formed into new Corps under British officers.

Military Preparations.

Negotiations with the Sultan of Mysore proving to be of no avail, a force was assembled at Wallajahbad, under Colonel the Honourable Arthur Wellesley, in November 1798, and in December the Governor-General himself proceeded to Madras to direct the military preparations in case the Sultan should continue refractory. Colonel Wellesley remained in command until February 1799, when General Harris

* 11,000 men were disarmed. the remainder being absent on detachment.

arrived at Vellore, to which place the army of the Carnatic had moved in the meantime. General Harris found the army in an excellent state of preparedness for war, and wrote to the Governor-General in Council on 2nd February—" Having had leisure since my arrival here to inspect the Division of the Army which has been since its formation under the orders of the Honourable Colonel Wellesley,* I have much satisfaction in acquainting Your Lordship that the very handsome appearance and perfect discipline of the troops do honour to themselves and to him ; while the judicious and masterly arrangements in respect to supplies, which opened an abundant free market, and inspired confidence into dealers of every description, were no less creditable to Colonel Wellesley than advantageous to the public service, and deservedly entitle him to my thanks and approbation. " On the 2nd February the Governor-General wrote to his brother— " Nothing has given me more pleasure than to hear from all quarters such unqualified commendations of your arrangements in your late command. I wish to God the whole were under your direction ; but even as it is, I think our success is certain. "

The Army was composed as follows :—

The Army of the Carnatic.

Army of the Carnatic under Lieutenant-General G. Harris.—

Cavalry	Major General Floyd.
1st Brigade (Colonel Stevenson.)	19th Light Dragoons. 1st Madras Light Cavalry. 4th Madras Light Cavalry.
2nd Brigade (Colonel Pater.)	25th Light Dragoons. 2nd Madras Light Cavalry. 3rd Madras Light Cavalry.
	Detachments Bengal and Madras Artillery. Corps of Madras Engineers. The Pioneer Corps.

*It is noteworthy that Wellesley advised a pacific policy towards Tipu, and on September 19th wrote to the Governor-General :—" I am very anxious to hear of the conclusion of your negotiations with the Peshwa and the Nizam, that you may make your proposition, whatever it may be, to Tipu as soon as possible, and that he may see that you are not bent upon annihilating. He is well aware of the bad consequences which resulted in the last war from his suffering us to make our preparations at our leisure and to attack him ; and you may depend upon it that if he is not convinced that we do not mean to go to war, he will endeavour to strike the first blow. Our great strength, to which an addition will have been made by the re-establishment of our allies and the total failure of his allies the French, will induce him to grasp at any favourable opportunity which a moderate proposition from you will give him of settling this difference. "

Infantry.

Right Wing	Major-General Bridges.
1st Brigade (Major-General D. Baird.)	His Majesty's 12th Regiment. His Majesty's 74th Regiment. Scotch Brigade. (Afterwards 94th Regiment.)
3rd Brigade (Colonel Gowdie.)	1st Battalion, 1st Madras Infantry. 1st Battalion, 6th Madras Infantry. 1st Battalion, 12th Madras Infantry.
5th Brigade (Colonel Roberts.)	2nd Battalion, 3rd Madras Infantry. 1st Battalion, 8th Madras Infantry. 2nd Battalion, 12th Madras Infantry.
Left Wing	Major-General Popham.
2nd Brigade (Colonel Sherbrooke.)	His Majesty's 73rd Regiment. The Regiment de Meuron.*
4th Brigade (Lieutenant-Colonel Gardiner.)	1st Battalion, Bengal Volunteers. 2nd Battalion, Bengal Volunteers. 3rd Battalion, Bengal Volunteers.
6th Brigade (Lieutenant-Colonel Scott.)	2nd Battalion, 5th Madras Infantry. 2nd Battalion, 9th Madras Infantry.

Before the army marched, it was joined by the Hyderabad Subsidiary Force, constituted under the provisions of a treaty with the Nizam, and by a contingent of the Nizam's Army, which the ruler of Hyderabad was bound by treaty to supply.

The Subsidiary Force was placed under the command of Colonel Wellesley, whose regiment was attached to it, and consisted of—

His Majesty's 33rd Regiment. 1st and 2nd Battalions, 10th Bengal Infantry. 2nd Battalion, 2nd Madras Infantry. 2nd Battalion, 4th Madras Infantry. 1st and 2nd Battalions, 11th Madras Infantry. Artillery.	Subsidiary Force.

* The Regiment de Meuron was a Swiss corps, which surrendered to the British when Ceylon was captured from the Dutch in 1795. The regiment was transferred to the British East India Company by a deed executed at Neuchatel in March 1796. Although raised in Switzerland, the corps was not under control of any of the Cantons, and the officers were nominated by the Count de Meuron. The Colonel-Commandant was the Count's brother, and most of the other officers were connected with him. It was composed of 10 companies, about 800 strong, when it arrived in Madras Presidency.

In 1808 the Regiment de Meuron was disbanded, when 133 men were transferred to the artillery, on which occasion the Court of Directors remarked :—"In consideration of the long and faithful services of the Regiment de Meuron under the British Government in India, and of the deficient state of your artillery corps, we do not object to the transfer of a part of that regiment to the corps alluded to, notwithstanding our disinclination, on general principles, to any large proportion of foreigners being admitted into that corps."

The Nizam's Contingent consisted of four battalions of infantry under Captain John Malcolm and 10,000 Nizam's cavalry under Mir Alam.

The Bombay Army.

A second force had been collected at Cannanore under Major-General Stuart to co-operate in the advance on Seringapatam. Exclusive of the Nizam's troops, General Harris had under his command a force of 30,959 fighting men, completely equipped and supplied, and, as Major Beatson, who took part in the campaign, wrote, "as well appointed, as perfect in discipline, and as fortunate in the acknowledged experience and ability of its officers in every department, as any that ever took the field in India. It comprised a more numerous and better appointed corps of cavalry than any European power in India had ever brought into action."

The strength of the Army in round numbers amounted to—

(1) Carnatic Army, 20,000 men including 4,300 Europeans and 2,600 Cavalry.
(2) Cannanore Army, 6,400 men including 1,600 Europeans.
(3) Nizam's Army, 6,500 British and British Sepoys, and 10,000 Native Troops.

The brunt of the fighting in this, as in other military campaigns in India, fell on the British troops. They took the posts of danger on all occasions, headed forlorn hopes, and generally led the native troops into action, the latter sometimes having a company of a British Corps placed at the head of each regiment to supply them with that *élan* in which they were deficient.

The Nizam's Army.

Regarding the Nizam's Army, the Governor-General wrote to the Court of Directors in March 1799—"This force under the general command of Meer Allum formed a junction with the Army on the 19th February; and it is with the greatest satisfaction that I remark to your Honourable Court the beneficial effects which the Company have already derived from the recent improvements of an alliance with the Court of Hyderabad. The Nizam's Contingent actually arrived in the vicinity of Chittur in a state of preparation for the field before General

Harris was ready to proceed on his march from Vellore.'' We are told that the sepoys of the late French Corps were taller and stouter than those of the Company on the Coast, a superiority maintained by the Hyderabad Contingent, which was subsequently evolved from these and other troops in the Nizam's Army.

Baggage of the Army.

The Roman word *impedimenta* is certainly more expressive than "baggage,'' for the baggage is surely the greatest impediment to the mobility of an army. This was particularly the case during the wars of the first half of the last century, when officers appear to have been allowed an unlimited quantity of impedimenta. The numerous camp followers of the armies in India also added to the incumbrance of supply and transport. With General Harris' army of 35,000 fighting men there were 120,000 followers, a number that was exceeded in the Mahratta War of 1817, when the Marquis of Hastings had a fighting force of 110,000 men accompanied by 500,000 camp followers. Every sepoy of the Madras Army took with him into camp his whole family, the members of which cheerfully shared with him the hardships of war.

The Brinjaras.

Supplies were in those days collected from different parts of the country by Brinjaras,* who carried their goods on pack bullocks, of which they possessed immense numbers. In the Wellington Despatches we find frequent mention of these nomadic supply agents, of whom Wellesley wrote in 1804—"These are a class of carriers who gain a livelihood by transporting grain or other commodities from one part of the country to another. They attend armies and trade in nearly the same manner as they do in common times of peace. They either purchase grain themselves in the country with their own money, or with money advanced to them by the Company, and sell it to the bazaar at the rates of the day on their own account, or they take grain at the Company's stores at certain reduced rates, and sell it on their own account in the bazaars; or they take up grain in the Company's stores and carry it with the army, and receive a sum of

* Appendix II. "The Brinjaras."

money for every march they make; or they hire their cattle by the month to the Company." Immense numbers of Brinjara cattle accompanied the army in the field, and we read in one place of a single convoy of 14,000 of these animals.

Tipu Sultan.

Tipu Sultan, commonly known as the "Tiger of Mysore" from the ferocity of his character, is generally represented as a monster in human form. It is said that he was in the habit of declaring that he would rather live two days as a tiger than 200 years as a sheep. He must not, however, be judged by European standards, but by the character of the age and country in which he lived. He had a great hatred of the English, which is not surprising in view of their attitude and the extension of their territories and interests which placed the existence of his state in a precarious position. This enmity was vented on the unfortunate prisoners who fell into his hands, many of whom were murdered after long confinement in the dungeons of Seringapatam, while others were hurled from the Tiger Rock to serve as food for vultures and jackals in the plains below.

Born in 1753, Tipu is described as being in 1799 of low stature, corpulent, with high shoulders, and a short, thick neck; but his hands and feet were remarkably small. His complexion was rather dark, his eyes large and prominent, with small arched eyebrows, and an aquiline nose. He had an appearance of dignity, or rather sternness, in his countenance, which distinguished him above the common order of his people. Not only was his nature comparable to that of the tiger, but that animal constituted the symbol of his state; his flag was a large square of light green, with a blazing sun in the centre, set off with the tiger streak on the sides and angles. His cipher represented a tiger's face, and his throne was thickly sculptured with the same device. A number of tigers were found chained in the courtyard of his palace, and had to be destroyed after the fall of Seringapatam.

The Sultan was brave and intelligent, but in the field was not the equal of his father Hyder Ali, one of the few natives of India who have exhibited the qualities of a great military commander.

To oppose the British Army he had a force of some 76,000 men, well armed and equipped, and composed as follows:—

Regular Cavalry	6,000
Irregular Cavalry	7,000
Guards (Slaves)	4,000
Regular Infantry	30,000
Pikemen	15,000
Carnatic Peons	8,000
Pioneers	6,000

These numbers include the lascars and gunners. Each regiment of regular horse had two three-pounder galloper guns, and each body of irregular horse had three six-pounders; these were drawn by mules. Each infantry brigade had two eighteen-pounders. Each brigade had an elephant attached to it, to assist the guns through difficulties. The cavalry and infantry were clothed alike in a striped blue and white stuff of country manufacture. The artillery were clothed in white cotton with large round blue spots. The pay of the regular cavalry troopers whose horses were furnished by the State was Rs. 12-0-0 monthly. The Muhammadan troopers of the irregular cavalry received Rs. 45-0-0 and the Hindus Rs. 40-0-0 monthly, having to provide and maintain their own horses. They were also entitled to half plunder. The infantry was divided into three classes, who received respectively Rs. 10-0-0, 8-0-0, and 7-0-0 monthly. There were about 120 Frenchmen at Seringapatam and some 70 men under Messrs. Dubuc and Chapuy, who had come over from Mauritius. The French auxiliaries were paid by contract; Lally as Commandant, Rs. 2,000-0-0; Rs. 500-0-0 for each gun, twelve pagodas* for an elephant; for a European horseman Rs. 90-0-0; a foot soldier Rs. 30-0-0; half-castes Rs. 20-0-0; sepoys Rs. 16-0-0. Under this contract the French Commandant was obliged to pay his officers, mount and maintain his cavalry, find clothes and arms for the infantry, and provide bullocks to draw the guns. The regular infantry were composed of men of large stature, who carried firelocks of French manufacture, with long bayonets.

* Pagodas varied in value; these were probably the equivalent of Star Pagodas, equal to three and a half rupees.

CHAPTER II.

THE FALL OF TIPU SULTAN.

The March from Vellore.

The Army of the Carnatic marched from Vellore on February 11th, and on the 18th effected a junction with the Nizam's Cavalry under Mir Alam at Kelamangalam. There it was delayed, principally by difficulties connected with the transport and siege train, until the 9th March. Meanwhile a force of some 5,000 men under Colonel Read was detached to protect the frontier of Baramahal, to collect provisions, and ultimately to co-operate with another force under Colonel Brown which had been assembled near Trichinopoly, and was about to march on Seringapatam by Karur, Erod, and Kaveripuram.

March of the Bombay Army.

General Stuart, with the Bombay Army, had left Cannanore on the Malabar Coast on the 21st February; and on the 2nd March encamped on the Coorg Frontier, the advanced brigade of 2,000 men, composed of three native battalions under Colonel Montresor, being at Sidesvara with the main body eight to twelve miles in rear at Sidapur and Amuntanur. This somewhat dangerous division of his force by General Stuart was unavoidable, owing to the enclosed nature of the country, which was covered with jungle and afforded little space for encampments. The occupation of Sidesvara was necessary as that place commanded a view of the Mysore country almost up to the gates of Seringapatam, and enabled the Cannanore Army to obtain communication with the Army of the Carnatic as soon as the advanced picquets of the latter made their appearance.

Action at Sidesvara.

On the 28th February Tipu Sultan marched from his camp at Chenapatam to oppose the advance of the Bombay Army, and arrived at Periapatam, within striking distance of General Stuart's advanced brigade, on the 5th March. His camp with several large tents including a green pavilion, which denoted the presence of the Sultan, was seen by a reconnoitring party from the summit of a hill. The enemy's approach being discovered, the British General sent another battalion to reinforce Colonel Montresor. On the morning of the 6th March Tipu advanced by jungle pathways into Coorg, and surrounding the British advanced force, which was only 2,000 strong, with his army of 11,800 men he suddenly attacked them on every side. There seems little doubt that the British would have been totally destroyed had not General Stuart sent a reinforcement of the 75th and 77th regiments, who turned the tide of battle, and by two o'clock the Mysore Army was put to flight with a loss of some 1,500 killed and wounded, including several officers of high rank. The British loss amounted to 31 killed, 93 wounded, and 16 missing. Tipu wrote the following somewhat inaccurate account of this action:—"On Wednesday the 30th or last day of the month of Razi of the year Shadeb 1226 from the birth of Muhammad, corresponding with the 29th of Ramzan, 1213 Hegira, or 6th March 1799, the victorious Army of the Sultan, having left their baggage at Periapatam, and formed themselves into three divisions or detachments, entered the forests of Coorg by three different roads, where the Army of the Christians had taken up a position, and, advancing, gave battle, fighting with firelocks and spears, and the whole army of the infidels was routed, some of the Christians taking to flight.

"In that battle Muhammad Reza and Muhammad Miran devoted themselves and drank the cup of martyrdom ; Mirza Bakar Bakshi and Muhammad Jahangir Bakshi became martyrs; and Moazim Khan Bakshi was wounded and taken prisoner by the Christians; and Ghulam Mohiuddin devoted himself a martyr."

Movements of the Enemy.

Repulsed at Sidesvara, Tipu returned to Seringapatam, and thence advanced to oppose General Harris, who left Kelamangalam on the morning of 10th March, moving by way of Anikal, Talghatpuram, and Kankaneli to Seringapatam. Parties of the enemy's horse were engaged in destroying villages and forage, and some of these attacked a company of sepoys belonging to the rearguard of the Nizam's Contingent, killing 20, wounding Lieutenant Reynolds and 36 men, while the remaining 9 were missing. On the 14th the army encamped near Bangalore, and on the 16th moved forward by Talghatpuram and Kankaneli, a route by which Tipu had not expected them. The march was consequently unopposed, while supplies were plentiful as these had not been destroyed along the Kankaneli road, as was the case elsewhere.

Battle of Malavelly.

On the 26th March General Harris' army encamped five miles east of Malavelly on open and commanding ground, from which some of the enemy's troops, with guns and elephants, could be seen on a ridge beyond the town. Next morning at daybreak the army marched on the great road to Malavelly, the Nizam's Contingent protecting the left flank and baggage, while five regiments of cavalry under Major-General Floyd covered the advance. On approaching Malavelly it was found that the enemy had occupied some ridges, his cavalry on the right flank and his infantry on the heights beyond the town.

The action that ensued was of short duration. Supported by some cavalry, Colonel Wellesley with his division, advancing in échelon of battalions, made an attack on the enemy's right flank, when a column of some 2,000 men moved forward in excellent order against the 33rd Regiment; this regiment reserved its fire with the utmost steadiness; received that of the enemy at a distance of sixty yards, and continuing to advance, the hostile column gave way and was thrown into disorder. Meanwhile the remainder of the British force was advancing against the hostile front; the enemy gave way at all points, and a charge of the cavalry under General Floyd completed the rout with great slaughter.*

Writing to his brother Henry, Wellesley says that Tipu's infantry "advanced and almost stood the charge of the bayonets of the 33rd and his cavalry rode at General Baird's European Brigade. He did not support them as he ought, having drawn off his guns at the moment he made his attack and even pushed forward these troops to cover the retreat of his guns. This is the cause of the

* For British Casualties see Appendix IX A.

troops he left behind him, and of the panic with which we have reason to believe all his troops are now affected."

After his defeat at Malavelly Tipu retired on Seringapatam, hoping to keep that stronghold against the attacks of his enemies. The British army continued its march unmolested, and on the 2nd April took up a position about two miles from the western face of the fortress, having the right resting on a height and the extreme left on the river Cauvery. In front were some ruined villages, while an aqueduct ran in an easterly direction to within 1,700 yards of the fort, and winding towards the right until it reached a grove of trees near Sultanpeth, 4,000 yards from the ramparts of Seringapatam, and about 900 from the place to which the British lines had been advanced. In this broken ground the enemy's skirmishers and rocket men found a safe cover, from which they could harass the advanced posts of the British army. On the morning of the 5th they occupied the grove and ruined village, from which they discharged rockets into the British encampment and kept up an annoying fusilade. No doubt the enemy should have been forestalled in the occupation of this place or it should have been attacked by daylight. No ground capable of concealing an enemy should be left unoccupied in the vicinity of one's troops.

March to Seringapatam.

Colonel Wellesley, with the 33rd Regiment and a battalion of Bengal Infantry, was ordered to make a night attack on the grove and establish a post there while Colonel Shawe with another force assaulted the ruined village. It is interesting here to quote a note written by Wellesley to General Harris on 5th April, after receiving his orders, from which it appears that he had a clearer view of the tactical situation than had his chief. "I do not know where you mean the post to be established, and I shall therefore be obliged to you if you will do me the favour to meet me this afternoon in front of the lines and show it to me. In the meantime I will order my battalions to be in readiness.

Wellesley's Attack on Sultanpeth.

"Upon looking at the *tope* (grove of trees) as I came in just now it appeared to me that when you get possession of the bank of the *nullah*, you have the *tope* as a matter of course, as the latter is in rear of the former. However you are the best judge, and I shall be ready.''

The night attack took place, but Wellesley was received by a tremendous fire of rockets * and musketry, and failed in his object. He lost his way and his force in the darkness, was struck on the knee by a spent ball, and only found his way back to camp after wandering about for some hours in the night. Some of his men were not so fortunate. Lieutenant Fitzgerald of the 33rd was killed and twelve grenadiers of this regiment were captured by the enemy, and cruelly put to death, some having nails driven into their heads, while others had their necks broken by Chettys, a caste who perform feats of strength.

The mistake had been in attempting to carry out a night attack without previously reconnoitring the ground, which was intersected by canals for irrigating the betel gardens, and it seems probable that Colonel Wellesley would have suffered severely professionally had he been a less distinguished personage than the brother of the Governor-General.† As he told Lord Mornington, he resolved after this never to attack by night a post which had not been reconnoitred by day, a lesson that holds good to our day, and embodies a recognised principle with regard to night operations of war.

The Duke of Wellington wrote to Colonel Gurwood (Editor of his Despatches) in 1833—"We had not reconnoitred the ground. The *tope* was on the enemy's side of the *nullah*, thus

* The rocket consisted of an iron tube about eight inches long and an inch and a half in diameter, closed at one end. It was filled in the same manner as an ordinary sky-rocket, and fixed to a piece of stout bamboo from 3 to 5 feet long, the head of which was armed with a heavy iron spike: at the extremity of the tube nearest the shaft was a match, and the man who used it, placing the butt end of the bamboo upon his foot pointed the spiked end in the direction of the object, and setting fire to the fuze pitched it from him, when it flew with great velocity, and on striking the ground, by a bounding horizontal motion acted with an almost certain effect in fracturing the legs of the enemy. It was frequently used against bodies of cavalry, which were thus thrown into confusion.

† Lord Mornington took a fraternal interest in his brother, and wrote to General Harris: "Do not allow Arthur to fatigue himself too much."

I had carried the *nullah* quite up to the mark O. My advanced guard under Captain West of the 33rd was beyond it and through the *tope*, and the lost prisoners on the enemy's side of it. But we could not maintain ourselves in it. In fact we knew nothing about the matter."

The following extract from General Harris' private diary is interesting and throws some light on the incident:—

"*5th April* marched to Seringapatam, rocketed a little on the march. Took up our ground ready for the siege. Concluded the arrangements for detaching General Floyd to General Stuart. Formed parties for the attack of the post occupied formerly by the Bombay troops, and the *tope* of Sultanpettah. Lieutenant-Colonel Shawe to command the detachment for the Bombay post. Colonel Wellesley that of the *tope* as being composed of his own people. Remained under great anxiety till near twelve at night, from the fear our troops had fired on each other. Lieutenant-Colonel Shawe very soon reported himself in possession of the post; but a second firing commenced, and as he had previously sent to know what had become of the two native battalions, I could not be satisfied but that, in the dark, they had mistaken each other. It proved that all the firing was from the enemy, His Majesty's 12th Regiment scarcely firing a shot the whole night. Near 12 Colonel Wellesley came to my tent in a good deal of agitation to say that he had not carried the *tope*. It proved that the 33rd, with which he attacked, got into confusion, and could not be formed, which was a great pity, as it must be particularly unpleasant for him. Altogether, circumstances considered, we got off very well. General Baird's expedition of last night so far answered our expectations, as he fell in with a small party of the enemy's horse and cut up 8 or 10 of them, which will tend to prevent their plaguing us with rockets, I trust. He missed his way on the road back, although one would have thought it impossible; no wonder night attacks so often fail."

The incident is of historical interest and of lasting utility as an example; yet we have seen in our time the failure of night operations, owing to similar causes, the neglect to reconnoitre. In modern war undoubtedly movements must frequently take place by night, but they should be carefully planned and should be undertaken only in case of necessity. It is easy to show that the hours of darkness should be turned to account in bringing troops close up to an adversary posted in a strong position, but great issues can only be fought out by daylight, and night marches and night operations exhaust the energies of the troops. Those who have failed in such enterprises can comfort themselves with the thought that with this historic example before them, they have erred in good company, and we may recall the dictum of Napoleon—"Speak to me of a General who has made no mistakes in war, and you speak to me of one who has not made war."

Night Operations.

By day on 6th April Colonel Wellesley carried the *tope* without difficulty and with trifling loss, and a post was established there.

While Wellesley was making his unsuccessful attack on the *tope*, Colonel Shawe had occupied the ruined village with the 12th Regiment and two battalions of Madras Infantry. The enemy was thus driven from the outward line of defensive posts, two miles in extent, reaching from the grove of trees to the river, and forced to take refuge within the walls of the fortress, of which the following description is given by Major Beatson, who took part in the campaign:—"The island of Seringapatam is three and a half miles in length and a mile and a half in breadth. It is formed by the river Cauvery, and rises considerably in the middle, from which there is a gradual slope towards the river. The fortress occupies two thousand yards of the west extremity of this island, and is a place of great strength. Covered upon the north and west by the river Cauvery, it was defended until the peace of 1792 by a single rampart; the east and west faces being considered weaker, were strengthened by double walls and ditches, by outworks before the gates, by a strong circular work upon the south-east angle and by several formidable

Seringapatam.

cavaliers within, and upon the southern rampart. Perhaps no place of the same extent of fortifications ever required so much labour in its construction. The rampart, which is thick and strong, varies in height from 20 to 35 feet and upwards, the whole of the revetment, except the north-west bastion, is composed of granite, cut in large oblong pieces, laid in cement, transversely in the walls. The western ditch has not been constructed with much less labour: it is formed by a strong mound or wall, of considerable thickness, parallel to the rampart and entirely built of stone.''

Investment of the Fortress.

The British Army took up a position to attack the north-west rampart of the fort. Batteries were established to bring a cross-fire to bear on this point, and the approach to the fortress was made by the construction of zig-zag trenches. The method of investment will be best understood from the accompanying plan. The Bombay Army effected a junction with General Harris' force on the 10th April. The course of the siege was generally uneventful until the 22nd, when a sortie was made by some 6,000 of the enemy's infantry and Lally's Corps of Frenchmen, but they were driven back with a loss of six or seven hundred killed and wounded. Tipu twice sent letters to General Harris, with a view to opening negotiations, but he would not accept the terms offered, which involved the surrender of half his territory, the payment of a large indemnity and the delivery of a number of hostages. Subsequently all the enemy's posts were driven in, principally by attacks carried out by parties of the 74th Regiment, and by the end of April breaching batteries were established. A practicable breach was made in the bastion in the course of a few days, and by May 3rd all was ready for the assault.

The Assault on Seringapatam.

During the actual assault Wellesley remained in command of the reserves in the trenches. Before daybreak on the 4th May the storming parties were assembled in the trenches. They amounted to 2,494 Europeans and 1,882 Native Infantry, under command of General Baird, and were divided into two parties. The right column under Colonel Sherbrooke consisted of flank companies of the Scotch Brigade, the Regiment de Meuron, the 73rd and 74th Regiments, eight flank companies of Madras and six of Bombay Sepoys and fifty artillerymen; who were destined to attack the southern rampart. The left column under Colonel Dunlop was composed of six European flank companies from the Bombay Army, the 12th and 33rd Regiments, ten flank companies of Bengal Sepoys, and fifty artillerymen, and was directed to assault the northern face. Each column was headed by a forlorn hope of a sergeant and twelve men, one of the 74th and the other of the 77th, followed by two subaltern's parties commanded by Lieutenants Hills, 74th, and Lawrence, 77th Regiment. The assault took place not long after midday, and in six minutes the breach was won and the British flag* waved on the ramparts. But on arriving at the top of the breach General Baird discovered a second ditch, full of water, within the outer wall, which appeared impassable. Leading his men along the ramparts, however, he found that some scaffolding had been left by workmen who had been engaged in repairing the wall, and by this means the troops crossed the inner ditch; the two columns joined on the other side of the fort and entered the body of the town. The firing continued until a little after two o'clock, by which time the whole of the works were in possession of the troops, and the British ensign floated from the flagstaff on the southern cavalier of the fort.†

A Single Combat.

Colonel Dunlop, at the onset, received a severe wound in a personal conflict with one of Tipu's officers, who about half-way up the breach made a desperate cut at him with his scimitar; this blow the Colonel parried, and in return mortally wounded his antagonist; but his opponent, as

* The flag was hoisted by Sergeant Graham, Bombay European Regiment, who received his death wound at the moment. When his party rushed forward to the breach, Sergeant Graham claimed the pre-eminence of being the first man who stood upon the top; and after hastily reconnoitring the disposition of the enemy within their works, he made a safe retreat to the column next in advance, which had then gained the midway ascent: here, anxious to secure to himself a still more distinguished honour, he obtained the colours from the officer who bore them, again ascended the ruins, over the bodies of his fallen comrades, and clambering upon the rampart planted for the first time the British ensign on the walls of Seringapatam. This act alone, by established military usage, entitled him, from that instant, to rank as a commissioned officer, and justly proud of its accomplishment, he held the colour staff with one hand, waved his hat with the other, and called out "Hurrah for Lieutenant Graham." He had scarcely uttered the words when a shot struck him to the heart, and this brave fellow dropped lifeless into the ditch of the fort.—*The Conquest of Mysore* (Anon.), 1800.

† Before a flag could be obtained, an English light infantry jacket was hoisted by some men of the 73rd and continued flying in sight of the whole army until the regiment came up, and the King's colour was substituted.

he fell, struck him across the wrist of the right hand, and nearly cut it through; he was instantly bayonetted by the grenadiers as they passed, and Colonel Dunlop, still endeavouring to head his column, had scarcely gained the summit of the breach when he sank from loss of blood, and had to be led off by a sergeant.

Last Stand of Tipu Sultan.

Meanwhile the final scene of the drama was being enacted at the covered gateway of the town, where the Tiger of Mysore was himself making a last stand. During the earlier part of the assault the Sultan remained in his palace, where from time to time he received information of the progress of the fight. At length he was told that the British columns were crossing the river and the news was confirmed by the roar of guns and musketry which he heard, like Brunswick's fated chieftain at Waterloo, "with death's prophetic ear." Mounting his horse, he rode proudly forth, never to return, and took up a position behind a traverse commanding the approaches from the breach, where he fired repeatedly at the assailants with deadly effect. But he was obliged to retire, accompanied by a few personal attendants, when the storming party entered the body of the place. "Fatigued, suffering from intense heat, and pained by an old wound, Tipu mounted his horse and retreated slowly along the northern rampart. The British were momentarily gaining ground, the garrison in every direction flying while a spattering fusilade, and occasionally a wild huzza, told that the victors were everywhere advancing. Instead of quitting the city as he might have done, the Sultan crossed the bridge over the inner ditch, and entered the town. The covered gateway was now crowded with fugitives vainly endeavouring to escape from the bayonets of their conquerors, who were heard approaching at either side. A random shot struck the Sultan: he pressed his horse forward, but his passage was impeded by a mob of runaways, who literally choked the archway. Presently a cross-fire opened, and filled the passage with dead and wounded. Tipu's horse was killed, but his followers managed to disengage him, dragged him exhausted from beneath the fallen steed and placed him in his palanquin. But escape was impossible; the British were already in the gateway; the bayonet was unsparingly at work, for quarter at this moment was neither given nor expected. Dazzled by the glittering of his jewelled turban, a soldier dashed forward and caught the Sultan's sword belt. With failing strength Tipu cut boldly at his assailant, and inflicted a trifling wound. The soldier, irritated by pain, drew back, laid his musket to his shoulder, and shot the Sultan dead. His companions, perceiving the struggle, rushed up; the palanquin was overturned, the body of the departed tyrant was thrown upon a heap of dead and dying, and the corpse, despoiled of everything valuable, left among the fallen Musalmans—naked, unknown, and unregarded."*

Death of Tipu Sultan.

Here the body was subsequently discovered by General Baird; Colonel Wellesley, and others. There was a bullet wound a little above the right ear, the ball lodging in the left cheek near the mouth, and there were three bayonet wounds in the right side. The corpse was handed over to the Muhammadans, who buried it beside the remains of Hyder Ali, and the evening on which the tomb closed over the departed Sultan was marked by a thunderstorm of remarkable violence, by which two officers, Lieutenants Barclay and Grant of the 74th, were killed.

No further resistance was experienced, and the town, palace, and fort were occupied by the British troops. From a return made out by one of Tipu Sultan's officers it appears that on the 4th May during the assault there were in the fort 13,739 regular infantry and outside in the trenches on the island 8,100. The number on the British side actually under arms was 4,376, including 1,882 natives.

The enemy's total loss during the siege was not ascertained, but some 8,000 were killed in the final assaults. The British casualties † amounted to 22 officers killed and 45 wounded; 181 European rank and file killed, 622 wounded and 22 missing; 119 natives were killed, 420 wounded and 100 missing.

Casualties.

* When the Sultan left the palace he was dressed in a light coloured jacket, wide trousers of fine coloured silk, a sash of dark red silky stuff and a turban with one or two distinguishing ornaments. He wore his sword in a wide belt slung over his shoulder, and a small cartridge box hung to another embroidered belt thrown over his left shoulder; the talisman was fastened under his jacket to his right arm.

† See Appendix IX B.

Loot of the Palace.

Immense treasure was found in the palace, but the troops broke in at the back and looted the greater part of it; valuable jewels were afterwards purchased for a few rupees. It is related that Dr. Mein purchased from a private of the 74th Regiment for a mere trifle two pairs of solid gold bracelets set with diamonds, the least valuable of which was valued by a Hyderabad jeweller at £32,000, and the most valuable pearls were frequently bought from the soldiers for a bottle of spirits.

Wellesley appointed Governor.

Wellesley was now appointed Governor of Seringapatam, and at once set about restoring order with such energy and method that the place was quiet in a comparatively short time. On the 6th May he was able to write to General Harris—"Plunder is stopped, the fires are all extinguished, and the inhabitants are all returning to their houses fast. I am now employed in burying the dead, which I hope will be completed this day." His care for the welfare of his troops is illustrated by the following passage from the same letter:—"I shall be obliged if you will order an extra dram and biscuit for the 12th, 33rd, and 73rd Regiments, who got nothing to eat yesterday and were wet last night." Later, on the 8th May, he wrote to Lord Mornington—"It is impossible to expect that after the labour which the troops had undergone in working up to the place and the various successes they had had in six different affairs with Tipu's troops, in all of which they had come to the bayonet with them, they should not have looked to the plunder of this place. Nothing, therefore, can have exceeded what was done on the night of the 4th. Scarcely a house in the town was left unplundered, and I understand that in camp jewels of the greatest value, bars of gold, etc., have been offered for sale in the bazaars of the army by our soldiers, sepoys and foreigners. I came in to take command on the 5th and by the greatest exertion, by hanging, flogging, etc., in the course of that day, I restored order among the troops, and I hope I have gained the confidence of the people. They are returning to their houses, and beginning again to follow their occupations, but the property of everyone is gone."

Restores Order.

The Sultan's children were removed to the fort of Vellore,* and the old Hindu family was restored to the *masnad* from which they had been deposed by the usurpation of Hyder Ali. The four eldest princes and their suite attended by Captain Marriott, and escorted by a detachment under Lieutenant-Colonel Coke, quitted Seringapatam on the 18th June. As they passed through the streets of the capital the procession attracted vast crowds to take a farewell look at the sons of their late sovereign, but they received no tokens of sorrow or regret at parting. The consequences of the campaign were of great political importance. Lord Mornington wrote on this subject to the Court of Directors—"The fall of Seringapatam under all the circumstances which accompanied that event has placed the whole kingdom of Mysore, with all its resources, at the disposal of your Government, and the only power in India to which the French could look for assistance, or which could be deemed formidable to your interests, is now deprived of all vigour, if not entirely extinct."

*Appendix III. "The Mutiny at Vellore."

CHAPTER III.

THE SETTLEMENT OF MYSORE.

Wellesley and the Administration of Mysore.

Having restored order in Seringapatam, Wellesley set about the establishment of tranquillity in Mysore, of which he was appointed civil administrator, besides being in command of the troops under the direct orders of the Governor-General in Council. It had been intended to associate with him a civil officer to undertake the administration of the country, but he very wisely refused to fall in with this arrangement, and was consequently given complete authority in both departments.

The duty of partition of the conquered territory was entrusted to five Commissioners, of whom Colonel Wellesley was one. In this capacity he was charged with the removal to Vellore of the family of the late Sultan, the Governor-General expressing the opinion "that the details of this painful but indispensable measure cannot be entrusted to any person more likely to combine every office of humanity with the prudential cautions required by the occasion; and I therefore commit to his discretion, activity, and humanity the whole arrangement, subject always to such suggestions as may be offered by the other members of the Commission."

Enthronement of the Raja.

The next duty that fell to Colonel Wellesley was the enthronement of the young Hindu Raja, who was selected for the succession by the Governor-General, and who was only five years of age. This accomplished, Wellesley set about the administration of the country, retaining the services of Purneah, the Minister of the late Sultan, and of many of the officers who had served the same master. The next twelve months were uneventful, being occupied with the settlement of the country, the assignment of pensions to those who had been in the service of the late Sultan, while a perusal of the Despatches shows that many small matters engaged his attention, such as the construction of a house for Colonel Barry

Close, the British Resident at Seringapatam. We find it recorded of this period of his work that "his active superintendence, discernment, impartiality, and decision in the arduous and important duties of the civil as well as the military administration of the command, were such as to have fully warranted his brother's judicious selection, and deserved and obtained the gratitude of the conquered people."

He was officially appointed to the command of the troops in Mysore in September 1799, and in March of the following year the forces in Canara and Malabar were also placed under him.

Dhoondiah Waugh, "King of the two Worlds."

At the commencement of 1800 a more serious matter began to engage his attention. When Seringapatam was captured, a number of prisoners, found languishing in the dungeons, were liberated by the victors without inquiry. Among them was Dhoondiah Waugh, at one time a Mahratta trooper in the service of Hyder Ali, who had deserted and become a freebooter on the death of that potentate. However, he subsequently entered the service of Tipu Sultan, but, incurring the displeasure of his new master, he was imprisoned, and made a Musalman. No sooner were his fetters struck off, than he hastened away from Seringapatam and soon assembled around him a band of adventurous spirits like himself, until at length he had a large and formidable army, with which, having assumed the high-sounding title of "King of the two Worlds," he established himself in the Bednore District, and commenced plundering the surrounding country. From this marauder there was more danger to be anticipated than that due to his profession as a mere bandit. Such adventurers had before then established states or even empires in India. The great Sivaji, founder of the Mahratta Empire, was of very similar personal character, crafty, cruel, and possessed of some personal courage, and considerable military skill. Hyder Ali commenced his career as a common soldier; why should not Dhoondiah become a second Sivaji or Hyder Ali, and establish a more permanent right to the title of his adoption ?

Defeat of Dhoondiah.

Against this bandit Wellesley found it necessary to concentrate his energies towards the middle of 1800. In August 1799 Dhoondiah was defeated by a force under Colonels

Dalrymple and Stevenson, and driven across the border with the loss of his guns and baggage. But he soon gathered renewed strength and fresh adherents, and in February 1800 we find him engaged in a bold plot to capture the British Commander, referred to in the following letter to Colonel Close:—"A fellow came here (Seringapatam) to-day and informed me that he had come from the Mahratta country, as far as Tumkur, with a gang employed by Dhoondiah to carry me off when I should go out hunting. He says that Dhoondiah proposes to collect a large gang in this neighbourhood and join them himself. In order to prove to him how little I fear his gang, I go out hunting to-morrow; but I have desired my friend to join his gang again; and I have promised him a reward if he will enable me to lay hands on them in this neighbourhood." He accordingly went out hunting next day, when his aide-de-camp said he saw about 20 horsemen, but the threatened attempt was not carried into execution, and Colonel Wellesley subsequently ascribed the information to a bazaar agent.

Plot to Capture Wellesley.

In May 1800 he was offered, by the Governor-General, command of an expedition destined for the Island of Batavia, but Lord Clive, the Governor of Madras, was so anxious to retain his services in Mysore, while the increasing strength of Dhoondiah Waugh was such as to cause alarm, that Colonel Wellesley decided to remain where he was.

The Batavia Expedition.

On the 7th May he wrote to Major Munro,* "I think that, upon the whole, we are not in the most thriving condition in this country. Polygars, Nairs and Moplahs in arms on all sides of us; an army full of disaffection and discontent, amounting to Lord knows what, on the northern frontier, which increases as it advances, like a snowball in snow. To oppose this we have nothing that ought to be taken from the necessary garrisons, and the corps we have in them are incomplete in men and without officers. If we go to war in earnest, however (and if we take the field at all it ought to be in earnest) I will collect everything that can be brought

Condition of Mysore.

*Afterwards Sir Thomas Munro, Bart, K.C.B., Governor of Madras.

together from all sides, and we ought not to quit the field as long as there is a discontented or unsubdued Polygar in the country."

Regarding Dhoondiah he wrote to the Marquis Wellesley—" he is certainly a despicable enemy; but from circumstances, he is one against whom we have been obliged to make a formidable preparation .... If we do not get him, we must expect a general insurrection of all the discontented and disaffected of these countries .... The destruction of this man is absolutely necessary for our tranquillity.''

Campaign against Dhoondiah Waugh.

Wellesley, accordingly, took the field towards the end of May, when the force was brigaded at Honore. The British Commander marched by way of Chitaldrug, Baramsagar to Harihar.

Colonel Stevenson, who subsequently co-operated with him in the Mahratta War, commanded the cavalry.

1st Brigade of Cavalry (Lieut.-Col. Torin)	His Majesty's 19th Light Dragoons. 1st Regiment Native Cavalry. 4th Regiment Native Cavalry.	
2nd Brigade of Cavalry (Colonel Pater)	His Majesty's 25th Light Dragoons. 2nd Regiment Native Cavalry.	
1st Brigade of Infantry (Lt.-Col. Montresor)	His Majesty's 73rd Regiment. His Majesty's 77th Regiment.	
2nd Brigade of Infantry (Lt.-Col. Tolfrey)	1st Battalion, 1st Regiment. 1st Battalion, 8th Regiment. 1st Battalion, 12th Regiment.	Madras Infantry.
3rd Brigade of Infantry (Major Capper)	2nd Battalion, 4th Madras Regiment. 2nd Battalion, 2nd Bombay Regiment. 1st Battalion, 4th Bombay Regiment.	

Co-operating with Wellesley, beyond the Malpurba river, was Gokla, one of the Peshwa's chiefs, with a force of 10,000 cavalry, 5,000 infantry and 8 guns, but he was attacked, defeated, and slain by Dhoondiah early in July, and on the 13th of that month Wellesley wrote to Colonel Close from his camp at Savanore that the "King of the two Worlds" was only 22 miles from him at Kundgul. Next day Wellesley marched to Kundgul and took by assault that place, which had a garrison of 600 of Dhoondiah's men; and on the 25th he stormed the strong stone fort of Damal, which was occupied by 1,000 men. The latter, a strong and well-built fort, was attacked in three places by parties of the 73rd, 77th, and 2nd and 4th Bombay Infantry, and taken by escalade with slight loss.

Marching from Damal, Wellesley encamped on the 29th at Alagawaddy, 15 miles from Sunduti, where he heard Dhoondiah was. He intended to await the co-operation of a detachment under Colonel Bowser, before attacking the enemy's camp. But Dhoondiah moved off with the intention of crossing the Malpurba on hearing of the proximity of the British force.

Attack on Dhoondiah's Camp.

Marching on the morning of the 30th July to Hoorgurgoor to the East of the Purghur hill, Wellesley surprised the enemy's standing camp on the river bank, opposite Manauli, and at once attacked it with his cavalry only. All the people in the camp were killed, captured or driven into the river, where some 5,000 were drowned, among them a chief named Babar Jung, who clad in armour leaped into the river and sank. Numbers of men, women, and children, elephants, camels, horses, and bullocks were taken, and all the baggage.

Dhoondiah's six guns had gone across the Malpurba prior to the attack, but they were dismounted by the fire of the British artillery, and were then captured, Lieutenants Fitchet and Jackson with some men of the 73rd and 77th having gallantly swum over the river, and seized and brought away from under the fort of Manauli a boat which carried the captain of the enemy's artillery.

Licentious Soldiery.

The following extract from a General Order of the 31st July is of interest, as showing the lawlessness of the soldiers of those days:—"Colonel Wellesley is concerned to observe the length to which the soldiers have carried plunder. Under the pretence of taking plunder from the followers, they have committed acts of which every good soldier is to be ashamed, and which, if continued, will tend to the ruin of the army. They have plundered the sepoys, the servants, followers, and baggage of their officers. The bazaar people and hircarrahs, and messengers coming with letters to Colonel Wellesley, and even their own servants and followers, have not escaped them. Under these circumstances it is absolutely necessary that this plunder should be stopped; and Colonel Wellesley accordingly declares his determination to punish, in the most exemplary manner, any man who may be found plundering." We shall see later how he put down plundering with a stern hand, and with salutary effect.

Pursuit of Dhoondiah.

The career of the "King of the two Worlds" was now drawing to a close. He got away over the Malpurba, having marched through the jungles, and turned the sources of that river, but many of his followers deserted him, and Colonel Stevenson, who pursued with the cavalry, found the track strewn with dead men, camels, horses and bullocks. Wellesley halted some days at Kittoor to construct boats, and on the 17th August wrote to Colonel Close that he was "going to give Dhoondiah one more run between Gutpurba and Malpurba, and, I think, I have a chance of picking up some baggage; it is clear I shall never catch *him*. His baggage has only one way to escape, and that is to recross the Malpurba near Badamy; but I guard against that by detaching two corps of Mahrattas and a brigade of infantry towards Jellahall, and I pursue him with my troops along the Malpurba, Stevenson's along the Gutpurba, and Goklah's and the Moghal's between us, as far as the junction of those two rivers with the Kistna. I think I shall make something of this plan, although I may not probably get hold of him."

Moving camp to Hubli on the 20th August, Wellesley remained there some days, and on the 23rd took 5 guns and a quantity of arms and ammunition left by Dhoondiah in possession of the Talloor Polygar while Colonel Capper took on one day the forts of Hooley and Syringhy. Dhoondiah crossed the Malpurba at Boodeyhaul on the night of the 24th August, making for the Nizam's country, and entered the Doab. Although many of his followers had deserted, he must still have had a considerable army, for he had with him early in September 40,000 Brinjaras, or nearly all that there were in that part of India.

Wellesley crossed the Malpurba at Jellahall and entered the Nizam's Dominions at Hanmansagar on the 5th September. On the 7th he was at Kanaghery, on the 8th at Baswapur, and on the 9th marched to Yepalparvy. Moving forward on the evening of the 10th he came up with Dhoondiah's army, consisting of 5,000 horse, at Conahgull, 6 miles off. The enemy was strongly posted, with his rear and left flank covered by the village and rock of Conahgull, but, forming his cavalry, consisting of the 19th and 25th Light Dragoons and the 1st and 2nd Madras Cavalry, in one line, the British commander at once charged, and bore down all opposition, pursuing the bandits for many miles. The "King of the two Worlds" was killed and his body brought into camp on a gun, his whole force dispersed, and all his baggage,* camp, elephants, etc., were captured. Wellesley's troops behaved admirably, and he himself wrote that, "if they had not done so, not a man of us would have quitted the field," for the so-called "victorious army" stood for some time with apparent firmness.

Defeat and Death of Dhoondiah.

This brought the campaign to an end. Wellesley after a halt of some days at Yepalparvy moved camp to Hubli, where he remained a month, being directed to maintain his position in the Mahratta territory until events settled themselves at Poona, where there was trouble between the Peshwa and Sindhia. Hostilities on this account were, however, postponed until 1803. He then returned to Mysore, marching by Harihar, Hooley, Honore and Chenapatam, having broken up his army on the Tungabhadra on the 16th November, leaving a portion of his force in the districts ceded under treaty by the Nizam.

The Red Sea Expedition.

In the middle of December he proceeded to Fort St. George, having been appointed to command a force, destined first for Batavia, but afterwards, on the abandonment of that projected expedition, for the Red Sea. This army was assembled at Trincomalee, where

* Among the baggage was found Salabat Khan, a son of Dhoondiah, about 4 years old. He was taken to Colonel Wellesley's tent, and most kindly and liberally treated by him. On his departure from India, Wellesley left several hundred pounds for the boy's maintenance in the hands of the Collector of Seringapatam. Salabat Khan grew up a fine handsome and intelligent youth. He was subsequently placed in the service of the Raja of Mysore, and died of cholera in 1822.

In December 1803 a Musalman assumed the character of a faquir and the name of Dhoondiah Waugh, and crossed the Kistna at Dharore at the head of 10,000 plunderers. These committed many depredations and were proceeding towards the Tungabhadra River and British territory. But they were pursued by General Campbell with a force of cavalry and infantry, and were attacked and dispersed on the 31st December, with a loss of nearly 3,000 killed and wounded.

Colonel Wellesley joined in December, and with his usual care and foresight at once set about arrangements for the supply of the troops. He then proceeded with his force to Bombay in H.M.S. *Suffolk*, having in the meantime been superseded by General Baird, to whom he was appointed second-in-command.

This supersession naturally was anything but pleasant to him, for, as he wrote to his brother Henry, Private Secretary to the Governor-General, "I was at the top of the tree in this country; the Governments of Fort St. George and Bombay, which I had served, placed unlimited confidence in me, and I had received from both strong and repeated marks of their approbation. I arranged the plan for taking possession of the Ceded Districts, which was done without striking a blow; and another plan for conquering Wynaad and reconquering Malabar, which I am informed has succeeded without loss on our side. But this supersession has ruined all my prospects, founded upon any service that I may have rendered."

However, he agreed to serve under General Baird, but was given permission to return to Mysore should he desire to do so. On the 3rd April 1801 he was attacked by fever, and was not able to embark with General Baird and the expeditionary force on the 5th. He accordingly remained some time in Bombay, and resumed command at Seringapatam on Sunday, the 17th May 1801.

Wellesley returns to Mysore.

During the next eighteen months Colonel Wellesley was fully occupied with the civil and military administration of Mysore.

In March 1800 a detachment under Lieutenant-Colonel Tolfrey had been sent against Kistnapa Naik, the Raja of Bullum, who had occupied one of the passes between Canara and Mysore and had long resisted authority. The Raja took up a strong stockaded position in the dense forest at Arrakhera, where he was attacked on the 2nd April, but the detachment was repulsed with a loss of 47 killed and wounded. On the 30th of the month, a reinforcement having arrived under Lieutenant-Colonel Montresor, the place was carried by storm after a stout resistance, the British force losing 37 killed and 104 wounded.

The Raja of Bullum.

Immediately after the departure of Colonel Montresor, the Raja reoccupied his position and recommenced his predatory incursions, but the operations against Dhoondiah Waugh prevented any notice being taken of him for some time. In January 1802, however, Colonel Wellesley marched against him from Seringapatam. On arriving in the neighbourhood of Arrakhera, he divided his infantry into three portions for the attack on the stockade :—

Right attack under Lieutenant-Colonel Spry.—19th Dragoons, Detachment of Artillery, Detachments, 77th Regiment, and Regiment de Meuron, 1st Battalions, 1st and 2nd Madras Infantry, and a party of Pioneers.

Centre attack under Lieutenant-Colonel Cuppage.—Detachments, 5th Cavalry, Artillery, 77th Regiment, and Regiment de Meuron, the 1st Battalion, 5th Madras Infantry, and a party of Pioneers.

Left attack under Major English.—Detachments, 77th Regiment, and Regiment de Meuron, the 2nd Battalion, 10th Madras Infantry, and a party of Pioneers.

The Mysore Infantry was disposed so as to cut off the retreat of the enemy towards the ghauts. The cavalry under Lieutenant-Colonel Macalister occupied all the open ground. The attack was successful at all points and the stockades were carried with trifling loss.

A detachment was left at Arrakhera while Colonel Wellesley proceeded towards the Bisleghaut to destroy other strongholds in that direction. On the 9th February the Raja was captured, and executed next day, together with six of his followers. Colonel Wellesley then returned to Seringapatam, leaving a detachment at Arrakhera to make a road down the Sissul Ghaut, to construct defensible posts at the heads of the passes, clear the jungle, and destroy the stockades. Another detachment was to establish authority in the Bellur district; the inhabitants were to be disarmed, roads made, and fortified villages dismantled.

Colonel Wellesley and his troops received the thanks of Government "for the judicious and spirited manner in which this service has been conducted and finally completed by the defeat and punishment of the rebel chieftain, and the entire establishment of the power of the Raja of Mysore throughout the province of Bullum."

Operations in the Wynaad.

On the 11th October 1802 a body of 400 Nairs attacked the post of Panamurtha Cottah in North Wynaad which was occupied by 70 men of the 1st Battalion, 4th Bombay Infantry, under Captain Dickinson and Lieutenant Maxwell. Both the European officers and 24 sepoys were killed, and 21 wounded, while the buildings were all destroyed. The head-quarters of the regiment were at Pulingal, some nine miles west of the post where this disaster occurred; but the officer in command remained inactive, drawing from Colonel Wellesley the following remonstrance addressed to the officer commanding the Bombay troops in Malabar:—"I beg that you will urge the officers to active measures. Let them put their troops in camp forthwith, excepting the number of men that may be absolutely necessary for the defence of the small posts against surprise. If the rebels are really in force, let a junction be formed, and then not a moment lost in dashing at them, whatever may be their force."

These instructions show what a complete grasp of tactical principles Wellesley possessed. A force consisting of the 1st Battalion, 8th Madras Infantry, and 200 Mysore Horse was at once sent from Seringapatam for the support of the Bombay troops. Captain Gurnell, who commanded this force, was directed to establish some posts, and keep the remainder of his battalion moving in the neighbourhood of Sungalee, and to attack the insurgents wherever met with, and so effective were these measures that Colonel Wellesley stopped the advance of a detachment of the 33rd Regiment and 1st Battalion, 4th Madras Infantry, which were moving towards the Wynaad. On the 12th November an action took place, thus described by Wellesley in his report to the Commander-in-Chief:—"Since I wrote to you on the 9th instant, a detachment of the 1st Battalion, 8th Regiment, has had a smart action with the Nairs in Wynaad, in which they sustained a considerable loss. They had marched to Manantawaddy with a despatch to Lieutenant-Colonel Lawrence, and on their return were attacked near a swamp at which the battalion had been hard-pressed heretofore. The Nairs took advantage of a *nullah* which was impassable, across which they fired at them, and killed nine and wounded eighteen. The officer in command of the battalion, however, at Sungaloo sent out three companies to the support of the other detachment, and the Nairs were driven off with considerable loss. Many of those on this side of the *nullah* were put to death in the road. By all accounts the troops behaved remarkably well on this occasion."

The troops were after this recalled from Wynaad as more momentous affairs were awaiting Wellesley's attention, owing to events which had come to a climax in the Mahratta Empire. At the end of November 1802 he received notice that it was probable that an army would be assembled on the Tungabhadra, with a view to operations in the Mahratta territory, and he at once began to prepare the troops under his command for the coming campaign. In March 1803 he marched to the Tungabhadra with his force, and there received his orders from General Stuart, under whom a corps of observation had already been assembled.

CHAPTER IV.

THE MAHRATTA WAR.

The Mahrattas.

The Mahrattas, originally a mere predatory horde, had in the seventeenth century become an organised nation under the rule of Sivaji. After Sivaji's death the government passed from the feeble hands of his successors, the Rajas of Satara, into those of the astute Brahmin Ministers, the Peshwas, who had their seat at Poona. Other Mahratta Princes combined with the Peshwa to form a Confederacy in some measure acknowledging the latter as their head, but in reality independent of each other. They were prepared to unite against a common enemy although at times quarrelling among themselves. This Confederacy consisted of the Peshwa at Poona, Holkar at Indore, the Gaikwar of Baroda, Sindhia,* who had his capital at Gwalior, and the Raja of Berar, who was chief of Nagpore, and also bore the title of Bhonsla.†

Affairs in the Mahratta Confederacy.

In reviewing the causes which led up to the Mahratta War of 1803, it is necessary to trace the relations of the British Government with the great Confederacy founded by Sivaji, for some years back since the period when, in 1792, the three great powers, the British, the Peshwa, and the Nizam, were banded together against Tipu Sultan.

After that campaign Lord Cornwallis, with a view to preventing dissensions between the allies, desired the Mahrattas to allow the British Government to arbitrate on the claims of the Peshwa on the Nizam, whose territory had always been subject to incursions of the predatory hordes.

But the Peshwa refused. Subsequently war broke out between the two native powers, and the Nizam's army was defeated at the battle of Kardla in 1795, in which the only troops that distinguished themselves on the Hyderabad side were the French Battalions under the celebrated adventurer Raymond.

* Properly Shinde.

† Properly Bhosle, the family name of Parsaji, a trooper of Sivaji, who established himself at Nagpur.

The Nizam and the Mahrattas.

The Nizam, as a result of this contest, was obliged to pay a large indemnity, and to cede half his territory to the Mahrattas. The ruler of Hyderabad took umbrage with the British, who had held aloof from their ally, with the result that the British subsidiary force of two battalions was withdrawn from Hyderabad, and the French party obtained the ascendancy, while their troops were largely increased. Sindhia also had a large corps of efficient troops officered by Frenchmen who had been mainly instrumental in establishing the ascendancy of that Chieftain at Poona; it thus came about that the Mahrattas, largely with the support of French adventurers, had become the predominant power in India. The Nizam, reduced in strength and subject to the constant menace of his powerful neighbours, was supported only by the French party, who were, moreover, in communication with their compatriots at the court of Tipu Sultan, the implacable foe of the British.

It was at this juncture that in 1798 the Marquis Wellesley arrived in India, firmly imbued with the necessity of reducing the power and the influence of the French. With this object in view he disbanded the French Corps at Hyderabad, and then turned the arms of the allies against Tipu Sultan, as we have already seen. It now remained to deal with the Mahrattas, against whose aggressions it was necessary to protect the Nizam, with a view to excluding the recrudescence of French influence at Hyderabad, which would arise in the absence of British support, while it was equally desirable to oust Perron and the other adventurers whose power was great in the North of India, where they had trained Sindhia's infantry on European lines.

Affairs at Poona.

Shortly after the peace of Kardla, a state of confusion arose at Poona on the occasion of the succession to the Peshwa's *masnad.* This resulted in the establishment of power in the hands of Daulat Rao Sindhia, who was ambitious of becoming the head of the Mahratta Empire and who also possessed the chief power in Hindustan, and the largest corps of regular infantry under foreign adventurers. It therefore became desirable for the British Government to relieve the Peshwa from the domination of Sindhia, whose ascendancy at Poona constituted a menace both to the British and to their ally the Nizam.

The latter was in 1800 taken under the protection of the British by a general defensive treaty, the consequence of which it was obvious must eventually be a struggle with the Mahrattas.

At the end of 1800 Sindhia was still at Poona with an army. It was scarcely to be expected that he would consent to the treaty, which put an end to his ambitious projects in the Deccan; while the Peshwa, being under his domination, was also helpless in the matter. It therefore became an object to release the Peshwa from his subordinate situation, and to conclude a treaty with him, so as to secure the *status quo* in the Deccan.

Sindhia.

Sindhia now became involved in a contest with Holkar, and the defeat of a detachment of his army by the latter at Ujjain demanded his presence in Malwa at the end of 1800. He defeated Holkar at a battle at Indur, and in the succeeding two years drove him from Malwa into the Deccan. Holkar then attacked the allied forces of Sindhia and the Peshwa, and defeated them under the walls of Poona on the 25th October 1802, whereupon the Peshwa fled to Bassein, where he landed on the 6th December, and there concluded a treaty with the British, under the terms of which he agreed to exclude foreign adventurers from his service, to have a permanent Subsidiary Force established in his dominions, and to co-operate with the British in return for their protection.

Holkar.

Treaty of Bassein.

In this crisis all the Mahratta powers urged the Governor-General to interfere in their affairs.

The state of affairs in the Mahratta Confederacy had already caused the assembly of a corps of observation, 20,000 strong, under General Stuart, at Harihar upon the North-West Frontier of Mysore, for the effectual defence of the British possessions during the convulsed state of the Mahratta Empire, and the eventual establish-

Assembly of a British Army.

ment of a subsidiary force at Poona, under the operation of the general defensive alliance concluded with the Peshwa.* Such was the aspect of affairs when the Peshwa sought the aid of the British, and entered into the treaty of Bassein.

Wellesley Detached to Poona.

In March 1803 Wellesley was detached by General Stuart with the following instructions :—

(1) To encourage the Southern Jagirdars to declare in favour of the Peshwa's cause; to employ every means to reconcile their mutual animosities and to induce them to unite their forces with the advancing detachment for the purpose of re-establishing the Peshwa's Government.
(2) To proceed to Merich, and form a junction with the Peshwa, or should that measure be deemed inadvisable on the part of His Highness, with such of his chieftains and troops as might be able to assemble there.
(3) To open communication and form a junction with the Subsidiary Force under Colonel Stevenson, and the contingent of the Nizam.
(4) To proceed eventually to Poona, and establish an order of things in that capital favourable to the return of the Peshwa and the attainment of the ends of the treaty.

In pursuance of these directions, Wellesley commenced his advance on the 9th March, was joined by a number of Mahratta Chiefs and Jagirdars during his progress, and effected a junction with Colonel Stevenson on the 15th April. He then, with his cavalry and the Mahratta horse, made a rapid march to Poona, covering 60 miles in 24 hours, entered the city on 20th April in time to save it from destruction, and established the Peshwa on the seat of Government, deposing the latter's brother, Amrat Rao, who had been installed by Holkar, and who subsequently sided with the British against Sindhia and the Bhonsla.

* Baji Rao was then Peshwa. He was the same who, in 1817, rose against the British, was defeated at the battle of Kirki and eventually surrendered. His territories were confiscated, and he was given an estate and allowance at Bithur, near Cawnpore, where he died in 1843. His adopted son was the infamous Nana Sahib who perpetrated the massacre at Cawnpore in 1857.

Movements of Holkar.

Holkar, after making a predatory excursion to Aurangabad, drew off to the north on the approach of Stevenson's force, which Wellesley detached to move up the left bank of the Bhima river for the protection of the Nizam's dominions, and, owing to his enmity with Sindhia, held aloof from the coming contest; nor did he take further action against the British until 1804, when the campaign in the Deccan had already been brought to a successful conclusion.

Sindhia and the Raja of Berar.

It was, then, with Sindhia and the Raja of Berar that the British had to deal, and for this purpose an army was assembled in Northern India under General Lake,* who beat the Mahrattas at Delhi and Laswari while the campaign in the Deccan was in progress, and released from the domination of the French adventurer Perron the once glittering puppet who sat in squalor on the Moghal throne. A second army consisted of Wellesley's and Stevenson's forces, with which alone we are here concerned, while a corps of observation was assembled in the Raichur Doab under General Campbell.

Negotiations.

The occupation of Poona was followed by protracted and fruitless negotiations with the two chiefs, who acted with the usual duplicity of their race, and procrastinated from day to day in the hope of concluding an alliance with Holkar. Wellesley was given full power in dealing with the Mahratta Chieftains, and his despatches prove how much patience, diplomacy, and skill he exercised in these negotiations. Of the character of these people he wrote— "In proportion as I gain experience of the Mahrattas, I have more reason to be astonished at the low, unaccountable tricks which even the highest class of them practise, with a view, however remote, to forward their own interest."

On the 4th June he marched towards the Godavery to watch Sindhia and the Raja of Berar who had assembled their forces at Barhanpur on the Tapti, with the intention of invading the Nizam's

* Appendix V. General Lake's Campaign.

dominions. On the 14th July it was ascertained that the Mahratta Chiefs were moving towards the Ajanta Ghaut, and the General informed them that unless the Raja retired to Nagpur and Sindhia crossed the Narbada war would be declared.

The Governor-General saw the uselessness of further attempts to attain, by peaceable means, the objects he had in view, and in investing General Wellesley with plenary powers wrote—" The effectual security of our interests in the Mahratta Empire is the strongest barrier which can be opposed to the progress of the French interests in India; the early reduction of Scindhia would prove a fatal blow to the interests of France. An imperfect arrangement with the Mahratta Powers, or a delay of active measures, might open to France the means of engaging with advantage in the affairs of the Mahratta Empire."

The Chiefs answered that if the British returned to their cantonments, they would retire toward Barhanpur, and at length, perceiving that the sole object of the Mahrattas was to gain time, Wellesley directed his envoy, Colonel Collins, to leave the Mahratta Camp, and on the 7th August 1803, having informed them that as they had refused the terms offered and chosen war, they were responsible for all consequences, issued from his camp near Ahmednagar a proclamation amounting to a declaration of war.

Proclamation by the Hon'ble Major-General A. Wellesley.

Proclamation of Hostilities.

" Daolut Rao Scindhia and the Raja of Berar having threatened with hostilities the British Government and their allies, Rao Pundit Purdhaun (the Peshwa), and the Nabob Nizam Aly (Nizam of Hyderabad); and, in pursuance of these threats, having advanced with their large armies to a position contiguous to the frontiers, and having refused to depart from it, notwithstanding the repeated representations and entreaties of Major-General Wellesley, as the only mode of preserving peace, he at last finds himself obliged to commence hostilities against these chiefs. He does not, however, intend to make war upon the inhabitants; and, accordingly, all *amildars* and others are required to remain quietly in their stations and obey the orders which they will receive; and if they do no injury to the British Armies, none will be done to them. But notice is hereby given that if any of the inhabitants of the country either abandon their dwellings or do any injury to the British armies or their followers, they will be treated as enemies, and suffer accordingly."

Wellesley's Army.

The strength and disposition of the opposing armies was :—

Wellesley in camp near Ahmednagar with :—

CAVALRY,	19th Light Dragoons	384 men.
	4th Native Cavalry	1,347 men.
	5th ditto	
	7th ditto	
ARTILLERY,	17 guns and	173 men.
INFANTRY,	74th Regiment	1,368 men.
	78th ditto	
	1st Battalion, 2nd Regiment, Native Infantry.	5,631 men.
	1st and 2nd do. 3rd ditto	
	1st Battalion, 8th ditto	
	2nd do. 12th ditto	
	2nd do. 18th ditto	
	Total	8,903 men.

He also had 603 Pioneers of the establishment of Fort St. George, 2,400 Cavalry belonging to the Maharaja of Mysore, and 3,000 Mahratta horse. The Native regiments were all of the Madras Army.

Stevenson's Force.

Under Colonel Stevenson at Aurangabad were :—

3rd and 6th Regiments, Native Cavalry	909 men
Artillery	120 men
His Majesty's Scotch Brigade (afterwards 94th Regiment)	778 men
2nd Battalion, 2nd Regiment, Native Infantry	6,113 men
1st do. 6th ditto	
2nd do. 7th ditto	
2nd do. 9th ditto	
1st and 2nd do. 11th ditto	
Total	7,920 men

together with 276 gun lascars and 212 pioneers. A contingent * of 7,000 Cavalry, 5,000 Infantry and 40 guns, supplied by the Nizam of Hyderabad under the terms of the treaty of 1800, also took the field at a later date.

* Appendix IV. The Hyderabad Contingent.

The Mahratta Forces.

An interesting memorandum by Colonel Collins, dated at Jalgaon, 25th July 1803, gives the following details regarding the Mahratta armies then in the field in the Deccan:—

Force with Daulat Rao Sindhia, Jalgaon, 25th July 1803.

	CAVALRY.		INFANTRY.		ORDNANCE.	
	Hindustani.	Deccani.	Sepoy Bns.	Matchlock men.	Heavy guns.	Field pieces.
Under command of Colonel Pohlman . .	500	..	7	500	8	40
Under command of Colonel Soliever, in the pay of Begum Sumroo* . . .	..	..	4	..	2	30
Under command of different Native Sirdars	12,000	2,000	..	..	..	..
Under command of Bapoji Sindhia Park of Artillery	4,000	..	..	..	25	100
	16,500	2,000	11	500	35	170

N.B.—The Sepoy Battalion consists of 700 rank and file.

The Forces of the Raja of Berar.

	CAVALRY.	INFANTRY.	ORDNANCE.			
			Heavy guns.	Field pieces.	Rockets.	Sutanants.
Under command of different Native Sirdars	20,000	..	..	..	..	..
Under command of Beni Singh . .	..	6,000	..	35	..	..
Camels carrying rockets . . .	..	..	..	..	500	..
Camels carrying sutanants . . .	..	..	..	..	..	500
	20,000	6,000	..	35	500	500

* Colonel Soliever is elsewhere spoken of as Colonel Saleur. The Begum Sumroo or Sombre was so-called from her first husband, Walter Reinhard, known by the *sobriquet* of Sombre, the perpetrator of the massacre of Europeans at Patna in 1763. She was a Mussalman of remarkable beauty and force of character, and later joined the Roman Catholic Church. She married Sombre at her native place Sardhana, where he settled until his death in 1778. During this period he organised a force under European military adventurers, and it was these troops, afterwards commanded by the famous George Thomas, then by the Begum's second husband Le Vassoult, and finally by Colonel Saleur, that fought under Sindhia's flag at Assaye in 1803. After Le Vassoult's suicide in 1795, the corps was raised by Colonel Saleur, a French officer, to six battalions. At Assaye only one battalion of the corps was destroyed; the remainder, being on guard over the Mahratta camp, made their escape. The Begum submitted to General Lake after the fall of Aligarh in 1803, and died in 1836. Among other deeds recorded of this amiable lady, she had two slave girls, who set fire to her houses at Agra, buried alive in a pit dug in front of her tent.

The Mahratta forces were encamped about 9 miles north of the Ajanta Pass.

Sindhia's Army.

Sindhia's regular infantry and artillery, under the instruction and command of European adventurers, among whom may be mentioned de Boigne and Perron, had been brought to a high state of efficiency. But this organised infantry in some respects detracted from the power of the Confederacy, as Wellesley observed when he wrote in November 1803:—"Sindhia's army had actually been brought to a very favourable state of discipline, and his power had become formidable by the exertions of the European officers in his service, but I think it is much to be doubted whether his power, or rather that of the Mahratta nation would not have been more formidable, at least to the British Government, if they had never had a European, as an infantry soldier, in their service; and had carried on their operations, in the manner of the original Mahrattas, only by means of cavalry. I have no doubt whatever but that the military spirit of the nation has been destroyed by their establishments of infantry and artillery, possibly, indeed by other causes; at all events it is certain that these establishments, however formidable, afford us a good object for attack in a war with the Mahrattas, and that the destruction of them contributes to the success of the contest; because, having made them the principal objects of their attention, and that part of their strength on which they place most reliance, they become also the principal reliance of the army; and therefore when they are lost the cavalry will not act." This was written after the experience of Assaye, but is quoted here in order to illustrate the military characteristics of the people with whom Wellesley had to contend. The British General might have added that the artillery and infantry of the Mahratta Army proved somewhat of an encumbrance, detracting from the mobility which rendered their predatory horsemen so famous in days gone by.

Mahratta Warfare.

In a letter to Colonel Murray, Wellesley wrote:—

"There are two modes in which the Mahrattas carry on their

operations. They operate upon supplies by means of thier cavalry; and after they have created a distress in the enemy's camp, which obliges the army to commence a retreat, they press upon it with all their infantry and their powerful artillery. Their opponent, being pressed for provisions, is obliged to hurry his march, and they have no fear of being attacked. They follow him with their cavalry in his marches, and surround and attack him with their infantry and cannon when he halts, and he can scarcely escape from them.

"That therefore which I consider absolutely necessary in an operation against the Mahratta power (indeed in any military operation in India) is such a quantity of provisions in your camp, as will enable you to command your own movements, and to be independent of your magazines, at least for that length of time which may be necessary to fulfil the object for which you may be employed.

"The Mahrattas have long boasted that they would carry on a predatory war with us: they will find that mode of warfare not very practicable at the present moment. At all events, supposing that they can carry their design into execution, unless they find the British officers and soldiers to be in the same corrupted and enervated state in which their predecessors found the Mussulman in the last century, they cannot expect much success from it. A system of predatory war must have some foundation in strength of some kind or other. But when the Chiefs avow that they cannot meet us in the field; when they are obliged to send the principal strength of their armies, upon which the remainder depend, to a distance, lest it should fall into our hands, they must have little knowledge of human nature if they suppose that their lighter bodies will act; and still less of the British officers if they imagine that, with impunity, they can do the smallest injury, provided only that the allies, who are to be first exposed to their attacks, are true to their own interests."

Season for Operations in the Deccan.

In 1801, foreseeing the probability of a conflict with the Mahratta powers, Wellesley had written a memorandum regarding operations in the southern portion of their territories, in the course of which he said:—"The season at which it is most convenient to commence a campaign with the Mahrattas is that at which the rivers, which take their rise in the Western Ghats, fill. This happens generally in the month of June. The reasons why I think that the most favourable season for operations against the Mahrattas are as follows:—

"*First.*—The Mahratta Army is principally composed of Cavalry, and their plan of operations against a British Army would be to endeavour to cut off its communication with the rear, and to impede the junction of its supplies from the Mysore country. As the rivers are not fordable, as there are no bridges and no means of passing them excepting by basket boats, which it is difficult and might be rendered impossible to procure, the fullness of the rivers operates as a barrier. It is certain that the enemy cannot pass them in large numbers, and it is probable that they would not venture to throw across a small body, or rather, that they would not be able to prevail on a small body to remain on a different side from the main body of their army. The inconvenience and delay which the British army experience in crossing the rivers by means of boats, when they are full, is trifling; and in fact they would experience no inconvenience or delay, if good pontoons were provided, and a bridge were thrown across each river for the passage of the army. The communication might afterwards be kept up by means of common basket boats. If the army should be thus equipped with a bridge, the Mahratta would never dare to detach a body across any river for the purpose of annoying our communications. Thus then we should enjoy all the advantages of a river not fordable, to shorten our line of communications, which river our enemy could not pass with a large body of troops, and over which he would not dare to detach a small body; and we should have it in our power to pass it with as much ease, and with as little inconvenience and delay as we should experience if the river were fordable.

'*Secondly.*—The Mahratta country in general is but ill supplied with water. The rains which fill these rivers, although not heavy at the beginning of the rainy season, are sufficient to fill many *nullahs*; and an army has at this time a chance of being supplied with water, of which, in the dry season, it is certain it would never find much, and frequently none. The inconvenience to be apprehended from the rains is trifling. It is true that heavy rain would ruin the cattle of the army, and would put the roads in such a state as to render them impracticable for wheeled carriages. But heavy rain for any long continuance is not to be expected in the Mahratta territory; and particularly not early in the season.

Supply of the Army.

"The produce of this fertile country is *jowari* (millet) principally, and other dry grains, but no rice. This is the great difficulty with which our army would have to contend. The rice which must be procured for them must be brought from the distant rice countries of Mysore or in Canara, with which country in the rainy season it is impossible to keep up a communication.

"The army also might depend upon procuring some sheep and bullocks in the Mahratta territory; but if its European force should be large, it will certainly require supplies of the former from Mysore and in any case supplies from thence of the latter.

"It is well known that *jowari* straw is the best kind of forage for horses and cattle, and of this there is an abundance everywhere, and besides this forage, it seldom happens that green forage cannot be found."

This memorandum is of great interest as showing the British Commander's foresight and that attention to detail which characterises all his despatches; as, for instance, when we find him specifying the amount of salt beef and *arrack* and other supplies required for the use of his troops during this campaign.

The Theatre of Operations.

Before proceeding further with this narrative, it is advisable to give some description of the country which was to form the theatre of operations in the coming campaign. The scene of the approaching conflict lay within that part of India known as the Deccan, situated between the Krishna and Tapti Rivers. It contained within its limits the Mahratta State of Poona and Satara; the territory of the Raja of Berar; and, about Ahmednagar, a portion of that of Sindhia; who had a garrison in the fort at that place; and the northern part of the dominions of the Nizam of Hyderabad, an independent prince, formerly subject to the Moghal Emperor. This extensive region consists in the main of an elevated plateau, from one to two thousand feet above the level of the sea. Its northern boundary, between the Tapti River and the plains of Berar, and Khandesh, is characterised by a lofty range of rugged hills known as the Satpuras, covered with dense forest, and rising to a height of 4,000 feet above sea-level. On the outlying peaks of this range, like sentinels guarding the passes to the north, stand the fortresses of Asirgarh, Narnala, and Gawilgarh, built of massive stone. Below the Satpuras stretches the fertile valley of Berar, formerly the territory of the Nizam, but ceded to the Mahrattas after the battle of Kardla, watered by many streams, and having a rich alluvial surface known as "black-cotton soil," which bears fine crops of millet, wheat and cotton. This expanse of plain is now nearly all under cultivation, but at the period of the war it was probably in part covered with jungle. The numerous villages dotted over the land testify to the prosperity of the inhabitants under British administration, whilst the fact that each hamlet contains a dilapidated mud fort proves that they date as far back as the turbulent times of a century ago, when the Naiks and Pindari hordes were attracted by the wealth of this fair province.

The south-west frontier of Berar, and the boundary of Khandesh which lies upon its border, is marked by a spur of the Western Ghats, traversed by the passes of Kesari, Ajanta and Rajura, which are steep on their northern outlet, but more easy of access where they debouch into the plains on the south. These hills, though not so lofty, wide, or well watered, are similar in nature to the Satpuras, whilst to the south of them the soil is not quite so rich, though the general aspects of the country are similar to Berar; but the level is frequently broken by low stony or rocky hills, a range of which stretches from near Aurangabad to Jalna. To the South of Jalna and Aurangabad the Godavery River, issuing from the Western Ghats, and receiving many streams during its course, rolls through fertile plains, until it enters the dense jungles of Nirmal, whose chief inhabitants are predaceous animals, from which it flows due east to Sironcha, before turning in a more southerly direction to mark the eastern limits of the State of Hyderabad.

During the rainy season the watercourses, after a heavy downfall, become rapid and turbulent streams, difficult for the passage of troops, and many of them which have previously been dry, or have contained only occasional pools of water, are transformed into unfordable torrents. When the rain ceases, however, and with it the supply of water, these rivers soon run off again, especially where there is no forest to assist the retention of the moisture by the soil, and most of them are generally passable, except the larger streams, which are fordable only in the dry season. In the summer and sometimes in the cold weather if the rainfall has been scanty, only the larger rivers and *nullahs* contain water, varying in quantity according to the prevailing atmospheric conditions. During the prevalence of the south-west monsoon, the black cotton soil characteristic of the whole region north of the Godavery, which, under the heat of the summer sun, has been burnt up and is cracked into innumerable fissures, is converted by heavy rain from an arid desert into a kind of quagmire, over which men and horses move with difficulty, whilst it is quite impassable for wheeled traffic; but the surface of the ground is soon dried by a few days of sunshine. The fields in this country have as a rule no fences or hedges; the villages are built of mud, sometimes on a foundation of stone, and are frequently surrounded by a few acres of gardens and cultivated enclosures.

Supplies.

From the nature of the country it will be understood that the most difficult problem which offered itself for solution by the British Commander was that of supply and transport, perhaps the most important question in all operations of war; and it is noteworthy that it was to the details of this matter that Wellesley devoted the most careful attention in this as in his other campaigns. He procured rice for his troops from Mysore, that being the staple food of the Madras Sepoy. He arranged for a supply of Government cattle, and enlisted a large number of Brinjaras* with their pack bullocks.

Opening of the Campaign.

Wellesley had already determined that the first act of the war should be the capture of Ahmednagar, the possession of which would ensure the safety of the line of communications with Poona and Bombay, whilst it would cut off from the hostile princes such of the Southern Mahratta Chieftains as were discontented with the order of things established by the British Government. On the 8th August he advanced to attack this stronghold, which was held by some 5,000 men, including a body of Arabs† and some cavalry. The fortress and *pettah*, or native town, were enclosed within the usual outer wall of mud and stone, about 18 feet high, with small bastions at every hundred yards. The fort was one of the strongest in India. It was nearly circular in shape, and was built of solid stone, having a wide ditch all round it. It had large bastions at short intervals,

* For an account of the Brinjaras see Appendix II. The following extract from the *Journal of Major-General Sir Jasper Nicolls*, written in the field, 5th October 1803, is interesting:— "General Wellesley has always made it a point to encourage these people, by promises, kindnesses, presents, indeed by every kind of liberality of which he possesses the means, to attend our camp, and collect grain for the army. He advances them money; takes their grain when not in our allies' territory; provides guards in camp or whenever required; whenever they meet extraordinary losses he balances them by the price; and not seldom has he ordered two or three rupees a head as a reward for each bullock brought. In the case above mentioned he was generous to the Brinjaras, as some unexpectedly joined his camp with 3,000 bullock loads of grain, having been induced to do so by the *Kotwal* (or Chief Magistrate). To the *Kotwal* he gave a heavy pair of gold bangles, of which he considerably enhanced the value by putting them on his wrists with his own hands."

† The Arabs were largely employed by the Mahratta Chiefs, particularly in holding fortresses, which they defended generally with remarkable valour. They are still employed by the Nizam of Hyderabad, but not being amenable to discipline they have never been enlisted in our Indian Army. Wellesley wrote of them on 14th October 1803:—"They are undoubtedly the bravest of all troops I have yet seen in the service of the Native powers. They are a high-spirited people, and are by no means amenable to discipline and order."

mounted with at least sixty guns, from 12 to 52-pounders. On a large tower or barbette stood the Mahalachmi, a brass gun about 22 feet in length, carrying a ball 17 pounds in weight.

Capture of Ahmednagar.

Colonel Welsh, who was present, gives in his *Military Reminiscences* the following description of the attack on the outer wall:—"We had not hitherto seen the face of an enemy, and now for the first time perceived the walls of both the *pettah* and the fort lined with men, whose arms glittered in the sun, whilst another body of troops was encamped outside, between them. As we stood with the General reconnoitring from a small elevated spot within long gun-shot range of both places, he directed the leaders where they were to fix their ladders; but unaware that there was no rampart, we were ordered to escalade the curtains without breaching. The fort lay on our right hand, and the *pettah* in front, within gun-shot of each other; when the first column was ordered to attempt a long curtain to the extreme left having a high building immediately in its rear. The ladders were speedily planted and the assault made; but each man as he ascended fell, hurled from the top of the wall. This unequal struggle lasted about ten minutes, when they desisted, with a loss of about 15 killed, and about 50 wounded; amongst whom were Captains Duncan Grant, Mackenzie, and Humberstone, and Lieutenant Anderson killed; and Lieutenant Larkins mortally wounded. The third party to the right advanced at nearly the same moment, but a gun-elephant, taking fright at the firing from the fort, ran down the centre of our column, which occasioned no little confusion and some delay, giving the enemy more time and means to oppose the first attack. Being furnished with two scaling ladders only, we reached the curtain and planted them at the re-entering angle formed by a small bastion, the enemy playing some heavy guns on us from the fort. Such a rush was made at first that one ladder broke down with our gallant leader and several men, and we were forced to work hard with the other. Captain Vesey was then a very stout and heavy man; but what impediment, short of death, can arrest a soldier at such a crisis? He was soon on the bastion, surrounded by men determined to carry everything before them. Our two European companies had all scrambled up and about 150 or 200 of the 3rd (Madras Infantry) when a cannon-ball smashed our last ladder, and broke the thigh of my Subadar. We were now a party of 300 men left solely to our own resources, and dashing down we scoured all the streets near the wall, the enemy only once making a stand, and suffering accordingly. At length, arriving near a gate, marked out for the centre attack, and a loud peal of cannon and musketry from within announcing the second party under Colonel Wallace, we drove all the defenders before us, and some of our men opened the gate while they were battering at it from the outside, by which one of our party was killed. Our loss was eleven killed and twenty-two wounded, including Lieutenant Plenderleath killed and Lieutenant Nielson wounded. Our two parties now uniting under Colonel Wallace soon succeeded in clearing the place of our opponents, who, we afterwards learned, were one thousand five hundred Arabs and about three thousand Mahrattas, few if any of whom reached the fort, but were forced to fly in the other direction. The second column had but few casualties; and thus we had the quiet possession of a very fine and rich town, with a few prisoners, by three o'clock ; our total loss in killed and wounded being one hundred and sixty men."*

It is related that "among the killed was Captain Grant of the 78th Regiment, who, at the time of the attack, was under arrest for having been engaged in a duel with a brother officer, who fell in the encounter. The opponents had been intimate friends till the dispute which caused the fatal event. Such was the effect on Captain Grant that he became careless of life, and, although incapacitated by his situation for military duties, he courted death on the first opportunity and was among the foremost that mounted the ladders."

All the survivors of the garrison, including the Arabs, except those required to man the fort, made their escape towards the north during the night after this assault. Next day the batteries opened upon the citadel, a breach was soon made, and the bombardment was continued for two days. But the enemy did not stand for another assault, and asked for and obtained terms of capitulation

* Casualties. See Appendix IX.-C.

under which, to the number of fourteen hundred, they marched out and were allowed to depart with all their private property. These men became a horde of lawless plunderers, but eventually met with retribution, as will be related hereafter.* Thus fell a place which Wellesley described as being the strongest fortress he had seen with the exception of the fort at Vellore. A wild scene of disorder followed, soldiers and sepoys all taking part in plundering Sindhia's palace and other buildings, nor did the looting cease until two native soldiers had been seized and summarily hanged in the gateway of the palace. This, says an officer who was present, was "a measure which it must be confessed created some disgust at the moment, but which, at the outset of a campaign, was perhaps a necessary example for the sake of discipline, and a proper indication of the British character for justice and good faith."

The capture of this fortress was not only important by reason of its situation and strength, but from the great moral effect it had upon the natives, doubtless determining many who were hesitating as to the side they would take. Gokla, a Mahratta chief in the British Camp, who had command of 2,000, wrote to his friends at Poona :—"These English are a strange people, and their General is a wonderful man; they came here in the morning, looked at the *pettah* wall, walked over it, killed all the garrison, and returned to breakfast! What can withstand them?"

The care of his wounded, the settlement of the conquered districts around Ahmednagar, and the difficulties of supply and transport, now as always his chief care, prevented Wellesley from quitting that place for some time. However, Stevenson had already

Stevenson's Movements.

been despatched eastwards, and was moving between Aurangabad and Jafarabad, keeping watch upon the enemy's movements, and guarding the passes through the Ajanta Hills.

Wellesley's Advance.

At length, on August 18th, Wellesley moved towards the Godavery, which was crossed between Sen bugaon and Toka, the passage occupying a week, for the river was wide, deep, and swift. The army

* They were dispersed by Wellesley at Munkaisar on the 5th February 1804. See page 88.

crossed in wicker boats made by the troops from the jungle, and covered with bullock skins. It is probable that these boats were constructed of a kind of willow known as *sambalu*, which grows abundantly in many parts of the Deccan, and makes also excellent gabions. There are in the despatches several memoranda relating to the construction and dimensions of basket boats.

Difficulties of Supply.

The difficulties of supply with which the General had to contend will be understood from the following extract from a letter he wrote to Major Shawe on 24th August:—" Twelve days have elapsed since I took Ahmednagar; and in that time I have marched nearly fifty miles, and have crossed the river Godavery: having settled our conquests south of that river. I hope to get on equally well in the future; but I tremble for the want of the common country grains for the followers and the cattle. . . . The country is completely exhausted, the villages depopulated, and large tracts of excellent land uncultivated. Indeed, I believe, that these facts are the principal causes of Holkar's keeping aloof from the confederates. We have lost such numbers of cattle by the length of our march and starvation, that we have none to carry grain for our followers, and I learn that we have lost vast numbers of those coming from General Stuart's army; I believe nearly one half of the whole number.

" However, large numbers of dealers attend the camp, who came with me from Mysore; and if the Nizam's servants afford us any supplies, we shall still do tolerably well. I have plenty for the troops, and it may be depended upon that I will do everything in my power to procure what is wanted for the followers."

Wellesley's Movements.

Wellesley's movements in this campaign have been described as complicated, though skilful. Skilful indeed they were, following every manœuvre of the enemy, yet a study of the map and of the British General's correspondence shows that his movements were exceedingly simple until after the battle of Assaye, when it becomes more difficult to follow them. On August 26th, he wrote to Colonel Murray:—" Since the beginning of the war Colonel Stevenson has been exposed, single-handed, to the united armies of Sindhia and the Raja of Berar. Not a Mahratta horseman has been able to show himself in the Nizam's territories, and Colonel Stevenson, on the 23rd, played the Mahratta trick upon them of cutting off some of their supplies." On the same day he wrote to Stevenson:—"I think it capital that you should have played their own game on the Mahrattas and should have been the first to cut off the supplies going to their camp."

The Mahrattas Cross the Ajanta Pass.

Nevertheless the Mahratta Chiefs, taking advantage of Stevenson's absence to the east, entered the Nizam's territories with their horse only on the 24th August, pouring like a torrent over the Ajanta Ghaut, and spread their Pindaris* over the country, concentrating their main force in the direction of Jalna. Wellesley now advanced to Aurangabad, and from thence moved south to the Godavery, and kept along that river in order to prevent the enemy from crossing it and carrying out their declared intention of marching on the city of Hyderabad, which lay some 250 miles to the south-east. It is interesting to find him writing on the 28th August:—"We were never in better marching trim, notwithstanding all our losses by rain, etc. The horses of the cavalry and the cattle in general are in excellent condition."

King Collins.

On the 29th, having arrived within a few miles of the city of Aurangabad, the General proceeded to that place in order to hold a conference with Colonel Collins, the late British Resident at Sindhia's court. An officer who accompanied him wrote:—"On reaching the tent of the Resident we were unexpectedly received with a salute of artillery, for such was the state maintained by this representative of John Company (known in Bengal by the nickname of King Collins), that he had a brigade of field-pieces, worked by native artillerymen, attached to his escort. In front of a noble suite of tents, which might have served for the Great Moghul, we were received by an insignificant little, old-looking man, dressed in an old-fashioned military coat, white breeches, sky-blue silk stockings, and large glaring

* Appendix VI. The Pindaris.

buckles to his shoes, having his highly-powdered wig, from which depended a pig-tail of no ordinary dimensions, surmounted by a small round black silk hat, ornamented by a single black ostrich feather, looking not altogether unlike a monkey dressed up for Bartholomew Fair. There was, however, a fire in his small black eye, shooting out from beneath a large, shaggy, pent-house brow, which more than counterbalanced the ridicule that his first appearance naturally excited. After the usual compliments, the principals retired into an inner tent, where matters not to be entrusted to vulgar ears were discussed. But the last words uttered by the little man, as they came forth from the tent, I well recollect. 'I tell you, General, as to their cavalry, you may ride over them wherever you meet them; but their infantry and guns will astonish you.' As, in riding homewards we amused ourselves, the General among the rest, in cutting jokes at the expense of 'little King Collins,' we little thought how true his words would prove."

Capture of Jalna.

Meanwhile Stevenson, advancing from Jafarabad, stormed and took the fort of Jalna* on the 2nd September and during the next few days made night attacks on several of the enemy's camps, and forced him to retire in a northerly direction. Wellesley at the same time moved northwards, and checked the enemy's movements to the south, forcing him towards the Ajanta Hills. Sindhia had in the meantime been joined by his infantry and heavy guns, and the whole of the strength of the two Mahratta Chieftains was now concentrated south of the Ajanta Pass near Bokardhan.

Advance on Bokardhan.

On September 21st Wellesley's and Stevenson's forces had converged to within twelve miles of each other, north of Jalna, and on that date the two British Commanders met and concerted a plan to attack the enemy's camp, simultaneously on the morning of the 24th. They marched on the 22nd, Stevenson by the western route by Husainabad and Wellesley round the low flat-topped hills between Badnapur and

* Jalna, which was then in Sindhia's possession, was handed over to the Nizam. It was a Cantonment of the Hyderabad Subsidiary Force and of the Hyderabad Contingent for nearly a hundred years, and was abandoned on the break-up of the latter force in 1903. The fort, battered by Stevenson's guns, still stands in a state of ruin.

Jalna. The enemy was reported to be at Bokardhan. Acting on this information, and hearing that the Mahrattas were moving off, Wellesley moved forward from Nalni, where he left his stores and baggage on Friday, September 23rd, intending to arrive within convenient striking distance of the enemy on the following day. But the intelligence related to the district and not to the town of Bokardhan, and, arriving on the ridge beyond Nalni, the British Commander suddenly found himself in the presence of the hostile armies, which were drawn up on a tongue of land enclosed by the Juah and Kailna rivers, their left resting on the village of Assaye, their right stretching towards Bokardhan.

Battle of Assaye.

It may at first sight appear that the duties of reconnoitring had been neglected by the Cavalry, but it was impossible to view the enemy's position until the main body of the army was brought up, as they were always surrounded by immense bodies of horse. Thus it was that, Stevenson being at a distance, Wellesley found himself called upon to face the alternative of attacking an enemy over 50,000 strong with a force of some 6,000 men, or else retreating to await Stevenson's arrival. To have retreated would have been to bring upon him a swarm of 40,000 Mahratta Horse, who would in all probability have destroyed his small force. With a determination that was a flash of genius worthy of a great commander, he at once resolved to attack, at the same instant perceiving the best mode of carrying out his intention.

The Enemy's Position.

The enemy's left and centre were composed of infantry drawn up in several lines, in front of which their guns stood ready to vomit forth death upon the assailants. A dense mass of horse was arrayed upon the right, stretching away towards the west as far as the eye could reach. In front of the hostile position the Kailna* river, with steep banks cut into by innumerable fissures, ran deep and swift, swollen by the rain that had recently fallen. Beyond it, at a distance varying

* This is incorrectly printed Kaitna in the Wellington Despatches—and the error is repeated in all previous accounts of the battle. The present writer ascertained the correct name on the spot.

from half a mile to a mile of undulating ground, flowed the Juah river, on the hither bank of which stood the village of Assaye. But between the hamlets of Pipalgaon and Warur on the Kailna river was a ford, which the enemy had neglected to occupy, betrayed at once to the eagle eye of the British Commander by the position of the villages on either bank. He at once perceived that he could turn the Mahratta left, forcing them to change front and to confine their line to a narrow space where superiority of numbers would give them but little advantage. Covering his left front with his cavalry, and favoured by the ground, Wellesley carried out this operation successfully, the Mysore and Moghul cavalry keeping in check two large masses of the enemy's horse which had crossed the Kailna.* Sindhia at once presented a new front, with his left resting on Assaye, and his right on the Kailna river. This new front was one huge battery, supported by infantry, the big guns being especially thick about the village. At the commencement of the action the British artillery was almost overwhelmed, nearly all the bullocks and men employed to drag the guns being shot down and the General's orderly dragoon had the top of his head carried off by a cannon ball, but the body being left kept its seat by the valise, holsters, and other appendages of a cavalry saddle, it was some time before the terrified horse could rid himself of the ghastly burden. Wellesley intended first to attack and drive in the enemy's right, before advancing on Assaye. But Colonel Orrock, the officer commanding the picquets which as usual led the advance, exceeded his instructions, and led his men into a terrific fire, straight upon the enemy's left. The gallant 74th followed the picquets and engaged in a fierce struggle with the enemy, losing heavily from artillery fire, which burst upon them with a storm from the village of Assaye, and with difficulty maintaining the unequal contest, as they

Wellesley's Tactics.

* An officer who was present wrote :—"I was particularly struck at this time with the beauty of the line formed by our cavalry, and with the steady movement of the column of infantry, so unlike the usual order of march. It seemed as if each individual felt that this was to be the test of discipline against numbers, and that nothing but the utmost steadiness and determination could make up for the appalling disparity of force, of which, from the view we had of the enemy's army, every one had an opportunity of judging. Not a whisper was heard through the ranks; our nerves were wound up to the proper pitch, and every one seemed to know and to feel that here was no alternative but death or victory."

were at the same time charged by the enemy's horse. Fortunately, the British cavalry was at hand, and by a timely charge saved the remains of the picquets and the 74th from destruction, but suffered so severely from the cannonade that it was subsequently unable to pursue the flying foe.

When the whole line was ready to advance, Wellesley gave the command and, as graphically related in Stewart's Sketches of the Highlanders, "this order was received with cheers and instantly obeyed. It was soon perceived, however, that the leading battalion, composed of the picquets, had diverged from the line of direction, which made it necessary to halt the whole front line. This was a critical moment. The troops had got to the summit of a swell of the ground which had previously sheltered their advance; and the enemy, believing that the halt proceeded from timidity, redoubled their efforts, firing chain shot and every missile they could bring to bear on the line. General Wellesley, dreading the influence of this momentary halt on the ardour of the troops, rode up in front of a native battalion, and, taking off his hat, cheered them in their own language and gave the word to advance again. This was received with cheers, and instantly put in execution. When the 78th was within 150 yards of the enemy they advanced to quick time and charged. At this instant some European officers in the service of the enemy were observed to mount their horses and fly. The infantry, thus deserted by their officers, broke and fled with such speed that few were overtaken by the bayonet; but the gunners held firm to their guns; many were bayonetted in the act of loading, and none gave way till closed upon by the bayonet."

Defeat of the Mahrattas.

It was not until the British centre and left came into action, and defeated the enemy's right, that the Mahrattas were driven from Assaye, and rolled back across the Juah stream, which now ran red with blood. A charge by the cavalry, headed by the 19th Light Dragoons, whose brave leader, Colonel Maxwell, fell in the hour of victory, completed the discomfiture of the enemy, who fled without halting for twelve miles from the field of battle, leaving 1,200 dead and many wounded, including Jadun Singh, Sindhia's principal minister, who died a few days later. Sindhia's regular infantry, to the number of 12,000, was present in this action. It was disciplined by European officers, but most of these had retired with the adventurer Perron. Only one European officer was found dead on the field. Among the trophies that fell to the victors were 7 stand of colours, 7 brass howitzers, 69 brass guns, and 22 iron guns. The victory was dearly bought, the casualties* including British—23 officers and 170 men killed, 31 officers and 442 men wounded, and 4 men missing; Natives—8 officers and 222 men killed, 28 officers and 668 men wounded, and 14 men missing. The 74th alone had 401 of all ranks killed and wounded. In one company of the picquets, composed of one officer and fifty men, all fell except six men. Wellesley himself had one horse shot under him and one piked and almost all the staff had their horses killed and wounded. Colonel Welsh relates that "Captain A. B. Campbell,† of the 74th, Brigade Major to the

Casualties.

* See Appendix IX D. There appears to be some confusion as to the casualties at the battle of Assaye. In the Wellington Despatches the following return is given:—

Europeans.

	F. O.	Cap.	Sub.	Serg.	Drum.	R. & F.	Total.	Horses.
Killed	1	6	7	9	..	141	164	77
Wounded	3	6	20	33	6	343	411	3
Missing	..	..	..	..	..	8	8	..

Natives.

	Sub.	Jem.	Hav.	Trum.	R. & F.	Total.	Horses.
Killed	5	3	13	..	224	245	228
Wounded	12	16	39	6	1,138	1,211	75
Missing	..	..	..	..	18	18	1

But a General Order of the Governor-General, 30th October, gives the names of 21 officers and 1 volunteer (Mr. Tew, who had been recommended for a commission for his conduct at Ahmednagar) killed.

It seems probable that the above is taken from an erroneous statement in Colonel Welsh's *Reminiscences.*

† Colonel Welsh, however, was not present at the battle, and appears to have made a mistake in the identity of the officer, who was Lieutenant Colin Campbell of the 78th; afterwards General Sir Colin Campbell.

Before leaving India Sir A. Wellesley wrote to Colonel Shawe as follows regarding this officer:—

"Upon my departure from hence, I am exceedingly anxious about the fate of my Brigade-Major, Lieutenant Colin Campbell, of the 78th Regiment, and my aide-de-camp Lieutenant Close, of the 4th Regiment of Native Cavalry, particularly the former, who has been with me much longer, and from whom I have received much assistance.

"You are aware that he is the nephew of Colonel Campbell, and he has already interested the Governor-General in his favour by the accounts which he has laid before him of the losses of his family in the sea and land services. To my certain knowledge he lost two brothers in the campaign against the Southern Polygars, and a brother and a cousin (Colonel Campbell's son) in the battle of Assaye. I did not know him by name when I saw him distinguish himself in the storm of Ahmednagar, and I immediately appointed him my Brigade Major; and in the battle of Assaye he had either two or three horses shot under him, and ever since he has rendered me most important service."

General, who had lost an arm in the Poligar War, and had since broken his other arm at the wrist by a fall at hunting, was in the thickest of the action with his bridle in his teeth and a sword in his mutilated hand, dealing destruction around him. He came off unhurt, though one of the enemy very nearly transfixed him with a bayonet, which actually pierced his saddle in the charge." Among the killed was Captain Mackay, 4th Madras Cavalry, Commissary of cattle in the army. He had previously asked permission of the General to lead his squadron in case of an action, and had been positively refused. Instead, however, of remaining with the baggage, he risked his commission and lost his life.

A Gallant Officer.

Regarding the conduct of the troops, the General wrote to the Governor-General :—" I cannot write in too strong terms of the conduct of the troops. They advanced in the best order, and with the greatest steadiness under a most destructive fire, against a body of infantry far superior in number who appeared determined to contend with them to the last, and who were driven from their guns only by the bayonet, and notwithstanding the numbers of the enemy's cavalry, and the repeated demonstrations they made of an intention to charge, they were kept at a distance by our infantry."

Conduct of the Troops.

In a letter to Major John Malcolm he said with regard to the Mahrattas :—" Their infantry is the best I have ever seen in India, excepting our own; and they and their equipments far surpass Tipu's. I assure you that their fire was so heavy that I much doubted at one time whether I should be able to induce our troops to advance, and all agree that the battle was the fiercest that has ever been seen in India. Our troops behaved admirably. Our sepoys astonished me." The number of British troops engaged in the battle is generally given as about 4,500, but an examination of the returns indicates that there cannot have been much less than 6,000 effective rank and file alone.

The Native Madras Army at this time possessed a fine spirit. Sir John Malcolm related that "a staff officer, after the battle of Assaye, saw a

Brave Sepoys.

number of the Mahommedans of the 8th Regiment assembled for a funeral. He asked them whom they were about to inter. They mentioned the names of five commissioned and non-commissioned officers of a very distinguished family in the corps. "We are going to put these brothers into one grave," said one of the party. The officer, who had been well acquainted with the individuals who had been slain, expressed his regret and was about to offer some consolation to the survivors, but he was stopped by one of the men. "There is no occasion," he said, "for such feelings or expressions; these men were sepoys; the Government they served will protect their children, who will soon fill the ranks they lately occupied."

A Tactical Error.

The loss in this hard-fought contest would probably have been much less but for the mistake of the officer commanding the advanced picquets, regarding which Wellesley wrote :—

"When the enemy changed their position they threw their left to Assaye, in which village they had some infantry, and it was surrounded by cannon. As soon as I saw that, I directed the officer commanding the picquets to keep out of shot from that village; instead of that, he led directly upon it; the 74th, which were on the right of the first line, followed the picquets,* and the great loss we sustained was in these two bodies. Another evil which resulted from this mistake, was the necessity of introducing the cavalry into the cannonade and the action long before it was time; by which that corps lost many men, and its unity and efficiency, that I intended to bring forward in a close pursuit at the heel of the day. But it was necessary to bring forward the cavalry to save the remains of the 74th and the picquets, which would otherwise have been destroyed. Another evil resulting from it was, that we had no reserve and a party of stragglers cut up our wounded; and straggling infantry, who had pretended to be dead, turned their guns upon our backs. However, I do not wish to cast any reflection upon the officer who led the picquets. I lament the consequences of his mistake, but I must

* The picquets were furnished by details from each corps, and generally formed the advance guard.

acknowledge that it was not possible for a man to lead a body into a hotter fire than he did the picquets on that day against Assaye."

Regarding the General's conduct in the fight, Mountstuart Elphinstone said :—" It is nothing to say of him that he exposed himself on all occasions, and behaved with perfect indifference in the hottest fires (for I did not see a European do otherwise, nor do I believe people ever do), but in the most anxious and important moments he gave his orders as clearly and coolly as if he had been inspecting a corps or manœuvring at a review."

The Village of Assaye.

The village of Assaye,* remote from all sounds of war and far from the busy hum of the life of cities, now slumbers peacefully on the bank of the Juah stream amid the mouldering ruins of its fort. No monument marks the last resting place of the forgotten dead. Only the rough leaden and hammered iron bullets turned up by the plough of the husbandman bear witness to the great battle which took place over a hundred years ago on that little strip of land between the Kailna and the Juah Rivers.

Flight of the Mahrattas.

It was near nightfall when the battle closed, and Wellesley's force was in no condition to follow up the victory. After the battle of Assaye the scattered Mahratta hosts fled towards the north, halting for the night twelve miles from the field of action, and continuing their flight beyond the hills into Berar next day on hearing of Stevenson's advance. But it was not until the 26th September that the latter was able to pursue, as his surgeons were required to attend the wounded, many of whom were not dressed for nearly a week, for want of the necessary number of medical men. The enemy continued their flight towards Barhanpur in a state of complete demoralisation. Sindhia's infantry was entirely disorganised, the only part of it that escaped being of the Begum Sumru's brigade with the baggage, and perhaps one of Pohlman's battalions. At Bar-

The Enemy's Recovery.

* The present writer encamped at Assaye on Christmas Day, 1898. The village is small and insignificant, with few inhabitants and a small mud fort tenanted by a colony of pigeons. The people had traditions of a great battle, in which 100,000 horse took part, and one of them produced some bullets, many of which are still found on the battlefield.

hanpur they were reinforced by two or three fresh corps of infantry and some guns; then marching westward along the Tapti, they turned southward, threatening to re-enter Hyderabad territory by the Kesari Pass.

Capture of Asirgarh.

Wellesley marched to Ajanta on the 30th September, and then to meet this new threatened invasion moved towards Aurangabad and encamped at Pulmarhi some thirty miles north of that place on the 11th October, while he despatched Stevenson, equipped for a siege, to invest the fort of Asirgarh. He was thus in a position to act against the enemy should they attempt to cross either the Ajanta or Kesari Pass, while Stevenson's march would draw off a portion of their forces to the north. In his advice to Stevenson as to his tactics in case of meeting with the enemy he said, "Do not attack their position, because they always take up such as are confoundedly strong and difficult of access; for which the banks of the numerous rivers and *nullahs* afford them every facility. Do not remain in your own position, however strong it may be, or however well you may have intrenched it; but when you shall hear that they are on their march to attack you, secure your baggage, and move out of your camp. You will find them in the common disorder of march; they will not have time to form, which being but half disciplined troops, is necessary for them. At all events you will have the advantage of making the attack on ground which they will not have chosen for the battle; a part of their troops only will be engaged; and it is possible that you will gain an easy victory. Indeed, according to this mode, you might choose the field of battle yourself some days before, and might meet them upon that very ground."

Hearing of Stevenson's advance upon Asirgarh, Sindhia separated from his ally with the intention of impeding the operation; whereupon Wellesley marched back to Ajanta on the 18th October, and next day descended the pass to Ferdapur to arrest Sindhia's progress.

In the meantime Stevenson entered Barhanpur without opposition on October 16th, and then invested Asirgarh, took the *pettah* on the 18th, with a loss of two killed and five wounded, and, having erected a battery against the fort, gained possession of it by capitulation of the garrison on the 21st.

After the capture of Barhanpur, 16 of the enemy's European officers surrendered to Colonel Stevenson, including Colonel Dupont, Captain Mercier, and Captain Mann.

In the fort at Asirgarh some property was found regarding which we find the General publishing a memorandum as follows in a General Order of 5th January 1804:—" Major-General Wellesley is very desirous of having some dogs which were found in Asirgarh and also some fowling pieces taken there; and he will be much obliged to any gentleman who may be in possession of those dogs or fowling pieces, if they will send them in to him. The full value shall be returned."

NOTE.—Colonel Welsh gives the number killed at the battle of Assaye as European officers, 23, European soldiers, 198; Natives, 428. The officers killed were—*19th Dragoons*: Lieutenant-Colonel Maxwell and Captain Boyle; *4th Cavalry* : Captain Hugh Mackay; *5th Cavalry* : Lieutenant Bonomie; *7th Cavalry* : Captain M'Gregor; *Artillery* : Captains Fowler and Steel, and Lieutenant Griffiths; *74th Regiment*: Captains Aytone, McLeod, Dyce, and Maxwell, Lieutenant J. Campbell, M. Campbell, and Lorn Campbell, R. Neilson, James Grant, Morrison Kerman, and M'Murdo. Volunteer Moore. *78th Regiment*: Lieutenant Douglas. *2nd Native Infantry* : Lieutenant Brown.

Of 1,200 horses which the cavalry took into action, 325 were killed and 113 wounded.

CHAPTER V.

THE MAHRATTA WAR—contd.

Wellesley's Marches.

On the 24th October, while at Ferdapur, Wellesley heard that the Raja of Berar had moved southward, and re-entered the Nizam's territory by the Kesari Pass from Khandesh, and was marching towards the Godavery. The British General at once ascended the Ajanta Pass, and marching 120 miles in eight days, succeeded in saving all his convoys and in driving the enemy back into Berar. On the 25th he was back at Ajanta, and next day wrote from Pahlud :—

"Since the battle of Assaye I have been like a man who fights with one hand and defends himself with the other. With Colonel Stevenson's corps I have acted offensively, and have taken Asirgarh; and with my own, I have covered his operations, and defended the territories of the Nizam and the Peshwa. In doing this, I have made some terrible marches, but I have been remarkably fortunate; first, in stopping the enemy when they intended to pass to the southward, through the Casserbarry (Kesari) Ghaut; and, afterwards, by a rapid march to the northward, in stopping Sindhia when he was moving to interrupt Colonel Stevenson's operations against Asseerghur, in which he would otherwise undoubtedly have succeeded; and I think that, in a day or two, I shall turn Ragojee Bhoonslah (the Raja of Berar), who had passed through to the southward. At all events I am in time to prevent him from doing any mischief. I think we are in great style to be able to act at all on the offensive in this quarter; but it is only done by the celerity of our movements, and by acting on the offensive or defensive with either corps, according to their situation and that of the enemy."

Pursuit of the Berar Raja.

These masterly movements were, as he predicted. entirely successful. Making a few rapid marches to the south, he arrived at Aurangabad on the 29th, and on the 31st was tantalised all the morning by the sight of the enemy's camp, pitched at a distance of 20 miles. But when he arrived at a distance of 6 or 7 miles of them, they went off in a southerly direction. The enemy had a vast quantity of baggage and a number of tents, and from fear of the British moved his camp five times between the 29th and 31st. On the latter date the Bhonsla detached a body of 5,000 horse to endeavour to intercept a convoy of 14,000 bullocks which was marching to join the troops on the frontier. The convoy was protected by three companies 3rd Madras Infantry with two 3-pounders, under Captain Baynes, together with 400 Mysore Horse, a company from the Subsidiary Force, and two companies from Hyderabad. They had marched from the Godavery in the early morning, and had reached Ambad at 2 P.M. when they were attacked. The enemy advanced repeatedly as though to charge, but were each time driven off by the fire of the guns. They continued throwing rockets until dark, when they retired, having suffered considerable loss. Captain Baynes had only a few men killed and wounded, and a couple of hundred bullocks driven off. As the General wrote, this successful defence afforded "another instance of what can be done by disciplined infantry, determined to do their duty against very superior numbers of cavalry." And in a General Order, dated the 2nd November, in thanking Captain Baynes and his troops for their services, he remarked on the ability of infantry, who preserve their order and reserve their fire, to repel numerous bodies of cavalry. It was the convoy under Captain Baynes which occasioned some delay on the part of the British General, who made some interesting remarks on the subject in a letter to his brother Henry in January 1804. Wellesley wrote:—"The necessity of taking care of this convoy was unfortunate. If I had not been under the necessity of directing the movements of the troops in such a manner as to protect it, at the same time that I pushed the Raja, I should have had it in my power to have destroyed him between the 29th and 31st October. But all the subsequent solid operations of the war

Attack on a Convoy.

depended on the arrival of that convoy,* and it was more important to secure it, than to gain a victory over a body of horse; in the attempt to obtain which I might have failed, and then I should have lost the convoy. The troops had now been in march nearly every day from the beginning of October, and it was necessary to give them some rest. Accordingly I left the Raja to go off to the eastward, towards Berar, and I halted till the 4th in the neighbourhood of Ambad.''

The convoy joined him in safety at Chichkhera on the 1st November and reached Colonel Stevenson at Balapur in Berar on the 25th. The Raja of Berar now fled eastward along the Godavery ''in a violent hurry'', as Wellesley wrote from Chicholi on the 6th November, and turning northwards, re-entered his own territory by the Rajura Pass, south of Akola. Following on his footsteps, the British General crossed the Rajura Pass on the 25th November and marched northwards into Berar.

Opposition of Hyderabad Officials.

In carrying out these operations the British General had not only the enemy but many difficulties to contend with. He had to cover the approach of his own convoys from the south, whilst from his allies he received no assistance, and frequently experienced opposition. The Government of Hyderabad was then no less effete and corrupt than that of the Mahratta States; and many of the officials were in league with the enemy. Although the very existence of the State depended upon the support of the British arms, obstruction of every kind was offered to the British General, who wrote to the Resident at Hyderabad in a tone of bitter remonstrance on the 25th October:—

''It is very obvious that His Highness the Soubah (the Nizam) is not aware of the benefits which he derives from his alliance with the British Government. In fact his Government could not stand, and would not have stood one day without the powerful support which it has received. The war in which the British Government is engaged is in support of the Government of the Soubah of

* The incident may be compared with the loss of the great British convoy during Lord Roberts' advance into the Orange Free State in 1900.

the Deccan. The immediate cause of the war was the refusal of the Mahratta Chiefs to remove from His Highness' territories, and the large armies which they had collected for the purpose of invasion."

The particular acts of obstruction on the part of the Nizam's officials were detailed in a letter to the Nizam and included (i) the refusal of the Killadar of Daulatabad to admit the sick and wounded of the British troops engaged in the battle of Assaye, on General Wellesley's requisition ; (ii) the firing by the Killadar of Badnapur on a British convoy; (iii) the refusal of Raja Sukrudar to allow the sale of grain, in the district under his charge, to British troops ; (iv) the refusal by the Killadar of Dharur to give protection under the guns of his fort to a convoy coming to the army.

The Nizam's Contingent.

Nor were the troops of the Nizam's contingent,* provided by our so-called ally under the provisions of the treaty of 1800, of any service to the British. The elements of which it was composed were so inefficient that it formed more of an incubus than an auxiliary, and it has even been related that while the British army was fighting the battle of Assaye in order to relieve Hyderabad territory of invaders, the Nizam's troops were employed in plundering the British Camp.

Marches of the British Army.

The marches of the British Army during October and November were among the most remarkable recorded in history, carried out as they were in pursuit of a mobile enemy, through a difficult country and encumbered with a heavy artillery train. Wellesley himself wrote:—"Marches, such as I have made in this war, were never known or thought of before." Towards the end of October the British General suffered severely from fever, but his despatches show that his work never ceased, and his energies were in no wise relaxed. With

* In view of the circumstances, the following extract from the Berar Gazetteer is interesting:—The Duke of Wellington, were he now alive, might be amused to learn that the Nizam gets from the present generation of Berar natives all the credit of the campaign. Well-informed people would tell him that the Mahrattas were driven out in 1830 by the Nizam, whose officers are distinguished in the Despatches for their sloth and incapacity for anything but plundering. But the country was held by the Nizam up to 1853, and half a century's incessant bragging seems to have overpowered the true knowledge possessed by contemporaries.

regard to the order of the march, the following from the *Journal of Sir Jasper Nicolls* is interesting :—

"The *general* was beat at half past four, the *assembly* at half past five, and we marched immediately after. Since the 8th September General Wellesley has left off the usual mode of announcing the march or halt of the army in order to prevent the enemy from having intelligence of the intended marches of this Division. At present no person can certainly foretell whether the army is to move or not, except when the General has positively determined that he will not, and then he acquaints the heads of departments that they may profit of the time.

"A body of Mysore Horse, about four hundred, leads the column of march ; this, at some distance, is followed by the cavalry ; the new picquets of infantry march in their rear, then the line of infantry followed by the pack, store and provision carts ; the guns of the allies close the line of carriages, the ammunition and park bullocks follow them, and the rear-guard, consisting of the old picquets, a squadron of cavalry, which moves on the reverse flank, and another body of four hundred Mysoreans, close the line.

"Detachments of pioneers attend the leading divisions of the cavalry advanced guard, the line, and the park. Guides are sent every morning before the assembly beating to the heads of the cavalry, advanced, and rear-guard. The baggage is ordered to be kept on the reverse flank entirely. The horsemen of the allies march on either flank, as most agreeable to their leaders. The Brigadier of Cavalry is ordered to halt whenever he may exceed the distance of three quarters of a mile in front of the infantry ; the long roll for a halt is to be beat by any corps on the march which may by accident be so long stopped as to occasion a break of one hundred yards ; this to be repeated from front to rear by every corps ; and when ready to move again the taps are passed, as before along the line which proceeds."

Intelligence.

This, and another extract from the same diary, which may be given, illustrates the care and attention of the Commander to all details on the march. "Here it may not be out of place to mention that, immediately on our coming to our ground each day, the neighbouring villagers are sent for, and the Captain of the Guides, after comparing their accounts, takes down all the necessary information relative to the roads to the front and flanks, where and in what quantity water is procurable; this is the main object of the enquiry, unless where Ghauts are to be passed over, or rivers forded; the latter, however, rarely occurs. After the camp has been pitched and the men been refreshed, the officers of pioneers examine the adjoining roads, and take care that a passage to the front and one to each flank are prepared, at least for the distance of one mile."

Convoys.

The difficulty of protecting convoys from the south against the depredations of the numerous Mahratta Horse has already been referred to, in the account of the attack on the convoy in charge of Captain Baynes.

On another occasion, Colonel Welsh relates, "A company of the 12th Regiment Native Infantry under Lieutenant Morgan, having been detached from camp to proceed to the Carnatic, in charge of drafts from various Native corps in our army, for new corps raising at Madras; along with this party, and taking advantage of their escort, were Captain O'Donnell and Lieutenant Bryant of the 2nd Native Cavalry, proceeding to join their corps with the force under General Campbell. They had reached the vicinity of a village called Kurjet Koriagaum, about seventy miles from Ahmadnagar, when they were suddenly attacked by a body of about one thousand five hundred men, the former garrison of Ahmadnagar, of whom at least one-third were Arabs. Captain O'Donnell, who, though small, was a truly gallant fellow, immediately assumed the command and led on his motley band, amounting to not more than one hundred men, to the charge. Lieutenant Bryant, a very powerful man, first saved the life of O'Donnell, who had snapped his pistol at the leader of the Arabs, and was about to be cut down by him, when Bryant put him to death; and then attacking their colour-bearer, cut him down also, and seized their standard. At this moment the enemy's cavalry appeared, and Captain O'Donnell drew off his little party into the village; but so closely were they pursued that they were forced to take post in a large choultry, from whence the enemy could not dislodge them. Here the extraordinary courage and strength of Bryant, if it did not entirely save their lives, at least conduced to their preservation from famine. He harangued the Sepoys in broken English, not knowing a word of any native language, and continually sallied out with a few volunteers in search of food, and as regularly killed some of their opponents. Amongst other feats, having broken his sword on some Arab's skull, the first day, he seized a musket and bayonet, which he always used afterwards; and so dexterous was he with this new weapon, that he frequently put the bayonet through one man, and knocked a second down with the butt-end. One day seeing a leader mounted on a beautiful mare, he singled him out for his prey; and running him through the body, seized the mare by the bridle, and bore her off in triumph. On this mare he rode all the time he remained in the Mahratta country. Such a man at such a season, if he was mad, as some asserted, was worth a dozen of sober, plodding fellows who, calculating difficulties, would have sat despairing at home, rather than run such imminent risks on every occasion. Of the hundred men collected and blockaded in this spot, all the native officers behaved ill and would have persuaded the men to capitulate, had not many of them taken courage by the behaviour of Lieutenant Bryant, to them a perfect stranger, and by the conduct of the other two European officers; who, though neither possessing sufficient bodily strength to cope single-handed with the Arabs, always showed a proper spirit when their exertions were necessary.

"Matters were in this state when Captain Lucas with four companies and two guns made his appearance and relieved them without striking a blow, for the enemy had withdrawn, aware of his approach."

Arrangement with Sindhia.

Towards the middle of November Sindhia made overtures of peace, and Wellesley, in an agreement concluded with his envoy at Rajura on the 23rd of that month, assented to the cessation of hostilities with him, provided he would keep at a distance of at least 40 miles to the eastward of Ellichpur.

He thus hoped to create dissension between the allied chiefs.

Pursuit of the Bhonsla.

But the Mahratta armies again united between Colonel Stevenson and Gawilgarh, and it was necessary to defeat them before the siege of the fort, for which Stevenson was equipped, could be undertaken.

Still pursuing the Bhonsla northwards through Berar, the British Commander was joined by Stevenson on November 29th at Patholi, near which place the latter had halted on his way to the investment of the fort of Gawilgarh. It was not until the afternoon of that day, after a march of 26 miles, that Wellesley's long pursuit ended, and the British army came into contact with the enemy, who were drawn up on a broad plain in front of the village of Argaum. This plain was intersected by innumerable watercourses, which drain the southern slopes of the Satpura Hills, and empty themselves into the Purna River. Approaching Argaum from the south, one passes through an area of almost unbroken cultivation, perhaps one of the richest cotton and wheat-growing districts in all India. But in those days it is probable that the principal product of the country was millet, which, growing to the height of 7 or 8 feet, would completely conceal the movements of an armed force. Although

Battle of Argaum.

late in the day, Wellesley, with his usual determination, resolved to attack at once, and advanced in one column, the British Cavalry leading, in a direction nearly parallel to that of the enemy's line. Emerging

Panic of Madras Troops.

from the cover into the open plain, two Madras Infantry Regiments, and the native portion of the picquets which were leading, came under the sudden fire of fifty pieces of cannon, and being seized with panic, broke and fled. Fortunately the British General was close at hand, and succeeded in rallying these regiments, which had fought so well at Assaye, whilst the supporting regiments passed through their disordered ranks, and advanced to the attack. With regard to this incident Wellesley wrote:—"I am convinced that if I had not been near them to rally them and restore the battle, we should have lost the day."

An officer who was present relates that "the General, who was close to the spot under a tree giving orders to the brigadiers, perceiving what had happened, immediately stepped out in front, hoping by his presence to restore the confidence of the troops; but, seeing that this did not produce the desired effect, he mounted his horse and rode up to the retreating battalions; when, instead of losing his temper, upbraiding them, and endeavouring to force them back to the spot from which they had fled, as most people would have done, he quietly ordered the officers to lead their men under cover of the village, and then to rally and get them into order as quickly as possible. This being done, he put the column again in motion, and leading these very same runaways round the other side of the village, formed them on the very spot he originally intended them to occupy, the remainder of the column following, and prolonging the line to the right.

"This was at once a masterpiece of generalship, and a signal display of that intuitive knowledge of human nature, only to be found in great minds. There is not one man in a million who, on seeing the troops turn their backs, would not have endeavoured to bring them again to the spot from which they retreated; in this attempt it is more than probable that he would have failed; and in that case the panic would most likely have extended down the column, producing the most disastrous consequences. As it was, the retrograde movement was mistaken by all, but the troops who actually gave way, for a countermarch. Indeed, it is very probable that, owing to the conduct of the general on this occasion, even the runaways might have flattered themselves into this belief, and thus have been saved from that sense of degradation which might have had a serious effect on their subsequent conduct during the day ... This circumstance produced in my mind the first clear idea of that genius which has since been so mainly instrumental, by its conduct and example, in achieving the deliverance of Europe. From the first moment I saw General Wellesley I formed a high opinion of him; but from this time forth I looked up to him with a degree of respect bordering on veneration. As fast as each battalion came into line, the General ordered the men to lie down." . . "While the General was thus employed in restoring order and forming his division, Colonel Stevenson* had begun to deploy to the left of the village; and by the time the General could with safety leave the right wing, this movement was effected. He was much pleased with the appearance of Colonel Stevenson's division in line; and no doubt a little pleased with himself also; for in riding back to the right wing he said to me, 'Did you ever see a battle restored like this?'"

The Enemy's Position.

"'The enemy's infantry and guns were on the left of their centre, with a body of cavalry on their left. Sindhia's army, consisting of one very heavy body of cavalry,† was on the right, having upon its right a body of Pindaris and other light troops. Their line extended above 5 miles, having in their rear the village and extensive gardens and enclosures of Argaum; and in their front a plain, which, however, was much cut up by watercourses. I formed the army into two lines; the infantry in the first, the cavalry in the second, and supporting the right; and the Moghul‡ and Mysore Cavalry on the left, nearly parallel to that of the enemy; with the right rather advanced, in order to press upon the enemy's left." (Wellesley's Despatch.)

Having made the signal of advance to the infantry, the General rode off to the cavalry, which, being drawn up in two lines on the right, awaited his orders. Putting himself at their head, he advanced against the main body of the enemy's horse, which, supported by a large rocket corps mounted on camels, appeared disposed to await his approach.

Halting the cavalry when within about six hundred yards of the enemy, he directed the galloper-guns to open upon them previously to the charge, which was to be made the moment the guns

* Colonel Stevenson was a brave and able officer who had served with distinction in the Mysore Wars; in the defeat of Dhoondiah Waugh, Wellesley attributed to him "the opportunity which was given of destroying the enemy's army." He was at this time weak and worn out, but this did not prevent his performing his duties in the most efficient manner. Seated on an elephant, he brought his division into action in excellent style, and by the coolness which he displayed under the enemy's fire, for which he was a conspicuous object, he set a gallant example to his troops. He died in 1805, on the voyage to England. Wellesley was god-father to his son, and forwarded Stevenson's interests on every opportunity, thus proving the respect in which he held him.

† His infantry had been practically destroyed at Assaye.

‡ The Nizam's Cavalry, composed of Hyderabad Musalmans of Moghul origin.

produced sufficient effect. The General then rode back to the infantry, which had advanced in beautiful order with all their guns in the intervals. These continued firing during the advance until within about musket-shot of the enemy, when, the charge being sounded, the whole line pushed forward at a rapid pace, and soon drove the enemy from the field.

Arab Charge.

The Arabs* alone, of whom there was a body of about two thousand, showed any fight, and with fierce shouts charged down upon the 74th and 78th Regiments, but were repulsed with terrible slaughter. Sindhia's cavalry attempted a charge against the 6th Madras Infantry on the left of the line, but were driven off, and the entire hostile army fled in disorder. The cavalry pursued for miles, continuing the pursuit by moonlight, and Wellesley wrote that but for an hour lost owing to the panic among the Native Infantry at the commencement of the action not a man would have escaped.† Immense numbers of the enemy were slaughtered, and 38 guns with a large quantity of stores and ammunition left on the field. Many camels, elephants, and standards were captured, and a rich prize was obtained by the seizure of the Bhonsla's jewels, valued at six lakhs of rupees. The Mahrattas were completely dispersed, but Beni Singh, escaping with his infantry, took refuge in the fort of Gawilgarh.

British Losses.

The total British loss amounted to 46 killed, 308 wounded and 7 missing. Of the enemy large numbers were destroyed, including Vittal Punt, who commanded the Bhonsla's cavalry. A picturesque incident is related by Colonel Welsh, who was present. During the action Lieutenant Langlands of the 74th had his leg pierced by a spear thrown by an Arab, who then rushed at him with a sword to complete his con-

A Single Combat.

* Wellesley terms them "Persians" in his despatch.

† The officer already referred to says—"I witnessed on this occasion a curious mode of attack adopted by the old 19th Dragoons, in their pursuit of the native horsemen, whose bodies were so defended either by armour or stuffed coats, that there was no getting a cut at them, while their heads were equally protected by a large turban, with a thick pad depending over the ears and neck. This being the case it became necessary to 'establish a raw' before any wound could be inflicted with the sword. To effect this, therefore, they first gave point at the turban, and, that being knocked off, they had a fair cut at the head."

quest. But Langlands seized the spear, and threw it with so true an aim that he transfixed his opponent, the weapon passing through his body at a few yards' distance. "'All eyes were for an instant turned on the two combatants, when a sepoy of our grenadiers rushed out of the ranks, and, patting the Lieutenant on the back, exclaimed, 'Achcha, Sahib! Achcha Kiya'! Well, Sir! Very well done! Such a ludicrous circumstance, even in the moment of such extreme peril, could not pass unnoticed, and our soldiers all enjoyed a hearty laugh before they concluded the work of death on the remaining ill-fated Arabs."

A Brave Native Officer.

The fine spirit of the native soldiers, so often exhibited since those days, may be illustrated by another anecdote related by Colonel Welsh:—"'Of three Native officers wounded, two died in hospital shortly after; of whom Subadar Ally Cawn, a man so uncommonly diminutive in person that we used to call him the little cock sparrow, was one of the best and bravest soldiers I ever knew. He was at this time far advanced in life, and had earned the respect and esteem of every European officer as well as of every native in the corps. In action he was the life and soul of those around him, and in devoted affection to the service he had no superior. The whole of the flesh and sinews of the hinder part of both thighs being torn away by a round shot, he fell, and could not rise again; but as soon as the action was over he requested his attendants to carry him after us, that his dear European comrades might see him die. We had halted on the field upwards of a mile in front of where he fell, when he arrived, and spoke to us with a firm voice and most affectionate manner; recounted his services, and bade us all adieu. We endeavoured to encourage him by asserting that his wound was not mortal, and that he would yet recover. He said 'he felt assured of the contrary but he was not afraid of death; he had often braved it in the discharge of his duty, and only regretted that he should not be permitted to render further service to his honourable masters.'"

In the despatch reporting this engagement, Wellesley says:—"'The whole advanced in the greatest order; the 74th and 78th regiments were attacked by a large body of Persians,* and all these were destroyed. Scindiah's cavalry charged the 1st Battalion, 6th Regiment, and was repulsed, and their whole line retired in disorder before our troops, leaving in our hands thirty-eight pieces of cannon and all their ammunition. The British cavalry pursued for several miles, destroyed great numbers, and took many elephants and camels, and much baggage. The Mysore and Mogul cavalry joined in the pursuit, and did much mischief, continuing the attack by moonlight." The General was on horseback from six in the morning until midnight.

Effect of British Victories.

The drama was now rapidly drawing to a close. The Mahratta hosts in the Deccan, broken alike in organisation and in spirit, had been scattered to the four winds, whilst the victories of General Lake in the north had not been without their effect in this part of India also. Already the Chieftains began to enquire concerning terms of peace. But the British Commander pursued his way relentlessly towards his goal. He would be satisfied with nothing less than the complete destruction of the hostile power. There still remained one stronghold to subdue, and on this the march of the victorious army was directed. The army arrived at Ellichpur on the 5th December, and a hospital was established there for the wounded.

The Fort of Gawilgarh.

North-west of Ellichpur, crowning one of the highest peaks of the Satpura Range, stands the great fortress of Gawilgarh, the walls of which can on a clear day be plainly distinguished from a distance of many miles. To this fortress there are several approaches. Some three miles from Ellichpur the road to the north-west splits into two branches, both of which lead to Gawilgarh; one, a somewhat circuitous way, through the villages of Dhamangaon and Mota; the other by way of the hamlets of Deogaon and Imlibagh. This path enters the hills through the valley of the Chandrabagha River, a considerable stream in the rainy season, but a dry, stony watercourse during the greater part of the year. There is a third and still more

* These were probably Gusains and Arabs—according to Colonel Welsh.

circuitous road which, winding up the mountains for 16 miles due north of Ghatang, turns abruptly to the west, and, passing through the dense Melghat Forest for another 16 miles, emerges on the plateau north of Gawilgarh. It is probable that this was the route taken by Stevenson, who was detached to attack the fort from the north, whilst Wellesley himself marched by way of Deogaon and Imlibagh, disposing his force to prevent the enemy from escaping to the south.

On the 6th December the villages of Dhamangaon and Deogaon were cleared of the enemy, whose advanced posts were driven into the fort, the following account of which is to be found in the General's despatch:—

"After the battle of Argaum, I determined to lose no time in commencing the siege of Gawilgarh. I accordingly marched on, and arrived at Ellichpur on the 5th instant (December) with both divisions, and halted there the 6th, in order to establish a hospital for the wounded in the battle of Argaum. The fort of Gawilgarh is situated on a range of mountains between the sources of the rivers Poorna and Tapti. It stands in a lofty mountain in that range and consists of one complete inner fort, which fronts to the south where the rock is most steep; and an outer fort which covers the inner to the north-west and north. This outer fort has a third wall, which covers the approach to it from the north by the village of Labada. All these walls are strongly built, and fortified by ramparts and towers.

"The communications with the fort are through three gates; one to the south with the inner fort; one to the north-west with the outer fort; and one to the north with the third wall. The ascent to the first is very long and steep, and is practicable only for men; that to the second is by a road used for the common communications of the garrison with the countries to the southward; but the road passes round the west side of the fort, and is exposed for a great distance to its fire; it is so narrow as to make it impracticable to approach regularly by it, and the rock is scarped on each side. This road also leads no further than to the gate. The communication with the northern gate is direct from the village of Labada, and here the ground is level with that of the fort; but the road to Labada leads through the mountains for about 30 miles from Ellichpur; and it was obvious that the difficulty and labour of moving ordnance and stores to Labada would be very great. However, after making enquiry at Ellichpur, it appeared, both to Colonel Stevenson and me, that this point of attack was, on the whole, the most advantageous, and we accordingly adopted it."

On the 9th December the General reconnoitred the fort, accompanied by his staff and escort. Mountstuart Elphinstone, who had ridden beside him at Assaye, and was with him on this occasion, says:—"There was steep rising ground between us and the fort, behind which we were quite concealed. We dismounted and ascended the rising ground, where from behind some stones the whole north side of the fort suddenly appeared. There was something of surprise and grandeur in this. The wall with battlements, the fort with tents, mosques, and other buildings all burst on our view at once. Between the fort and us on the right some houses were burning; and some of the enemy, who had set them on fire, were still there. They were very near; we had not time to look carefully at the fort. I did not like to look long for fear of drawing a fire on the General. . . In going off the General rode to rising ground to take a look at the fort, and all his troops rode after him. We thought it would draw a fire, but did not. As we went off the fort began firing, but without effect."

Siege Operations.

By dint of great exertions the troops managed to drag some of the guns through the forest, by roads which they themselves made to Labada. This operation occupied five days, and the difficulties that had to be overcome, and the manner in which they were met, will be understood from an anecdote related by Colonel Welsh:—

"We had been one night working very hard at a battery half-way up the hill, and afterwards cleared a road up to it, but no power we possessed could move our iron battering guns above a few hundred yards from the bottom, so steep and rugged was the ascent.

"I was just relieved from working by a fresh party, and enjoying a few moments' rest on some clean straw, when the officer commanding the working party came up to Colonel Wallace, and reported that it was impossible to get the heavy guns up to the battery. The Colonel, who was Brigadier of the Trenches, exclaimed :—'Impossible! hoot mon! it must be done; I've got the order in my pocket!' With such a spirit animating the force it is not surprising that even obstacles which appeared insuperable were overcome. Batteries were erected at Labada, and by the evening of the 14th December a practicable breach was made in the wall of the outer fort.''*

Orders for the Attack.

The following orders were issued for the assault:—

G. M. O. Camp at Deogaon, Thursday,

15th December 1803.

The breach having been reported practicable, the troops will advance to the attack at 10 o'clock.

Storming party to be commanded by Lieutenant-Colonel Kenny, and to be formed as follows:—

The advance to consist of a sergeant and 12 volunteers of His Majesty's 94th Regiment. First party under the command of Lieutenant-Colonel Kenny, to be composed of one flank and two battalion companies of the 94th Regiment, and the flank companies of the 2nd Brigade. Second party under the command of Lieutenant-Colonel Desse, to consist of one flank and two battalion companies of His Majesty's 94th Regiment, and the flank companies of the 1st Brigade. Third party, the remainder of His Majesty's 94th Regiment under Major Campbell. The 2nd Brigade, under the command of Lieutenant-Colonel Haliburton, will follow the storming party, advancing from the right. The first party, after entering the breach, will turn to the right, and the second party to the left, to drive the enemy from the ramparts, while the 94th Regiment

* During the siege a European officer belonging to one of the native regiments laid a bet that he would, in open daylight, walk from the breaching battery up to the ditch of the fort, a distance of about four hundred yards, and back again, without breaking into a run. He accordingly started about noon, while the batteries were silent, and walked slowly up to the edge of the ditch, which was within pistol shot of the walls; when, having taken off his hat, and made a low bow to the enemy, he deliberately retraced his steps, and won his bet uninjured. As long as he continued to advance, although the enemy crowded the ramparts to view him, they did not offer to fire, thinking he came to parley; but the moment he turned his back they opened upon him a shower of musketry and shot, which did not cease until he was safe in the trenches.

and the 2nd Brigade will advance and take possession of the heights and of the enemy's guns. A detail of artillery to accompany each party, to take possession of the guns, and turn them upon the enemy. . . . . .

Pioneers and scaling ladders will be allotted to each party."

At the same time two parties of Wellesley's Division were ordered to co-operate with the main attack, one, under Colonel Wallace, on the southern gate, and one, under Colonel Chalmers, on the north-west gate.

Capture of the Fort.

The outer wall was soon carried by the storming party. The wall of the inner fort was then escaladed by the light companies of the 94th, who opened the gates for their comrades, and in spite of the desperate efforts of the garrison, who made a determined resistance, the stronghold was soon in the hands of the British. In attempting to escape from the north-west gate, a party of the defenders was met by Colonel Chalmers' force, who drove them back, and entered by that way. Great numbers of the enemy were slain, including the Killadar of the fort and Beni Singh, whose body was found under a heap of dead at the gate. Beni Singh had directed that his wives and daughters were to be slaughtered, so that they should not fall into the enemy's hands, but the work of assassination was not thoroughly carried out, owing either to the humanity or carelessness of those to whom the performance of the deed was entrusted, and only three of the unfortunate women were killed and a few slightly wounded.

In an order dated Deogaon, Thursday, 15th December 1803, the General wrote:—

"Major-General Wellesley has great satisfaction in congratulating the troops under his command upon the brilliant success of this day.

"In the course of this short but laborious siege, Major-General Wellesley has with pleasure observed in all a most anxious and zealous desire to forward the service, the most steady perseverance in the performance of laborious services which would be thought impracticable by other troops, and that gallantry which they have shown so frequently during the campaign, and which has carried them with honour through so many difficulties.

"The most laborious and brilliant part of the siege of Gawilgarh fell to the lot of the Subsidiary Force serving with the Soubah of the Deccan, under the command of Colonel Stevenson, and Major-General Wellesley adopts this mode of declaring that he never witnessed such laborious and persevering exertions as were made by this corps to bring their ordnance and stores to the point of attack.

"The gallantry with which the attack was made by the detachment under the command of Lieutenant-Colonel Kenny has never been surpassed."

The General also thanked Lieutenant-Colonels Desse and Lang and Captain Campbell for their services.

Casualties.

The British loss amounted to one officer (Lieutenant Young, 7th Madras Infantry) and five European rank and file killed, two British officers and 59 rank and file wounded. Natives—8 killed and 51 wounded. Colonel Kenny died of his wounds in April 1804.

The Fort.

But little of value was found, although the Raja of Berar was said to keep his treasure there, and it is said that the jewellery of the women and other valuables were thrown into one of the tanks in the fort, where they may lie to this day. The turreted walls of Gawilgarh are still in an excellent state of preservation, while about a dozen guns which formed its armament rest on the battlements or lie among the rank undergrowth that springs beneath. The fort is abandoned and uninhabited, save for a few families residing in some squalid huts within the northern gate, who are perhaps descendants of those who so bravely defended it over a hundred years ago. But, lifting its time-worn pile on the summit of the hills, it remains a lasting monument to the skill of the British Commander, and to the valour of his troops. Wellesley stood triumphant on the summit of the Satpuras, and discerning men might already appreciate the genius which carried him to victory on a greater arena ten years later, when, in the words of Napier, "the English General emerging from the chaos of the Peninsula struggle, stood on the summit of the Pyrenees a recognised conqueror. From those lofty pinnacles the clangour of his trumpets pealed clear and loud, and the splendour of his genius appeared as a flaming beacon to warring nations."

This brilliant enterprise brought the war in the Deccan to a speedy conclusion. On the fall of this place, which had hitherto been deemed impregnable, the Raja of Berar at once sued for peace, which was concluded at Deogaon on December 17th, 1803. By the terms of this treaty, the province of Cuttack and the province of Berar were ceded to the British and their allies, whilst the Bhonsla engaged "never to take or retain in his service any Frenchman, or the subject of any other European or American power, the Government of which may be at war with the British Government; or any British subject, whether European or Indian, without the consent of the British Government." The submission of the Raja was soon followed by that of his ally Sindhia, with whom a similar treaty was concluded at Anjangaon a fortnight later.

Treaty of Deogaon.

The treaty of peace with the Raja was signed on the 17th December, but the General continued his march for three days eastwards in the direction of Nagpur, "in order to keep alive the impression under which it was obvious that the treaty had been concluded." On receipt of the Raja's ratification he marched westward to Anjangaon and there concluded the treaty with Sindhia on the 30th December. In his comments on the treaty with the Raja of Berar, the Governor-General wrote—"Your treaty is wise, honourable, and glorious, and I shall ratify it the instant a copy can be made."

With regard to the effects of the war, Wellesley wrote to the Governor-General—"The power of Sindhia is gone. The Raja of Berar will never dare to venture into another war with the Company; and if he does, we know that we can destroy him. Holkar alone remains of all these Mahratta chiefs, and he will be formidable only as a freebooter." No doubt this prediction would have been fully verified but for the fatuous policy which followed on the departure of the Marquis Wellesley from India, which resulted in another great war with the Mahratta Confederacy fourteen years later.*

Writing to Major Kirkpatrick on the 16th January 1804, General Wellesley said:—"The British Government has been left, by the late war, in a most glorious situation. They are the sovereigns of a great part of India, the protectors of the principal powers, and the mediators, by treaty, of the disputes of all. The sovereignty they possess is greater, and their power is settled upon more permanent foundations than any before known in India; all it wants is the popularity which, from the nature of the institutions, and the justice of the proceedings of the Government, it is likely to obtain, and which it must obtain, after a short period of tranquillity shall have given the people time and opportunity to feel the happiness and security which they enjoy."

On his return march to Poona, the British General was fully occupied with the settlement of the country that had formed the theatre of the recent operations. Amongst other undertakings was that of the dispersal of a body of freebooters at Munkaisir on the 5th February, who were principally composed of the garrison which had been allowed to escape from Ahmednagar when that place was taken. Marching all night with his cavalry, the 74th Regiment, and some Madras Infantry, he came up with the enemy at 9 o'clock in the morning, after one of the most remarkable marches recorded in history, and dispersed them completely, taking all their guns, baggage and bazaar. Regarding this operation he afterwards wrote:—"This was the greatest exertion I ever saw troops make in any country. The infantry was in the attack, although we marched 60 miles between the morning of the 4th and twelve o'clock at noon on the 5th of February; and yet I halted from noon till eight at night of the 4th." Many years afterwards he said to Earl Stanhope regarding this exploit:—"The most surprising march, I believe, ever made was one of mine in India—seventy-two miles

Freebooters Dispersed at Munkaisir.

Return to Poona.

* See Appendix XVII. The Last Mahratta War.

from 5 one morning to 12 the next, and all fair marching; nor could there be any mistake as to distance, for in India we always marched with measuring wheels."

Having completed his work, Wellesley arrived at Poona on the 27th February 1804, thus bringing to a successful conclusion an enterprise that had been so productive of important results to the British Empire, and of glory to the British arms. The close of this campaign marked an era in the progress of the British Empire in India. It signalised the commencement of the disintegration of the Mahratta Power,* and of the policy of establishing protectorates over foreign states, some of which were subsequently absorbed under the British Government. The Governor-General was, on his return to England, subjected to some criticism on account of the so-called aggressive policy which characterised his term of office. He was censured by certain of those narrow-minded politicians, whose counterparts may be found to-day, whose mental horizon is limited by their own interests or those of the unpatriotic clique to which they belong and who see good in every country but their own and are ever the friends of their country's enemies, whilst the General had his measure of blame for the part he had played in furthering his brother's policy. But the consensus of public opinion was not in favour of such purblind cavillers. And we, in the bright light cast by a hundred years of history and a century of progress in the policy they inaugurated (even were such illumination necessary) can rightly judge of the great qualities of the statesman and of the soldier, and of the immeasurable and lasting service they performed for their country and for mankind. The perspective lent by time enables us to view things broadly, with a due regard to the proportion of events, and their effect on succeeding generations. A contemplation of this peaceful and prosperous land, long in a state of anarchy, where no man's life or property was at one time safe, but where no clash of arms has now resounded for many decades; where the fort contained in every village, behind the walls of which

British Policy.

* Appendix VII. The Last Mahratta War

was at one time the only place of safety, is mouldering into dust, is alone sufficient to prove the righteousness of the policy that led to the overthrow of the Mahratta power in the Deccan, and to the eventual establishment of a permanent peace under the beneficent rule of the British Government.

The elimination of baneful states, the destruction of harmful and effete polities which constitute in themselves a danger to mankind and a barrier to the progress of the human race, are objects sufficient to justify measures such as those which led to the gradual construction of our Empire in the East, and will, most assuredly, be the cause of the establishment and consolidation of other Empires, in other parts of the world, and in future times.

Comments on the Operations.

Before bringing to a close the narrative of Wellesley's career in India it may not be unprofitable to indicate briefly the main features of his campaign in the Deccan, and of the means which the British General employed to ensure such signal success.

Those who have carefully studied the course of Wellesley's operations, and have followed on the map the progress of the British Army, step by step, from victory to victory, until the end came in the complete overthrow of the enemy, cannot fail to perceive that the main cause of success lay in the attention paid to detail by the British Commander. A perusal of his despatches and correspondence during the war will reveal the fact that no matter, however apparently trivial, escaped his notice, that every care possible was taken both as regards the details of supply and transport, and information of the enemy's movements, and measures to frustrate those movements. It has been well said that "the success of almost all great enterprises depends on small details." To leave undone or unthought of no matter, however small, which may contribute to success, to neglect no precaution that may tend to obviate failure, is to ensure the attainment of one's object if such attainment is possible. And just as success in war, as in other affairs, apart from the element of chance, is due to such attention to detail, so in the history of all campaigns, failure and disaster may generally be traced to its neglect.

Strategy.

The main strategical features of the operations that have been described consist in the utilisation by the British General of the natural objects that offered themselves, rivers and mountains. This we see at every turn, whether such obstacles are made use of to frustrate the manœuvres of the enemy and prevent his predatory incursions into the territory of the allies, to protect the army from the raids of the Mahratta Horse, or to cover the approach of convoys from the south. Thus the British Commander made use of the impediment offered to the enemy by the river Godavery in flood, which he well knew the Mahrattas were afraid to cross, whilst he could pass his army to and fro across the stream in the boats he was careful to provide. The use he made of this river, both as an obstacle and as an advanced base, forms one of the most prominent features of the campaign. Again, he took full advantage of the Ajanta Hills, as evinced by his marches and countermarches subsequent to the battle of Assaye, when the few passes through the mountain range facilitated the operations undertaken for the defence of the Nizam's dominions. The skilful employment of the two forces at his disposal from Ahmednagar to Argaum, where he was so opportunely joined by Stevenson on the eve of battle, is worthy of note from a strategical point of view, when, as Wellesley described it, he was "like a man who fights with one hand and defends himself with the other," using Stevenson's or his own force for attack or defence, or combining the two armies as occasion arose.

Tactics.

His conduct of the operations immediately preceding the battle of Assaye, and his temerity in attacking a force so vastly superior on that occasion, without awaiting the arrival of Stevenson, have been subjected to some criticism. Certainly he would appear to have contravened a military principle in separating his forces on the eve of battle, and in selecting for concentration a point so near the presumed position of the enemy. But he explains his reasons in a letter to Colonel Munro:—

"Your principal objection to the action is, that I detached

Colonel Stevenson. His was a separate corps, equally strong, if not stronger than mine. We were desirous to engage the enemy at the same time, and settled a plan accordingly for an attack on the morning of the 24th, he to march by the western, I by the southern route, round the hills between Badnapur and Jalna; and I have to observe that this separation was necessary; first, because both corps could not pass through the same defiles in one day; secondly, because it was to be apprehended that if we left open one of the roads through these hills the enemy might have passed to the southward while we were going to the northward, and then action would have been delayed, or probably avoided.

"Colonel Stevenson and I were never more than twelve miles distant from each other, and when I moved forward to the action of the 23rd we were not much more than eight miles. As usual we depended for our intelligence of the enemy's position on the common *hircarrahs** of the country. Their horse are so numerous that without an army their position could not be reconnoitred by an European officer; and even the *hircarrahs* in our own service, who are accustomed to examine and report on positions, cannot be employed here, as, being natives of the Carnatic, they are as well known as an European.

"The *hircarrahs* reported the enemy to be at Bokardhan. Their right was at Bokardhan, which was the principal place in their position and gave the name to the district in which they were encamped; but their left, in which was their infantry, which I was to attack, was at Assaye, which was six or eight miles from Bokardhan.

"I directed my march so as to be within twelve or fourteen miles of their army at Bokardhan, as I thought, on the 23rd. But when I arrived at the ground of encampment, I found that I was not more than five or six miles from it. I was then informed that the cavalry had marched, and the infantry were about to follow but were still on the ground. At all events, it was necessary to ascertain these points, and I could not venture to reconnoitre without my whole force. But I believed the report to be true, and I determined to

* *Hircarrahs*—Messengers or guides, employed to carry letters, and obtain information.

attack the infantry if it remained still upon the ground. I apprised Colonel Stevenson of this determination, and desired him to move forward too. Before marching on I found, not only their infantry, but their cavalry encamped in a most formidable position, which, by the by, it would have been impossible for me to attack, if, when the infantry changed their front, they had taken care to occupy the only passage there was across the Kailna.

"When I found their whole army and contemplated their position, of course I considered whether I should attack immediately, or should delay till the following morning. I determined upon the immediate attack, because I saw clearly that if I attempted to return to my camp at Naulniah, I should have been followed thither by the whole of the enemy's cavalry, and I might have suffered some loss; instead of attacking, I might have been attacked there in the morning; and at all events I should have found it very difficult to secure my baggage as I did in any place so near the enemy's camp, in which they should know it was; I therefore determined upon the attack immediately."

Tactics were simpler in those days of short-ranging arms when the battlefield was so limited in area. The difficulty of reconnoitring an enemy provided with a numerous mounted force is noteworthy, and has often been experienced in our own time. The swift decision to attack, especially necessary when dealing with an Asiatic or savage foe, followed by the crushing blow at Assaye, and the skilful use made on that occasion of the obstacle offered by the Kailna river in flood, afford valuable lessons. Wellesley has been criticised for making a flank march with his left exposed to the enemy, and for crossing the ford under artillery fire. What else could he do? Moreover, his flank was protected by the river, and the result proved that his estimation of the enemy and his measures for defeating him were correct. Hesitation or retreat would probably have been followed by destruction, as was exemplified the following year when Monson's force was destroyed by Holkar on the Chambal river.

The action itself, when once it had commenced, was a soldiers' battle, the result depending entirely on hard fighting and on the valour of the troops. The great loss on the British side was due to a subordinate officer having exceeded his instructions, and having, when he should merely have held the enemy until the attack had developed on the other flank, become so desperately engaged that the reserves and cavalry had to be used up in extricating him. But for this error it is possible that the battle would have had more decisive results, and perhaps it would not have been necessary to have fought again at Argaum. All these lessons are useful and applicable to more modern war. Of the battle of Argaum, there is not much to be said. The enemy was disheartened by his previous defeat, and it was only necessary to attack him boldly and vigorously in order to ensure his flight. It was, however, an event of great importance, as the Mahrattas were then vanquished in their own territory, and not merely in a State which they had invaded, as was the case at Assaye. It was thus proved that they could be pursued into their own country, and there defeated. After this campaign the Mahratta Horse never stood again, and its effects were felt in the war of 1817-18, when at Kirki, at Nagpore, and at Mehidpur they fled from the field of action without attempting to strike a blow.

The siege of Gawilgarh was a well-conceived and skilfully executed operation, and exemplified the value of a turning movement in dealing with a mountain stronghold, whilst its fall had a great moral effect, as it had hitherto been deemed impregnable. Indeed, one has only to behold its great grey walls crowning the rugged heights, and the difficulty of the approaches, to wonder how it could have been taken at all. But the British soldier is a marvellous man, as many strongholds in this country, which have fallen before his irresistible assault, bear witness to this day. The difficulty, with a force composed principally of infantry, of coming to terms with an enemy whose army consisted in a great part of horsemen, is evident throughout this war, and has been experienced again in recent times. This lesson might have been learnt a hundred years ago, though it is now spoken of as something new and unexpected. Finally there is the lesson, which we may profitably take as an example, of the valour of the British soldier, which, let us hope, is no less in our time than when the Highlanders fought so bravely at Assaye, and the 19th Light Dragoons scattered twenty times their number of Mahratta Horse like chaff before the wind. Without such valour, indeed, all the skill of Commanders, all the examples of history, all experience and theoretical knowledge of the art of war, however well applied, can avail but little on the day of battle.

CHAPTER VI.

THE LAST YEAR IN INDIA.

Wellington and Rewards to his Subordinates.

It is a frequent reproach to the memory of the great Duke that he was indifferent to the prospects and the merits of the officers under his command, that he treated his army as a mere machine, and that, as one distinguished writer * puts it, "he was somewhat chary of bringing to notice the meritorious services of individual regiments, officers, and soldiers." Certainly a hundred years ago it was not the custom, as it has been in our time, to grant orders and medals innumerable, and to mention in despatches a great number of officers, the special merit of the majority of whom is that they have merely performed the duties that were required of them. It may be a matter of opinion whether it is better to minimise the value of such distinctions by the cheapening process of publishing in a despatch a list containing the names of nearly every staff officer, and many of the regimental officers, who have taken part in the service, or to make a mention in despatches a coveted honour.

Even before our day this custom of bringing large numbers to notice was becoming too prevalent, for we find an officer writing in 1820, with regard to some operations in the Mahratta War of 1817, that "there was more paper consumed in the compliments on those occasions than was expended in the cartridges discharged. . . . We should be glad to see the copious stream of public encomium in India somewhat curtailed and confined to hardy and essential services. A public acknowledgment by Government should be a rare and distinguished mark of public approbation ; whereas of late, from the mass of names contained and re-echoed in the general order, it is as difficult to discover as to remember the particular merit of any individual." The Court of Directors of the East India Company, commenting on the despatches of that war (1817-1818)

* "The Rise of Wellington." By General Lord Roberts, V.C.

remarked—"It is natural that in weighing the effect of a recommendation, not only the rank and command of the superior officer by whom it is bestowed should be considered, but also the facility or cautiousness with which such an officer bestows his praise. The Commander who imagines that by mentioning in laudatory terms every field officer who has done his duty, he is rendering justice or even doing a favour to them all, is essentially mistaken. He is, on the contrary, perhaps doing a great injustice to the meritorious few."

It would appear, then, that if the Duke of Wellington was not as lavish in bestowing distinctions as other Commanders either of his own or our time, he was not therefore in the wrong.

Nor, at any rate during his Indian career, did he ignore the meritorious services of those under his command, and if a mention in despatches was not easily to be earned, it was all the more valuable on that account. After each of the actions recorded in these pages we find him thanking his troops in General Orders, and mentioning in his despatches the names of especially meritorious officers. In a General Order thanking the troops for their conduct in the defeat of Dhoondiah, he said:—"The effect of their exertions has fully proved what determined valour and discipline can do against a superiority of numbers." After the battle of Assaye he specially applauded the conduct of the cavalry, and particularly of the 19th Light Dragoons. After the capture of Ahmednagar he brought to special notice the services of six officers, and specially wrote to General Lake, the Commander-in-Chief, recommending for a commission Mr. Tew, who served as a volunteer with the 74th and was killed at the battle of Assaye. His discrimination is marked by another special letter, written to General Lake, on 30th September 1803, commending Lieutenant Campbell, 78th Regiment, for his conduct both at Ahmednagar and at Assaye, where he had two horses killed and was himself wounded. This officer was afterwards General Sir Colin Campbell, K.C.B. Both after Argaum and Gawilgarh, 11 officers were mentioned in despatches; and letters recommending particular individuals to notice are too numerous to mention. So frequent and numerous were his recommendations that we find him writing to General Stuart on 21st May 1804 "I hope you will excuse the liberties I take in so frequently recommending to your favour officers of the army, but their services give them undoubted claims upon me."

Wellington as a Disciplinarian.

As for his treatment of his soldiers, he was undoubtedly a hard disciplinarian, and to that his success in war must be largely ascribed. But every page of his despatches shows his care for the comfort and well-being of his troops, and it is well known that after Assaye he provided the wounded with wine and other luxuries from his own stores.

In putting a stop to plunder and resulting disorder among the troops he was pitiless, as every General should be, with the result that after the storming of a place order was soon restored, and after the capture of Gawilgarh his troops "marched out with as much regularity as if they had only been marching through it." We find him on the 2nd December 1803 writing to Colonel Murray in Gujarat :—"If my Mahratta allies did not know that I should hang any one that might be found plundering, not only I should have starved long ago, but, most probably, my own coat would have been taken off my back."

Characteristics of Wellington.

His principal characteristic appears to have been attention to all details, so that nothing is omitted that can contribute to success, and a stern and pitiless conduct of war, without which military operations cannot succeed. He, in fact, recognised the axiom of Napoleon that "War to be successful must be terrible." There is no weakness, no dallying with the enemy, but the pursuit of a campaign to its legitimate end with all possible celerity. In fact, we find in Wellesley, even in his early days in India, all the qualities of a great commander, and none of the weaknesses that have delayed or prevented success and led to prolongation of war in more recent times, and under the direction of lesser men. An officer who served under him throughout the Mahratta War said :—"The appearance and demeanour of General Wellesley were such as at first sight to inspire confidence, which feeling was not diminished on a closer acquaintance. All those who served under him looked up to him with that degree of respect, I might almost say awe, which, by combining an implicit obedience to his commands with an unbounded confidence in the wisdom of his measures, was calculated to draw forth all the energies of man in the execution of his orders."

With regard to his appearance, another officer who served with him says he was " a little above the middle height, well limbed and muscular, with little encumbrance of flesh beyond that which gives shape and manliness to the outlines of the figure; an erect carriage; a countenance strongly patrician, both in feature, profile and expression, and an appearance remarkable and distinguished: few could approach him on any duty, or any subject requiring his serious attention, without being aware of something strange and penetrating in his clear light eye."

His Views on Military Establishments in India.

The remainder of General Wellesley's career in India, after the conclusion of the campaign in the Deccan, was uneventful, but his despatches contain a great deal that is of interest. Writing to Major Shawe on 26th February 1804, the day before his arrival at Poona, he gives at length his views on the question of the military establishments of the Native Princes of India. He says:—" Bengal, the paradise of nations, enjoys the advantage of a civil government, and requires its military force only for its protection against foreign enemies. All the other barbarous establishments called governments, without excepting even that of Fort St. George, have no power beyond that of the sword. Take from them the exercise of that power, and they have no other; and can collect no revenue, can give no protection, and can exercise no government. The Native Governments, I mean those of the Nizam and the Peshwa, are fifty times worse than ours in this respect. They do not choose to keep armies themselves, their territories are overrun by a race of armed men, who are ready to enlist with anyone who will lead them to plunder; and there is no power in the country to support the Government and give protection to the industrious classes of the inhabitants except the British troops." This letter throws an interesting light on the state of India a hundred years ago. The *Pax Britannica* and the annexation of fresh territory was at first of doubtful benefit, although it ultimately made for good. In every village there were 20 or 30 horsemen, who had been dismissed from the service of the State, and who had no means of living except by plunder. Wellesley foresaw the anarchy of the succeeding 15 years, which ended only with the suppression of the Pindaris, when he wrote in this same letter :—

State of India 100 years ago.

"I think that we run a great risk from the freebooter system. It is not known to the Governor-General, and you can have no idea of the extent to which it has gone ; and it increases daily . . . no inhabitant can nor will remain to cultivate, unless he is protected by an armed force stationed in his village."

The remedy for this state of affairs was, as Wellesley foresaw, to oblige the Native Governments allied to the British to keep up bodies of regular troops with which to preserve order within their territories, a policy that was subsequently carried into effect.

The following passage from a letter written on 2nd March gives expression to views which he himself adhered to in practice :—

"It is necessary for a man who fills a public situation, and who has great public interests in charge, to lay aside all private considerations, whether on his own account or that of other persons." It would be well if his noble example were always followed.

On the 26th February a meeting of the principal officers of Wellesley's Deccan Army took place, at which it was decided to present him with a gold vase, while the following letter was written to him :—

Presentation to Wellesley by his Officers.

"The officers who served with the division of the army under your immediate command in the Deccan, are desirous of presenting you a pledge of their respect and esteem ; and to express the high idea they possess of the gallantry and enterprise that so eminently distinguish you, they request your acceptance of a golden vase of the value of 2,000 guineas, on which it is proposed to record the principal event that was decisive of the campaign in the Deccan." A service of plate was afterwards substituted for the gold vase, bearing the inscription:—" Battle of Assaye, September 23rd, 1803. Presented to Major-General the Hon'ble A. Wellesley, by the officers of the Division of the Army who served under his immediate command in the Deccan, in commemoration of the campaign in 1803." In replying to this letter, Wellesley wrote that he would never " lose the recollection of the events of the last year, or of the officers and troops, by means of whose ability, zeal, and disciplined bravery, they have in great measure been brought about in this part of India; but it is highly gratifying for me to be certain, that the conduct of the operations of the war has met with the approbation and has gained for me the esteem of the officers under my command."

His Views on the Peshwa's Government.

In a long and interesting letter to the Governor-General, dated 7th March 1804, Wellesley gives his views on the Government of the Peshwa, and describes an interview he had with the minister of that Chief, who, complaining of the conduct of his brother Amrat Rao, said that " his name was so odious to His Highness, that if it were only mentioned in his presence, it would be necessary for His Highness to perform his ablutions." In a letter of the same date to Major Shawe, he had given his opinion of the Peshwa Baji Rao, which was fully justified by subsequent events.* In this letter he says:—" the Peshwa . . . will commence his intrigues immediately with Sindhia's Durbar . . . or he will intrigue in any other manner to distress the British Government. . . . The Peshwa is callous to anything but money and revenge. He will call upon the British Government to gratify the latter passion, but he will make no sacrifices unless to procure money."

* Appendix VII. The Last Mahratta War.

NOTE.—It is interesting to find Wellesley writing to Colonel Stevenson on the 11th February 1804:—"I had reason to believe that all parties in England had agreed that it was absolutely necessary, at last, that Great Britain should really have an army, and not the skeleton of one, as had been the case hitherto . . . Everybody appears to be convinced of the necessity of having an army, but nobody appears to be inclined to adopt the measures which are necessary for that purpose. The same little temporary expedients are adopted that have been before practised, and they will equally fail." These lines might have been written in our time.

On the 8th March we find the General at Khandalla, where he stayed some days before proceeding to Bombay, where he had a great reception on his arrival from Panwell in the Governor's Yacht. When the harbour was reached, a salute of 15 guns was fired from the Indian Man-of-War *Elphinstone*, and repeated on the arrival of the General. The troops in the garrison lined the streets from the Dockyard to Government House, and the following public address was made by the 124 British inhabitants:—

Wellesley at Bombay.

"We might be justly deemed insensible to the signal benefits which your late brilliant career has conferred upon your country, if we did not avail ourselves of the opportunity which your temporary residence in this island affords, to express the high sense we entertain of your memorable and important services. To you, Sir, in an eminent degree, are owing, not only the immense advantages resulting from a successful campaign in the Deccan, but, those having been attained, the blessing of an early peace in India. The enemy's systematic inclination for desultory and protracted warfare was met on your part as it likewise was, with equal energy and success, in another quarter, by a wise and gallant resolution to bring affairs to a speedy as well as to a glorious issue. And the battle of Assaye, which displayed how justly you relied on the disciplined valour of your troops, and the zeal, courage, and conduct of every officer under your command, struck a damper on the hopes of the adverse powers, which may almost be said to have decided the fate of the campaign.

"But it is not in your military career alone that we have observed the effects of an active, able, and determined mind. The difficult negociations which you carried on with two hostile powers, when at the same moment your attention was occupied by the operations of the field, do the greatest honour to your talents as a statesman, and display a happy union of military science and political skill. Your victories have taken place in our neighbourhood; they immediately affect our future interests, and are intimately connected with our future prosperity. They lay the foundation of a peace to us and our successors, which is no longer to be interrupted by the feuds and combinations of a Mahratta Confederacy. They open to the trade and to the industry of Bombay, the resources of an extensive and populous country.

"Under these circumstances, when assembled to express our gratitude towards your noble and illustrious relative, we should have felt our duty only half discharged, if we had omitted this tribute of respect to one who is so justly dear to him, and under whose auspices the troops of every description have shown themselves worthy of such a leader, and of their former renown."

Wellesley as a Commander.

It was, perhaps, the union of military science and political skill referred to in this address that proved that this was no ordinary general. And in this connection it is interesting to quote a passage from the work of one of the best known of modern military writers:—

"The best officers must be on the same political level as the best men in the other professions and in public life. The men at the head of an army, the typical products of its corporate existence, ought to be intellectually and spiritually the peers of the leaders in other branches of life, on what Matthew Arnold called 'the first plane,' and in touch with the movement of national policy, and of literature, science and art. Only on the first plane can any man be a statesman, and unless the chief men of an army are statesmen, a nation will fight its own battles in vain. The battles may be won, but the fruits of victory will be lost."*

British Good Faith.

Wellesley was indeed a man on the first plane, even at this early period of his career, and the negotiations, which proved him to be a statesman, with Sindhia and the Raja of Berar were no less important than his victories over them on the field of battle. This combination of soldier and statesman is rare in our army, where few men on the first plane rise to distinction. Wellesley's appreciation of the requirements of our national policy are indicated in a passage of a letter he wrote to Major Malcolm:—"I would sacrifice Gwalior, or every frontier of India, ten times over, in order to preserve our

* "The Brain of an Army." By Spencer Wilkinson.

credit for scrupulous good faith, and the advantages and honour we gained by the late war and the peace; and we must not fritter them away in arguments, drawn from overstrained principles of the laws of nations, which are not understood in this country. What brought us through many difficulties in the war, and the negociations of peace? The British good faith and nothing else." There spoke the statesman, and his words hold good to-day, and embody the principle which forms the keystone of our Indian Empire.

General Wellesley spent two months in Bombay, where he had gone with Mr. Josiah Webbe, Secretary to Government, to confer with Lieutenant-Colonel Close* concerning the affairs of the Southern Mahratta States. His letters of this period contain many interesting passages, as, for instance, the following, dated 17th March 1804, evidently referring to the superiority of the Bengal over the Madras Native Army.† "I did not mean to compare the state of discipline of the Bengal troops with that of the troops of the Madras Establishment. They are not to be compared at all, I imagine; but I gave the preference to the Bengal troops on account

The Bengal and Madras Armies.

* Afterwards Sir Barry Close.

† It is interesting to compare this opinion with that of a contemporary, the author of "Twelve Years' Military Adventure," who says:—"The Bengal sepoys are mostly Rajpoots, who, next to the Brahmins, are the highest caste of the Hindoos. To those, therefore, who are unacquainted with their religious prejudices, and the consequent privations and hardships they undergo on boardship, it is surprising to see them come forward to make such sacrifices, when not bound to do so by the conditions of their enlistment. There cannot be a stronger proof of their attachment to service. To cherish this feeling should be the paramount policy of our Indian Government; for though we must rely chiefly on the valour of our European troops for conquests, yet the maintenance of our Eastern Empire depends altogether on the fidelity of our native army, that of Bengal in particular, which may truly be said to be the rampart of British dominion in India. This army is composed of a much finer race of men than the native troops of either of the other Presidencies. In fact, one Bengal sepoy would make two of Madras." Another officer wrote in 1820:—"The Madras and Bombay corps are generally composed of men who are as fit for boxers as they are for soldiers; many of them not equalling in muscular strength an European boy of 12 years old, and scarcely able to stand the shock of a musket. The whole of the native cavalry on these establishments are subject to the same observation; many of whose accoutrements, sword, and dress would nearly equal the weight of the man himself." Nevertheless the Madras sepoy contrived to give a very good account of himself in many campaigns. With regard to the Bengal sepoy, we find Wellesley writing on the 14th February 1804:—"Supposing all consequences to be equally convenient, I acknowledge that I should wish to see the Bengal troops composing all the subsidiary forces . . . the natives have more respect for them than they have for the Coast or Bombay troops. They have proved in this campaign that they yield to none in bravery; and they have long been notorious for their contempt of their enemies on horseback." This is no doubt the passage referred to in the quotation, given above, from his letter of 17th March.

of their superior size and appearance, and their caste; and I conceived them not to be objectionable on the score of discipline."

Holkar.

In the same letter, which is addressed to Lieutenant-General Stuart, he comments on the hostile attitude of Holkar, who in a letter to Wellesley had styled himself "the slave of Shah Mahmoud, the King of Kings," who "had seized the Government of Kabul after having defeated Zemaun Shah two or three years ago, and put out his eyes; but he was in his turn defeated and dethroned very lately by another brother, assisted by the King of Persia. Holkar had taken this title, either to frighten us with the prospect of an invasion of India by the Afghans, or he has really communicated with and entered the service of Mahmoud Shah."

As an instance of General Wellesley's administrative ability, the following extract from a letter to Major Graham, dated 11th

Wellesley on Famine Relief.

April 1804, is interesting. It is noteworthy that this letter embodies what are now recognised as the correct principles of famine relief, and it shows the remarkable grasp of affairs of widely different nature proposed by the great soldier and administrator. "The delivery of provisions *gratis* is, in my opinion, a very defective mode of providing against the effects of famine. It is liable to abuses in all parts of the world,* but particularly in India; and at Ahmednagar, the consequence of its adoption would be, that crowds of people would be drawn there from other parts of the country in which the distress is equally felt; and they would increase the distress at Ahmednagar to such a degree as to render all the efforts to remove it from its immediate inhabitants entirely fruitless; and it might at last reach our own troops and establishments. The principle, therefore, of the mode in which I propose to relieve the distress of the inhabitants is not to give grain or money in charity. Those who suffer from famine may be properly divided into two classes; those who can and those who cannot work. In the latter class may be included old persons, children, and the sick women; who,

* The truth of this has lately been exemplified in Russia.

from their former situation in life, have been unaccustomed to labour, and have been weakened by the effects of famine." The letter goes on to point out that those who can work should be employed by the public, and the others fed at the public expense. He directed the organisation of work under proper superintendence, and the institution of hospitals under medical supervision. The letter is a most striking one, and would apply to the organisation of famine relief to-day.

Wellesley's Career.

It is well known that Wellesley was not satisfied with his progress in the service, first in having been superseded by General Baird in command of the expedition to the Red Sea, and secondly that his appointment to the Staff in India, made on his promotion to Major-General, had not been confirmed by the Commander-in-Chief in England. No doubt, also, he felt that he had been long enough abroad, and that the state of affairs in Europe gave promise of more opportunity of advancement to a distinguished soldier than was offered by a career in the East. In those days, as in ours, India attracted but little attention or interest at home, the affairs of the country being directed by the oligarchy of Leadenhall Street. Wellesley's and Lake's victories over the Mahrattas were scarcely noticed in England, and India was entirely overshadowed by the progress of great events in Europe. Thus it is that we find Wellesley, in April 1804, asking permission of General Lake, the Commander-in-Chief in India, to relinquish his appointment and return to Europe. In forwarding the application to the Governor-General Lake wrote :—"I shall feel most exceedingly the loss of his abilities and experience should the war continue with Jeswant Rao Holkar, both in his military and political knowledege of affairs in this country."

But Wellesley's labours were in no wise relaxed by reason of his impending departure, and on the day he submitted this application we find him giving a full account, in another despatch to General Lake, of the military situation in the Deccan. His correct views with regard to both political affairs and war are evinced throughout his subsequent correspondence concerning the war with Holkar; thus we find him

On the War with Holkar.

writing to Captain Wilks :—"If General Lake attacks Holkar vigorously and with activity, the war will not last a fortnight. If the General should stand on the defensive, the contest will be long and may lead to unpleasant consequences."

Soon after the middle of May, General Wellesley moved into camp to rejoin his army which he had completely clothed, armed, and equipped in anticipation of the war with Holkar, but it was not found necessary for his forces to take part in the contest. It would, no doubt, have been difficult for him to do so, as famine was raging in the Deccan, and in consequence the country would yield no supplies for an army. Writing from Poona on the 1st June he says, "We lose 50 persons every day at Ahmednagar, where we feed to the number of 5,000. What must it be where the people are not fed?" However, as he pointed out in a despatch to the Governor-General, the famine that precluded the movement of his army also prevented the incursion, on the part of Holkar, into the Deccan, whose possessions in that region were consequently at the mercy of the British. Wellesley's method of supplying his army must always be a subject of great interest, and some light is thrown on it by the following order issued by him on the 4th June 1804 :—

Supply of the Army.

"In order to relieve the distress in camp for want of grain, and that of the followers on account of its high price, it is intended to supply the bazaars with rice from the stores in the depôt.

"2. The mode in which this must be effected is to bring rice from the depôt to the army by means of the grain dealers, and to sell it to the bazaars at a reasonable rate.

"3. The commanding officers of corps and heads of departments must take care that the public followers of their corps and departments are supplied by arrangements which they will make; the former with the *cutwals* * of their regimental bazaars, and the latter with the *cutwal* of the grand bazaar."

There follow other minute instructions on matters of detail. Grain was brought from Hyderabad, Mysore, and other parts of the country.

* *Cutwal*—*Kotwal*—Superintendent.

On the 8th June we again find him expressing a very strong desire to return to Europe . . "My principal reason for wishing to go is that I think that I have served as long in India as any man ought who can serve anywhere else, and I think there appears a prospect of service in Europe, in which I should be more likely to get forward. Another reason is that I have been a good deal annoyed at the rheumatism in my back, for which living in a tent during another monsoon is not a very good remedy; and a third is that I do not think I have been very well treated by the King's Government. It is now about two years since I have been Major-General, and nearly as much since I was appointed to the Staff at Fort St. George, by General Stuart. Since that time it has been perfectly well known that I have led a body of British troops into the Mahratta territories; and supposing that I had no other pretentions to be placed on the Staff, I might have expected a confirmation of General Stuart's act, under those circumstances."

His Return to Europe.

Another reason for wishing to leave India is given in a letter to General Stuart :—"I think it desirable that I should leave this country. The Peshwa has manifested a most unaccountable jealousy of me, personally; and has refused to adopt certain measures, evidently calculated for his advantage, only because I recommended them. He has allowed their benefit, and has avowed this motive for refusing to adopt them. We have always found it very difficult to manage him, but it will be quite impossible if this principle is allowed to guide his conduct. I, therefore, think it best that I should go away as soon as possible: and I am certainly very desirous of getting some rest."

At the same time he had made many staunch friends in India, and did not leave the country without regret. On the 26th February 1805, we find him writing to Malcolm—"I cannot express to you how much distressed I am at going away and parting with my friends in this country." A few days later, writing to Purneah, Dewan (Minister) of Mysore, a state with which he had been so long and so intimately connected, he gives some good advice—"Upon the occasion of taking my leave of you, I must take the liberty to recommend you to persevere in the laudable path which you have hitherto followed. Let the prosperity of the country be your object, protect the *ryots* (peasants) and traders, and allow no man, whether vested with authority or otherwise, to oppress them with impunity; do justice to every man; and you may depend upon it that your Government will be as prosperous and as permanent as I wish it to be."

On the 30th May 1804 the Governor-General wrote to General Wellesley, directing him to proceed to Fort William, either by land or by sea as he chose, and by whatever route was convenient for him, in order to confer with him and the Commander-in-Chief "upon the various important political and military questions now depending in India."

Native Address at Seringapatam.

He accordingly proceeded to Seringapatam, being entertained on the way by the native Commandant of Dharwar Fort and other Mahratta Chiefs, where he received the following eloquent address from the native inhabitants on his arrival:—

Address of the native inhabitants of Seringapatam to Major-General the Hon'ble A. Wellesley, commanding the troops in Mysore, etc., on his return from the field.

"*Seringapatam*, 16*th July* 1804.

"We, the native inhabitants of Seringapatam, have reposed for five auspicious years under the shadow of your protection.

"We have felt, even during your absence, in the midst of battle and of victory, that your care for our prosperity had been extended to us in as ample a manner as if no other object had occupied your mind.*

* That this was not a mere compliment due to oriental hyperbole is evident from the despatches which prove Wellesley's continued interest in the welfare of Seringapatam during his absence on field service. As an example of this we may quote from a General Order issued in camp on the 8th January 1804, in the course of which the General says:— "Major-General Wellesley has experienced during the late war the greatest benefits from the protection which he has uniformly given to the inhabitants of Seringapatam, and he is determined to continue it. He requests, therefore, from the Commanding Officer at Seringapatam the support of, and co-operation with, the civil magistrate in the exercise of the duties of his office, as the foundation of the system, at that place, from which such extensive and important public benefits have been derived."

"We are preparing to perform, in our several castes, the duties of thanksgiving and of sacrifice to the preserving God, who has brought you back in safety, and we present ourselves in person to express our joy.

"As your labours have been crowned with victory, so may your repose be graced with honours. May you long continue personally to dispense to us that full stream of security and happiness, which we first received with wonder, and continue to enjoy with gratitude; and, when greater affairs shall call you from us, may the God of all castes and all nations deign to henceforth favour our humble and constant prayers for your health, your glory, and your happiness."

In his reply to this address, Wellesley said:—"In every situation in which I have been employed, it has been my uniform wish and endeavour to conduct the public affairs entrusted to my management, according to the orders and intentions of the Government which I am serving, and under whose protection you are living.

"I have always been particularly interested in the welfare and prosperity of the inhabitants of Seringapatam, and have been anxious that they should enjoy the full benefit of the security which the laws and regulations by which the British Government is administered afford to every individual.

"The attention which I have given to your affairs, in every situation in which I have been placed, has been a part of my duty, and a necessary consequence of my desire that you should not cease to feel the benefit of the Company's Government; and it is very gratifying to my feelings to find that my conduct has been satisfactory to you."

Bullock Transport.

Having remained ten days at Seringapatam, he proceeded to Fort St. George, where he wrote an interesting and instructive letter to General Stuart, regarding the transport of his army, in the course of which he said:—" In former wars the utmost exertion which it was possible for the army to make was to draw its train of artillery to Seringapatam. It was not possible, and never was expected, that the guns and carriages which were drawn there, should be brought away again: and accordingly, notwithstanding the undoubted talents and the great reputation of the officers who have at different times led British armies to that place, it has invariably happened that by far the greater part of the train and carriages have been left behind when the army marched away. Those who have seen the mode in which those armies made their marches, and were acquainted with the system under which cattle were, and must necessarily be, procured for the service, will not hesitate to allow that the slowness of all our operations, and the necessity to which I have above alluded, of leaving our guns after they had been drawn above 300 miles, were to be attributed entirely to the faults of the system under which the cattle were procured for the service. All the carriages attached to the division under my command were drawn by the public cattle; and I shall advert to a few facts, to point out the difference between this part of the equipment of the troops in the late and former wars.

"We marched to Poona from Seringapatam, the distance being nearly 600 miles, in the worst season of the year, through a country which had been destroyed by Holkar's army, with heavy guns, at the rate upon an average of 13½ miles a day . . On this march we lost no draft cattle . . it has frequently been necessary for the troops to march, for many days together, a distance of from 15 to 20 miles daily, the heavy artillery always accompanied them, and I always found that the cattle could go as far as the troops. Upon one occasion I found it necessary to march a detachment 60 miles in 30 hours, and the ordnance and provision carriages drawn by the Company's bullocks accompanied this detachment. Instead of being obliged, as the Commanders-in-Chief of armies in former wars have been, to leave guns and carriages behind, such was the state of efficiency of this Department throughout this severe service, that I was able but with little assistance to draw away the guns which the troops took.

"It must be obvious to every man, that in a war, such as the late war, there could be no success unless the officer commanding the troops was able to move, at all times, with the utmost celerity of which the troops were capable, and to continue his movements so long as was necessary. Rapid movements of guns and carriages cannot be made without good cattle, well driven and well taken care of. ''

This shows that Wellesley fully appreciated the advantage of mobility. His remarks are made in the course of a letter recommending the grant of a gratuity of a month's pay to the persons of the Bullock Department, who " were present in the actions which were fought; some of them were killed and others desperately wounded." The General had every consideration evidently even for the humblest individuals serving under his command.

After a short stay at Madras, General Wellesley proceeded to Calcutta, where the following gazette extraordinary was published prior to his arrival, by the Governor-General :—

Reception at Calcutta.

In honour of the eminent services of Major-General the Hon'ble Arthur Wellesley, in command of the forces in the Deccan during the late memorable and glorious campaign, and as a testimony of respect to the gallant officers and troops who, under the command of Major-General Wellesley, have contributed to the splendid success of the war against the Mahratta Confederates, the Governor-General will proceed down the river to meet Major-General Wellesley, and to conduct that distinguished officer publicly to the Presidency of Fort William. The usual salute to be fired when the Doonamookee yacht, with the Governor-General on board, shall pass Fort William in proceeding down the river, and also on her return.

The General arrived on the 12th August, and landed with the Governor-General and his suite at six o'clock in the evening. The Governor-General was received by Major-General Cameron and the staff of the garrison of Fort William; all the principal civil officers of the Government and the principal European inhabitants of Calcutta had also assembled to congratulate Major-General Wellesley on his arrival; a vast concourse of natives was present on this occasion.

A street of troops was formed from the Governor-General's ghaut to the north front of Government House, through which the Governor-General's carriages, with the Governor-General, the Hon'ble Major-General Wellesley, the Hon'ble Chief Justice,

Sir George Barlow, Mr. Udny, Major-General Dowdeswell, and the Governor-General's suite, proceeded to Government House; the Governor-General was received with the usual honours as he passed the different corps.

On the arrival of Major-General Wellesley at Government House a salute of thirteen guns was fired from Fort William, and in the evening the Hon'ble the Chief Justice, the Members of Council, and all the principal civil and military officers of the Presidency dined at Government House. (Despatches of the Marquis Wellesley.)

The British inhabitants of Calcutta had already, in February, voted him a sword of the value of £1,000, as a testimony of the sense which they entertained of the services rendered by him to the East India Company, and to his country.

At Calcutta General Wellesley's advice regarding the conduct of hostilities then proceeding with Holkar was most welcome, and the views and opinions expressed in his despatches during this period are of the greatest interest. Colonel Monson's disastrous retreat* from Holkar had taken place, and Wellesley's comments on this event are instructive.

We find him writing to Major Malcolm on 24th August:—

On Monson's Disaster.

"I have read with the greatest attention all Monson's letters, and all the information which has arrived respecting the late misfortune; and I am decidedly of opinion that Monson advanced without reason; and retreated in the same manner; and that he had no intelligence of what was passing five miles from his camp. It is a curious circumstance that Monson and the Commander-in-Chief should attribute their misfortunes to Murray's retreat, and that Murray should attribute his retreat to a movement of the same kind made by Monson. At any rate both parties appear to have been afraid of Holkar, and both to have fled from him in different directions. I do not think that the Commander-in-Chief and I have carried on the war so well by our deputies as we did ourselves."

* Appendix VIII. Monson's Retreat.

Offensive Tactics.

Both Wellesley and Lake had learnt the lesson, inculcated by Clive at Plassey, that it is best to attack an Asiatic enemy, however numerous, and that retreat or a show of fear is liable to lead to disaster. Sir Charles Napier, after fighting his battles in Sind, acknowledged his indebtedness to "the great Master" (Wellesley) for this lesson of Asiatic warfare.

On the Treaty of Bassein.

One of the most interesting and valuable documents from Wellesley's pen during his stay in Calcutta is his Memorandum on the Treaty of Bassein, a lucid exposition of the political events which led up to that compact and to the rupture with the Mahratta Powers. Other documents of interest treat of the systems of supply and intelligence in the army of the Deccan.

Appointed to Political and Military Power in the Deccan.

On the 9th November 1804 Wellesley was directed by the Governor-General to resume command of the army, with "the chief command of all the British troops, and of the forces of our allies serving in the territories of the Peshwa, of the Soubahdar of the Deccan, or of any of the Mahratta States or Chiefs, subject only to the orders of the Commander-in-Chief at Fort St. George, or of His Excellency General Lake." He was at the same time vested with "the general direction and control of all the political and military affairs of the British Government in the territories of the Soubahdar of the Deccan, of the Peshwa, and of the Mahratta States and Chiefs."

Wellesley Proceeds to Madras.

In pursuance of these orders, he embarked on board the *Bombay* frigate on the 14th November, and, having been joined by Major Malcolm, reached Madras a week later. There are several interesting despatches written from Fort St. George. The following extract from a letter to Colonel Montresor indicated a policy which Wellesley always pursued, both in India and in the Peninsula, and notably in France after passing the Pyrenees:—"As I have served much in the Mahratta territory, and must have acquired some knowledge of the people, I take the liberty of suggesting to you to preserve the most strict discipline among your troops and their followers; and to make them pay for everything which they may want. You will do well to keep up and encourage, by mild treatment, a constant intercourse with the natives of the country through which you will pass, as the best means of drawing from them the resources which the districts can afford."

Return to Seringapatam.

On the 30th November he arrived at Seringapatam. He had intended to proceed northwards to join the army at once, but was detained by an attack of fever and ague. In the meantime Holkar had been defeated by Generals Lake and Fraser, this event rendering unnecessary the advance of the Army of the Deccan, so Wellesley remained at Seringapatam until the 9th February 1805, when he returned to Fort St. George.

On the 17th February ships arrived from England bearing Wellesley's appointment as Knight of the Bath, dated 1st September 1804.* Having permission of the Governor-General to resign the political and military power in the Deccan, he decided to return to England, and had taken a passage in the *Marchioness of Exeter* when the Admiral offered him a passage in H. M. S. *Trident*, which he accepted. His interest in affairs did not, however, cease owing to his decision; for we find him on the 24th February writing long letters to Colonel Haliburton and Colonel Close regarding political and military affairs in the Deccan, and his correspondence continued up to the moment of and even subsequent to his embarkation. The frequent reproach that he did not sufficiently acknowledge the services of those under him is not borne out by the evidence of his despatches, and the following order published by him at Fort St. George on the 9th March 1805, one of many similar orders, supports this contention:—

Departure from India.

"Major-General Sir A. Wellesley informs the troops under his command that he has received the permission of His Excellency the

* On the 3rd May 1804 the House of Commons passed a vote of thanks "for the many important, brilliant, and memorable services achieved by General Wellesley as the commandant of the separate army within the Deccan."

Governor-General to resign the political and military powers with which he had been lately entrusted in the Deccan, and the leave of His Excellency the Commander-in-Chief to proceed to England. He cannot avoid expressing the regret which he feels upon taking leave of officers and troops with whom he has served so long.

"In the course of the period of time which has elapsed since Major-General Wellesley was appointed to the command of a Division of this army, various services have been performed by the troops, and great difficulties have been surmounted, with a steadiness and perseverance which have seldom been surpassed. Upon every occasion, whether in garrison or in the field, the Major-General has had reason to be satisfied with their conduct; and he once more returns them his thanks, and assures them that he shall never forget their services, or cease to feel a lively interest in whatever may concern them. He earnestly recommends to the officers of the army never to lose sight of the great principles of the military service, to preserve the discipline of the troops, and to encourage, in their respective corps, the spirit and sentiments of gentlemen and of soldiers, as the most certain road to the achievement of everything that is great in their profession.

"Upon the occasion of taking leave of the troops who have been so long under his command, Major-General Wellesley cannot avoid noticing and recording the assistance which he has received from officers commanding districts and divisions under his orders; and the officers of the staff appointed to assist him; of the former some distinguished characters are now no more, and others have gone to Europe, and all are sufficiently known to the troops; but in noting the assistance he has received from the Staff, he must record particularly his obligations to Major Barclay, Captain Bellingham, and Lieutenant Campbell of the 78th Regiment."

Prior to embarkation he received addresses from the officers of the 33rd Regiment, from the native inhabitants of Seringapatam, from the officers of his Division, and from the European inhabitants and military officers of Fort St. George, and he received from England the thanks of the King and Parliament and of the Court of Directors.

On the 5th March a grand entertainment was given in his honour in the Pantheon of Madras, and a few days later he embarked for England, "leaving his great name and example as an imperishable monument, exciting others to like deeds of glory, and serving at once to adorn, defend, and perpetuate the existence of our Empire among the ruling nations of the Earth."

APPENDICES.

APPENDIX I.

NAPOLEON AND ORIENTAL CONQUEST.

Napoleon had always been attracted by the Orient, and already at Campo Formio, prior to his Egyptian Campaign, he had remembered the "Philosophical and Political History of the two Indies" when he said, "Europe is a mole-heap; only in the East have there ever been great Empires and great cataclysms; in the East there are six hundred millions of human beings." And he remarked after his first Italian Campaign:—"My glory is already at an end; there is not enough of it in this little Europe. I must go to the East; all great glory comes from there." A sentiment worthy of the man who had said:—"I hold the immortality of the soul to be the remembrance we leave behind us in the minds of men. This thought is an inspiring one; it were better never to have lived at all than to leave no trace of one's existence behind."

From childhood the East had been opened to his fertile imagination by the study of the expeditions of Alexander the Great, the works of Plutarch, Herodotus, Strabo, and Diodorus. It has been even said that he had applied for service under the British East India Company. Certainly the idea had been entertained, for Lucien Bonaparte tells us in his Memoirs that in 1793 Napoleon had spoken longingly of India, and of the English Empire there, destined to spread with every year, and of the career thus opened for good artillery officers, who were scarce in the British Service; and he said at this time:—"If ever I choose that career, I hope that you will hear from me. In a few years I shall return thence a rich Nabob and bring fine dowries for our three sisters." Yet we find him paying little attention to the famous adventurers de Boigne and Perron, the latter of whom he received coldly on his return to France in 1806. It was natural that, in his visions of Oriental Empire, the thoughts of Napoleon Bonaparte should first be directed towards Egypt. That country lay on the threshold of the Orient, and had been connected with India and the East from times that were lost in dim antiquity. Alexander, on his way to the conquest of the East, had founded on the banks of the Nile the great city which bears his name. Napoleon would follow in his footsteps, first conquering that fertile land on the borders of the Desert, where from the summits of the Pyramids forty centuries would look down upon his deeds. Beyond, the Red Sea and the Persian Gulf bore the vessels and commerce of the Indian coasts; the Euphrates and the Tigris watered the western portion of the ancient empire of Darius, while a canal across the Isthmus of Suez had been suggested by d'Argenson in 1738, and was a possibility of the future to Bonaparte, who located the canal of Sesostris.

On April 12th, 1798, the Directory ordered the preparation of the Army for Egypt, and the "Citizen Bonaparte, at the moment General-in-Chief of the Army of England," was named "General-in-Chief of the Army of the Orient." In orders issued on the same day the right of the French to keep open the road to India is insisted upon.

The expedition, 30,000 strong, equipped as though for a permanent occupation of Egypt, set sail from Toulon on May 19th. Bonaparte was ready either to return to France "when the pear was ripe," or to carve out for himself an Empire in the East. He said to his brother Joseph:—"I go to the Orient with every means to ensure success. . . . If the Republic is successful in war, if a political general like me appears and centres the hopes of the people in himself; well, still in the East I shall perhaps do greater service to the world than he." On July 21st the Mamelukes were defeated in the battle of the Pyramids. Next day the French entered Cairo, and Bonaparte saw fulfilled the first stage on his way to Oriental Empire. On the march to the great city of Egypt his imagination took a bold flight:—"I saw myself freed from the fetters and constraints of civilisation; I dreamt all sorts of things, and saw the means of carrying out what I dreamt. I pictured myself on the road to Asia on an elephant, a turban on my head, and holding in my hand a new Koran, which I had written myself from my own inspiration. I should have combined in my enterprises the traditions of the two worlds, putting under contribution for my own advantage the whole domain of history; I should have attacked the British Empire in India, and restored my connection with old Europe by that conquest." Nor were these merely the dreams of a visionary, for he took a practical view of a move on India. On the 30th August, he wrote to the Directory:—"Mistress of Egypt, France will by and by be Mistress of India;" and in January 1799 he addressed the following letter to Tipu Sultan:—"You have been instructed as to my arrival on the borders of the Red Sea with an innumerable and invincible army, filled with the desire to deliver you from the iron yoke of England. I hasten to request you to give me, by way of Muscat or Mecca, news as to your political situation. I would like you to send to Suez some able man in your confidence with whom I could confer."

Moreover, in November the Directory had urged him to march towards India, and join Tipu Sultan, or else to march on Constantinople. Meanwhile the French fleet was destroyed at the battle of the Nile by Nelson on July 31st, and the army was cut off from its base and deprived of all supplies and reinforcements. But the great General was nothing daunted by this misfortune. "This is the moment," he said, "when characters of a superior order assert themselves;" adding on another occasion, "The English will compel us to do greater things than we intended." Thus isolated, he would march towards the rising sun, and would return from a tour of Eastern conquests at the head of Eastern nations. He continued to consolidate and strengthen his position in Egypt. Attempts were made to conciliate the people. Some of the French embraced the Musalman religion, and Bonaparte himself pronounced the creed of the Prophet in the Tomb of Cheops, and received from the natives recognition as El Kebir, The Exalted. On the eve of the last assault on St. Jean d'Acre, he said to Bourrienne,—"If I succeed I shall find in the town the Pacha's treasure and arms for 300,000 men. I stir up and arm all Syria. . . . I march on Damascus and Aleppo; as I advance in the country my army will be augmented by the discontented. I proclaim to the people the abolition of slavery, and of the tyrannical government of the Pashas. I reach Constantinople with armed masses. I overthrow the Turkish Empire; I found in the East a new and grand empire, which assures my place with posterity, and perhaps I return to Paris by way of Adrianople, after having annihilated the house of Austria." But his repulse before Acre dissipated, for the time being, his ideas of Oriental Empire, and he returned to France.

He did not, however, cease to be attracted by the glamour of the East. In the year 1800, a treaty of peace was concluded between France and Russia, and experts were appointed by the Emperor Paul to consider the question of a combined Franco-Russian invasion of India. In 1801, two expeditions were proposed, a Russian one through the Ural Mountains to the Indus (a rather vague proposition), and a French one through Persia, of which it is recorded that "the plan for the latter was worked out in the minutest detail, and every item was carefully commented upon by Bonaparte."

Again, in January 1805, when prepared for the invasion of England, we find Napoleon proposing to attack the East Indies with the Brest squadron and 30,000 men. In 1802, Sebastiani had been sent to the Levant to enquire into Persian affairs, and the results of his expedition were published in the *Moniteur* of January 30th, 1803. Early in 1807, a treaty was concluded with the Shah, under the terms of which, the historian Sloane tells us, "France promised to drive Russia from Georgia and to supply Persia with artillery; in return the Shah was to break with England, confiscate British property, instigate the peoples of Afghanistan and Kandahar to rebellion, set on foot an army to invade India, and in case the French should also despatch a land force against India, he was to give them free passage along a line of march to be subsequently laid out, together with means of sustenance." Consequent on these intrigues, more than one British Embassy was despatched to Persia, the best known being the mission of Sir John Malcolm, who had commanded the Nizam's Infantry during the last war in Mysore.

From this time onward the idea of Oriental empire continued to grow in the mind of Napoleon. It was discussed at Tilsit with Alexander of Russia, who wrote in February 1808, proposing to march into Asia by way of Constantinople, saying that "the Euphrates would not be reached before England would begin to tremble. One month after an agreement we could be on the Bosphorus. . . . By May 1st our troops could be in Asia." An expedition to Egypt was to sail from Corfu, while the united armies of Russia, France and Austria were to march on India. Napoleon studied the history of Persia, and after his surrender to England we find him comparing himself to Themistocles, who took refuge in that country. In 1808, he writes to his librarian: "The Emperor would wish M. Barbier to occupy himself, in conjunction with one of our best geographers, with the task of collecting memoirs about the campaigns which have taken place on the Euphrates and against the Parthians, beginning with that of Croesus down to the 8th century, and including those of Antonius, Trajan, Julian, etc.; he is to mark off on maps of suitable size, the route which each army followed, together with the ancient and modern names of the countries and principal towns, and add notes on the geographical features, and historical descriptions of each enterprise." This is of interest, showing not only that Napoleon still aspired to Oriental Empire, but that he appreciated the value of military history, a science so neglected in our time. Again in 1811, we find him issuing orders for expeditions to Egypt and Ireland. If these succeeded he would extend his empire far to the East and West. "They wish to know where we are going, where I shall plant the new pillars of Hercules. We will make an end of Europe, and then as robbers throw themselves on others less bold, we will cast ourselves on India which the latter class have mastered." "Three years more," he exclaimed to the Bavarian Minister, "and I am lord of the Universe."

Probably he looked on his expedition to Russia as a prelude to conquests further East, led on by a spirit of adventure, and attracted by the glamour of an unknown and mysterious land. But his visions of Oriental conquest were quenched for ever in the snows of Russia, and on the plains and mountains of the Iberian Peninsula, where the sun, shorn of the glory of Austerlitz, was setting on the ruins of his arms.

APPENDIX II.

THE BRINJARAS.

The Brinjaras deserve more than a passing notice, for they acted a large part in the operations of the war, and were at one time the principal means of transport throughout India. They are commonly supposed to be identical with the gypsies of Europe, and, like them, their origin is surrounded in mystery. The name is by some derived from the Sanscrit *Bunij*, a merchant. They are indicated by Arrian as one of the classes of Indian society. They are met with in wandering encampments from the Himalayas to Southern India, whilst there are also some settled communities in Rohilkhand and in other parts of the country. There was at one time a colony of these people in the vicinity of the ruined city of Mahoba in the North-West Provinces, where they dwelt in substantial stone houses, but have long since disappeared. In the Deccan I have found them in small settled communities, but they are almost entirely nomadic, seldom occupying their temporary hamlets for any extended period. The following from Wilks' "History of Mysore" is interesting —"Much has been conjectured and little ascertained regarding this extraordinary class of men, whose habits and history were at that period (1792) entirely unknown to the British Army. Every man and many of the women were armed with a variety of weapons, and though moving with their whole train of women and children, who would scarcely be classed among the impedimenta, proved themselves capable, in several instances, not only of military defence but of military enterprise, as was particularly evinced in the assault and plunder of the lower part of Cabal Droog." After a discussion with an assembly of chiefs regarding their descent and pressing for some traditional account of their original country and home, "That is our country," said the eldest of them, pointing to the tent which covered his grain bags, "and where-ever it is pitched is our home; my ancestors never told me of any other." Wilks, who wrote a hundred years ago, adds :—"After a war, in which of course many of their cattle are destroyed, they seek for some forest inhabited only by tigers, worthless to its government, and the terror of the neighbourhood, which they obtain permission to occupy, and enter it fearlessly, waging war with its former inhabitants until it becomes a safe nursery for the increase of their herds."

Since the days of Muhammad bin Tughlak in 1340, the Brinjaras have figured in the supply of armies in all campaigns in India. They are still to be found with their droves of pack bullocks employed as carriers in the remoter parts of the country. But with the spread of railways and other means of communication their occupation has almost gone, and they are fast disappearing or settling down, although their encampments, with the women dressed in picturesque parti-coloured skirts and a profusion of ornaments, are doubtless known to all who have wandered about the wilder parts of the country. "Their social system is unique, and they are guided exclusively by their own laws and customs; each community is governed by a priest, who exacts and receives implicit obedience, and who exercises, under the cloak of religion and supernatural agency, the undisputed power of life and death over them. They maintain the closest secrecy regarding their customs, and would sooner forfeit life than divulge them. Infanticide, human sacrifice, witchcraft, sorcery prevail amongst the different communities, who can recognise one another by masonic signs."

They have never been enlisted in our army, but, in class regiments under their own headmen or Naiks, they might make good irregular soldiers. They are generally of fine physique, manly, plucky, and in their own tribal organisation are accustomed to the strict discipline of their Naiks. They possess, moreover, more intelligence than most of the tribes and castes of India, whilst their nomadic habits of life render them in many respects peculiarly fitted for military service. In the Deccan, I have everywhere found the Brinjaras amongst the best of shikaris, and have always been glad to have them when beating for dangerous game, when they are plucky and trustworthy. They are themselves much addicted to the chase ; assisted by their fierce breed of dogs and armed with spears they hunt down their game. In my wanderings in the jungles in search of big game, I have often had considerable assistance from the Brinjaras. The haunts of tigers are frequently known to them, owing to the depredations committed by these animals upon their herds and sometimes upon themselves, and they are always ready to assist in bringing to bag the great beasts of prey. In this respect they are not secretive as to the presence of wild beasts, as are the generality of villagers in the Deccan, who almost invariably display a remarkable reluctance in giving any information regarding tigers and panthers, although these animals may be carrying on considerable depredations on their live stock. The Brinjaras are remarkably truthful, a virtue to which the mild Hindu is not generally addicted.

In beating for tigers I have always been glad to get a Brinjara Naik and his following; for they can be trusted as "stops," and relied upon to beat the jungle thoroughly, and not miss out dense patches of bush where the beast might be lurking. I recollect how one great tiger, trying to break out of the beat, rushed up the side of a ravine, scattering the beaters in all directions ; but a Brinjara Naik was fortunately at hand with some of his men, and, seeing that the tiger was likely to escape, he led them in a charge against the beast, uttering fierce shouts, and drove him grumbling down the slope again. Such incidents might be multiplied, and in most of my excursions in pursuit of big game this fine and manly race has figured largely. The following memorandum on Brinjaras and the supply of the Army in the Deccan is interesting.

Memorandum by Major-General the Hon'ble A. Wellesley, detailing the system for regulating the supplies of an army in the Deccan.

FORT WILLIAM,
The 3rd November 1804.

There are in every army four descriptions of persons and animals to be supplied with food, *viz.* :—

(i) European Soldiers.
(ii) Native Troops.

(iii) Horses of the Cavalry.

(iv) Followers of all descriptions, including horses, cattle, servants, etc., of officers, departments, soldiers, etc.

(*i*) *To feed the European soldiers, a Commissary of provisions is appointed.*—The quantity of provisions necessary for the number of men for any given period of time (two or three months) is issued to him from the public stores, or he purchases them, according to the orders which he may receive. Carriage is allotted for this provision, either carts or bullocks. In this quantity of provision the Commissary of provisions has only five days' grain, and the carriage allotted for that quantity ; and he indents on every fifth day on the Commissary of grain for that grain which will be necessary for the European troops for the following five days. The object of this arrangement is to keep the account of the grain clear, and that it may always be known what length of time the quantity of grain in camp will serve for the whole army.

(*ii*) *The Native Troops receive grain only.*—When the army is assembled a quantity of grain which will last the troops, including the Europeans, a given period of time (two or three months), is issued from the public stores to the Commissary of grain. Carriage is allotted for it, *viz.*:—bullocks, either the property of the company or hired for the purpose, and under the immediate charge of the Commissary of grain. When the Commissary of grain makes an issue, he replenishes it, either by drawing again upon the stores, if he can communicate with them, or by purchases in the country, or the bazaar, according to the orders which he may receive from the Officer Commanding the Army.

(*iii*) *The horses of the cavalry.*—When the number of horses to be fed is ascertained, a quantity of grain is issued from the public stores to the Gram Agent General. The Gram Agent General has under his charge and superintendence bullocks in sufficient number (either hired or belonging to the Company) to carry the remainder of the grain. When he makes an issue to the Quarter Master, he replaces it either by drawing again upon the stores, or by purchases in the bazaar or the country, according to the orders he may receive from the Commanding Officer of the Army.

(*iv*) *Followers of all descriptions.*— These persons live by the daily purchases they make in the bazaar, the supply of which becomes an object of the greatest importance. What follows is the mode of supplying the bazaar which I have seen practised. The bazaars are placed under the charge and superintendence of an officer called the Superintendent of Supplies, and in him the whole business of the internal police and supply of the camp rests. The following modes are adopted to supply the grain required for it.

I. *Brinjaras.*—These are a class of carriers who gain a livelihood by transporting grain or other commodities from one part of the country to another. They attend armies, and trade nearly in the same manner as they do in times of peace. They either purchase grain themselves in the country with their own money, or with money advanced to them by the Company, and sell it in the bazaars at the rates of the day on their own account, or they take grain at the Company's stores at certain reduced rates and sell it on their own account in the bazaars; or they take up grain in the Company's stores and carry it with the army, and receive a sum of money for every march they make, and the grain is sold in the bazaars on account of the Company; or they hire their cattle by the month to the Company, and take up grain from the public stores and carry it with the army, where it is sold in the bazaars on account of the Company. It is the business of the Superintendent of Supplies to settle all these various accounts, and to see that the Brinjaras get fresh loads as fast as they can empty them, and to know always, as nearly as possible, the quantity of grain which this description of people have got.

II. *Biparries.*—This is another description of dealers. They do not go in large flocks like the Brinjaras, to such distances, to look for grain. They are generally attached to the camp bazaar, and they go out to the villages and towns in the neighbourhood of the camp, and purchase grain and bring it in immediately for sale. These are a more civilised, industrious, and useful people than the Brinjaras; they are much more active, and if the country is open, the supply which they bring in is more plentiful.

III. *The Biparries of the country.*—These are of the same class with the second, only not immediately attached to the camp. They bring grain to the camp from the neighbouring villages, when ordered by the Amildars and Government, or excited by their own interests; but their attendance is not so constant. Besides these three principal descriptions, there are others, but they may all be classed under one of the three general heads.

From this statement it is obvious that when the communication between the army and the country is not free, that alone upon which the bazaar can depend is the Brinjaras, who are generally assembled in large numbers, and attend it when the campaign is opened. It frequently happens, as was the case with me in the last campaign, that the Brinjaras desert the army. The communication with the country may be cut off from many causes; the enemy, the swelling of a river, bad roads, rainy weather, etc. On the other hand, the army may outmarch the supplies which might be expected from Biparries, etc. In any of these cases it is useful for the Commissary of grain to issue to the Superintendent of Supplies any quantity of grain that may be required to supply the consumption which falls upon the bazaar. The Commissary of grain makes his purchases again from the bazaar when it fills. The Gram Agent General issues, by order, gram to the Superintendent of the bazaar when that article is wanted for officers' horses and cattle. He frequently issues it by order to the Agent for the public draught bullocks, when the supply of grain in the bazaar is not sufficient for the cattle in his department.

In this manner the army can never be in want. The camp stores are always kept complete, and supply the bazaars occasionally while the bazaars, in more plentiful times (which under good arrangement must occur frequently), supply the camp stores.

APPENDIX III.

THE MUTINY AT VELLORE.

It is interesting to follow the fortunes of the family of Tipu Sultan after they were interned in the fortress at Vellore, where they were the cause of a remarkable outbreak which occurred there seven years later.

The family, which consisted of four sons and some daughters, were provided with an establishment of a magnificence more in accordance with their former state than their present condition; their quarters in the fort resembled a palace, and large numbers of their followers had been allowed to migrate to Vellore, while husbands for the princesses came from different parts of the country. In these circumstances it is easy to understand that a nucleus of disaffection was formed, and that the Muhammadan sepoys were subject to temptations to rebel against their British officers.

But in November 1805, a further cause arose for disaffection among the native ranks of the Madras Army involving Hindus as well as Muhammadans. In that month an order was issued for the introduction of a new fashion of turban, patterns of which were sent to Vellore, as well as to other stations between April and June 1806. The sepoys objected to these head-dresses, as they bore a resemblance to the hats worn by the Eurasian drummers, and a rumour spread that this was a measure preparatory to enforcing conversion to Christianity.

Nor was this all. An order was shortly afterwards promulgated to the effect that "a native soldier shall not mark his face to denote his caste, or wear ear-rings when dressed in his uniform, and it is further directed that at all parades, and upon all duties, every soldier of the battalion shall be clean shaved on the chin. It is also directed that uniformity shall, as far as is practicable, be preserved in regard to the quantity and shape of the hair on the upper lip."

It is not surprising that such inconsiderate orders, prejudicial to the sentiments and religion of both Hindus and Musalmans, should cause the smouldering discontent already existent to break out into open mutiny. The garrison of Vellore in July 1806 consisted of four companies of His Majesty's 69th Regiment; three companies 1st Battalion, 1st Madras Infantry; and the 2nd Battalion, 23rd Madras Infantry, the whole under the command of Colonel Fancourt. At Arcot, 16 miles distant, Colonel Robert Rollo Gillespie had under his command the 19th Light Dragoons, and their comrades of Assaye and many another battlefield, the 7th Madras Cavalry, known in those days as the "Black Nineteenth" from their close connection with the Dragoons.

Gillespie was one of the most energetic and bravest officers of his time. Born at Comber, County Down, on 21st January 1760, he was appointed Cornet in the 3rd Regiment, Irish Horse (now 6th Carabineers), on the 25th April 1783. In 1787 at Kildare he fought a duel across a handkerchief with a brother of Sir Jonah Barrington, whom he shot dead. In 1792 he was promoted to a Lieutenancy in the 20th Light Dragoons, which was raised for service in Jamaica. In the attack on Port-au-Prince he distinguished himself by swimming across a harbour infested with sharks, with a flag of truce, and his sword in his mouth, under fire from the land. During his residence in San Domingo, his house was attacked one night by eight desperadoes, who murdered his servant, when Gillespie, hearing the noise, fell upon the assassins with his sword, killed six of them, and was dangerously wounded by the other two, who then made their escape. Later he exchanged into the 19th Light Dragoons, then stationed at Arcot, and proceeded to India through Germany, Austria, Servia, Constantinople, Aleppo, and Bagdad, a hazardous journey in those days. At Constantinople he fought a successful duel with a French officer. It was fortunate that such a brave and determined officer was at hand when the mutiny broke out.

At Vellore the 69th were quartered in the fort; the sepoys mostly lived in the native town outside, providing certain guards within the precincts of the fort, where also the arms were kept. Some of the guards were composed of mixed native and British soldiers.

On the night of 10th July 1806 the greater portion of the 23rd Madras Infantry were given permission to sleep in the fort, so as to be ready near their arms for a field day which had been ordered for the next morning. At half past two in the morning the sepoys of the main guard suddenly attacked their British comrades, and murdered all except four, who contrived to escape. At about the same time an attack was made on the barracks of the 69th, and continued throughout the night. In the meantime eight officers and a sergeant, alarmed by the firing, met at the house of Lieutenant Ewing, 1st Madras Infantry, who had secured the arms and ammunition of four men on guard at his quarters. After an attack had been repulsed, these officers proceeded to the adjoining house of Surgeon Jones, which offered greater facilities for defence. From here Sergeant Brady went out to reconnoitre and returned in an hour with information that the Commandant of the garrison and all the Europeans on guard had been killed, and that the Mysore flag had been hoisted, whilst the barracks were being attacked by the fire of two six-pounders as well as musketry. At 8 A.M. the sepoys broke in at the back of the house, and the officers effected their retreat to barracks by the front. There they found many killed and wounded, especially by the fire of the two guns, which were playing on them from short range. The men had but few cartridges left, having originally been provided with only six rounds; but a sally was made by about 200 who survived out of the 372 forming the detachment of the 69th; a position was taken up on a bastion, and an advance then made along the ramparts to the main gateway, under a heavy fire from the palace, by which several officers and many men were killed or wounded. A party being left to keep the gateway, the remainder drove the sepoys from the south-east bastion and cavalier, and obtained possession of the grand magazine, only to find that it contained nothing but gun-powder. All the officers had now fallen, with the exception of Surgeons Jones and Dean, who gallantly led the survivors. After visiting the magazine, the soldiers wished to go and attack the sepoy barracks, but this was not permitted, as so many had fallen. The party then returned to the gateway, the Mysore flag being pulled down *en route* under a heavy fire by Sergeant McManus and Private Philip Bottom of the 69th.

At daybreak that morning Colonel Gillespie rode out on the way to Vellore, where he had an engagement to breakfast with Colonel Fancourt. He was not gone far when he was met by a messenger galloping from the fort, who had been despatched with news of the outbreak by an officer who resided outside the walls. In a very short time Gillespie, with a squadron of the 19th* under Captain Wilson, and a troop of Madras Cavalry, was thundering along the road to Vellore, leaving orders for the galloper guns and the remainder of the 19th to follow.

The 69th had been in Jamaica four years before, and when the relieving party approached, Sergeant Brady, who was with the survivors over the gateway, exclaimed—"If Colonel Gillespie be alive, God Almighty has sent him from the West Indies to save our lives in the East!" The moment was critical, for the survivors had expended their last cartridge, and the sepoys were

* The author of "Twelve Years' Military Adventure" (1829) relates—"The old 19th Dragoons, excepting that their habits were not the most temperate, were a fine specimen of what a regiment ought to be. By almost constant service, and the manly game of long bowls which the old Indian regiments used to practise under the hottest sun, these men had become perfectly bronzed, and were as hard as iron, being proof against sun without and arrack within. They used to call themselves the 'Terrors of the East.' Indeed such was the respect in which they were held by the natives that, when they embarked for England, all the Black Town of Madras was emptied to see them off."

gathering to destroy them, but, seeing the approach of the troopers, the greater number retired to the further ramparts, leaving the gateway and one bastion to Sergeant Brady's party of the 69th. There were four gates, of which the two outer ones were open, and the drawbridge was down. The third gate was opened by men of the 69th, who were lowered by their belts, but they lost several men during this operation, and were unable to force the fourth gate. Gillespie then broke open the wicket, and entering the fort with Captain Wilson and three men on foot, attempted to open the last gate from inside, being all the while exposed to a heavy fire, but could not do so, as it was strongly locked and barred. At this moment Gillespie found a rope, which he threw up to the men over to the gateway, who hauled him up on to the ramparts. Seizing a pair of regimental colours, the gallant colonel at once headed a bayonet charge against a battery, turned the guns on the mutineers, and although there was no ammunition, kept them in check for a time. At this moment, when it seemed as if the fate of the party could no longer be averted, the remainder of the 19th and the galloper guns appeared at the gate, which was commanded by two guns, while the sepoys had assembled to dispute the entrance. Placing himself at the head of the survivors of the 69th, Gillespie headed a bayonet charge to clear the way for the cavalry; the gate was blown open by a shot from one of the galloper guns, the cavalry charged into the fort and the mutineers were slain to the number of 350, while others who escaped through the sally-port were cut down outside. By 10 o'clock all was over. The 69th lost 115 killed and 76 wounded; the 19th had one trooper killed and three wounded, and Colonel Gillespie was ridde down and badly bruised in the mêlée.

Thus ended one of the most stirring episodes not only in the life of a gallant man of action, but in the history of India. Gillespie in 1811 was chiefly instrumental in the conquest of Java. In 1814 he was shot through the heart during the Nepal War when attacking the fort of Kalunga in Dehra Dun, a fitting termination to his whole career, and was buried at Meerut. "By the irony of fate on the 10th May 1857, the first shots of the great Sepoy Mutiny were fired within a mile of the monument over his grave, and were the beginning of events that at one time threatened to involve British power in the East in ruin, and that have changed the whole course of Indian history. If that gallant spirit was still permitted to take interest in the events of that day, how it must have chafed at the exhibition of incapacity and indecision that led to such disastrous consequences. In view of what happened at Vellore, it is allowable to believe that the great Mutiny of 1857 would never have assumed the proportions it did, had the first outbreak been met by the same display of energy and resolution as was shown, under similar circumstances, fifty-one years earlier."*

* "The Nineteenth and Their Times." By Colonel John Biddulph.

The great services of this gallant soldier received tardy recognition. On the 2nd January 1815, before the news of his death reached England, he was gazetted a K.C.B., and a monument by Chantrey was erected to his memory in St. Paul's. An obelisk was also put up in his native place.

The Mysore Princes were removed to Calcutta; and the obnoxious orders, which were one of the principal causes of the outbreak, were cancelled.

Vellore had for some time a considerable garrison, and fifty years ago the ditch, which was full of water, contained a number of crocodiles. There was then a garrison order forbidding the killing of these reptiles, but the British subaltern—always bent on sport—used to catch them surreptitiously by an arrangement of hooks, baited with a goose, or used to shoot them when they came to the surface, a pariah dog, soundly beaten on the bank, serving as a dinner-bell to the hungry monsters. It is even said that no less a person than the Brigadier had been seen looking on at the sport from a place of concealment, although it was indulged in contrary to his orders. It is also related that when the gun was fired nightly after "Last Post," the crocodiles all sank to the bottom of the moat, probably owing to the noise and concussion, and soldiers wishing to break out of barracks were in the habit of taking advantage of this to swim across in safety, and so escape for the night, returning in the same manner when the morning gun was fired at réveille.

The Fort of Vellore is now abandoned, and its massive granite walls are the sole witnesses of the stirring past. But, standing at the gateway one can hear in fancy Gillespie and his galloper guns come thundering up the road from Arcot.

APPENDIX IV.

THE HYDERABAD CONTINGENT.

The contingent of troops supplied by the Nizam in alliance with the British Government was first furnished under the terms of the Tripartite Treaty of 1790. This treaty was entered into between the British, the Nizam of Hyderabad, and the Peshwa. Under its provisions the Nizam was obliged to furnish 10,000 troops, which took part in the campaign against Tipn Sultan in the following year, and included two battalions of regular infantry disciplined by the famous French adventurer Raymond.

The Nizam's cavalry at this period is thus described in Wilks' *History of Mysore*:—"They were rated at 15,000 and really amounted to 10,000 men, well mounted on horses in excellent condition; and to those who had never before had an opportunity of observing an Indian Army, their first appearance was novel and interesting. It is probable that no national or private collection of ancient arms in Europe contains any weapon or article of personal equipment which might not be traced in this motley crowd : the Parthian bow and arrow, the iron club of Scythia, sabres of every age and nation, lances of every length and description, and matchlocks of every form, metallic helmets of every pattern, simple defences of the head, a steel bar descending diagonally as a protection to the face; defences of bars, chains, or scale work, descending behind or on the shoulders, cuirasses, suits of armour, or detached pieces for the arm, complete coats of mail in chain-work, shields, buckles and quilted jackets, sabre-proof. The ostentatious display of these antique novelties was equally curious in its way; the free and equal use of two sword-arms, the precise and perfect command of a balanced spear eighteen feet long, of the club which was to shiver an iron helmet, of an arrow discharged in flight, but, above all, the total absence of every symptom of order, or obedience, or command, excepting groups collecting round their respective flags; every individual an independent warrior, self-impelled, affecting to be the champion whose single arm was to achieve victory; scampering among each other in wild confusion; the whole exhibition presenting to the mind an imagery scarcely more allied to previous impressions of reality than the fictions of an Eastern tale, or the picturesque disorder of a dramatic scene."

After the campaign of 1791 Raymond's corps was gradually increased until, at the battle of Kardla, between the Nizam and the Mahrattas in 1795, it amounted to some 7,000 men. These troops, however, do not appear to have distinguished themselves, although they fought in the presence of the Nizam's corps of Amazons, known as the *Zafar Paltan*, or victorious battalions, who did not behave any worse than the remainder of the army on that occasion. It does not appear whether the Amazons earned the distinguished appellation of *Zafar Paltan* by the glory of their deeds, or whether it was merely a tribute to what should have been the gentler sex. They have long since been disbanded, the place of muskets on their shoulders being taken by smiling infants. The Nizam took umbrage at the absence of assistance from the British in this war with the Mahrattas, and from this time the French began to gain an undue and dangerous ascendency at the Court of the Nizam.

By 1798 we find the French corps amounting to 14,000 men, who bore the Colours of the French Republic and had the Cap of Liberty engraved upon their buttons. This corps was divided into ten battalions, and had a train of Field Artillery, an ordnance park of forty pieces, and a troop of 60 Dragoons. The British Government beheld with jealousy and apprehension the recrudescence and progress of French influence in the councils of the Nizam, and when, in 1798, hostilities were impending with Tipu Sultan, it was feared that the French battalions might rise in aid of that potentate, who had the support of a corps of their fellow countrymen. Accordingly, under agreement with the Nizam, a British force marched to Hyderabad, and took up a position to coerce the French troops, which were disbanded; the French officers being deported to their own country. Such of the men of the disbanded corps as were fit for service were drafted into battalions which, under British officers, formed the contingent furnished by the Nizam in the last war with Tipu Sultan.

On the conclusion of the Mysore War, a fresh treaty was entered into between the British Government and the Nizam, under the terms of which the latter was bound to furnish, in the event of a war between the contracting parties on the one hand and a third state, a force of 6,000 infantry and 9,000 cavalry. A quota of troops was accordingly, after a great deal of delay, furnished by the Nizam to co-operate with the army under General Wellesley in the Mahratta War of 1803. These troops, however, proved so inefficient, that we find General Wellesley writing to the British Resident at Hyderabad on December 2nd, 1803:—"I think it possible that at the conclusion of the war some means may be devised to place the public force of the Nizam's Government upon a better footing, and it is very desirable that you should turn your thoughts to the subject. In its present state it is of no use whatever. The Soubah (Nizam) can do nothing without the assistance of the British Government. This inconvenience will increase daily unless some remedy is applied, and in a greater proportion as the extent of the Soubah's territories may be greater. The consequence will be that the British troops will always be in the field; and, indeed, if the Soubah's military establishments are not improved, the Subsidiary * Force as at present constituted will not be equal to the duties which will be required from it." As a consequence of the delay on the part of the Hyderabad Government in furnishing their contingent in the Mahratta War, and of its inefficiency when furnished, it was found necessary to effect a thorough reform of the regular troops of the State. It was recognised that, in order to provide a satisfactory force in time of war as required by treaty, it would be necessary to organise, train, and maintain them in time of peace. With this object in view it was decided to form the Nizam's Contingent into a regular force, commanded by British officers, some of whom were locally appointed and some lent by the East India Company. The work of reform was commenced by Mr. (afterwards Sir Henry) Russell, by the raising of the Russell Brigade of two battalions at Hyderabad in 1813. Subsequently six other battalions of Nizam's infantry were formed in Berar, and a large body of cavalry was trained under British officers, and eventually formed into four regiments, and four batteries of Field

* The Subsidiary Force consisted of British and Native troops supplied under treaty and quartered in Hyderabad territory.

Artillery were also raised. This force became the famous Hyderabad Contingent, which consisted of :—

1st Nizam's Cavalry, became 1st Lancers, Hyderabad Contingent, now XX Deccan Horse.

2nd Nizam's Cavalry, became 2nd Lancers, Hyderabad Contingent, now 29th Lancers, Deccan Horse.

3rd Nizam's Cavalry, became 3rd Lancers, Hyderabad Contingent, broken up in 1903.

4th Nizam's Cavalry, became 4th Lancers, Hyderabad Contingent, now 30th Lancers, Gordon's Horse.

5th Nizam's Cavalry, disbanded in 1853.

Artillery, Russell Brigade, became 1st Field Battery, Hyderabad Contingent. Disbanded in 1903.

Artillery, Aurangabad Division, became 2nd Field Battery. Hyderabad Contingent. Disbanded in 1903.

Artillery, Hingoli Brigade, became 3rd Field Battery, Hyderabad Contingent. Disbanded in 1903.

Artillery, Ellichpur Brigade, became 4th Field Battery, Hyderabad Contingent. Disbanded in 1903.

Russell Brigade { 1st Battalion became 1st Infantry, Hyderabad Contingent, now 94th Russell's Infantry.
2nd Battalion became 2nd Infantry, Hyderabad Contingent, now 95th Russell's Infantry.

1st Battalion, Berar Infantry, became 3rd Infantry, Hyderabad Contingent, now 96th Berar Infantry.

2nd Battalion, Berar Infantry, became 4th Infantry, Hyderabad Contingent, now 97th Deccan Infantry.

3rd Battalion, Berar Infantry. Disbanded in 1853.

4th Battalion, Berar Infantry. Disbanded in 1853.

1st Battalion, Ellichpur Brigade, became 5th Infantry, Hyderabad Contingent, now 98th Infantry.

2nd Battalion, Ellichpur Brigade, became 6th Infantry, Hyderabad Contingent, now 99th Deccan Infantry.

The Hyderabad Contingent thus became a very efficient fighting force, and was placed under the Resident of Hyderabad, and eventually subject direct to the orders of the Government of India. It was paid for by the Nizam until 1853, when, the payment of the troops having fallen in arrears, and a large sum being due to the British Government on this account, the province of Berar was made over to British administration, and the Contingent paid out of its revenues.

The services of the Hyderabad Contingent were very distinguished, and no other portion of the Native army has seen more fighting than did this force, at least up to 1869. In the early part of the last century the country was infested by turbulent spirits, who viewed with dismay and opposed with force the establishment of effective power in the land where they had been so long accustomed to carry on with impunity their lawless mode of life. The early history of the conquest and pacification of this country is apt to be forgotten, and the enforced state of comparative inactivity of the Hyderabad Contingent during the past forty years, induced by its local character, appears to have earned for it in some quarters in recent years the reputation of being a force that has always slumbered in cantonments. It is only the student of history who, in the course of his researches, becomes aware of the progress of events which have led to the pacification of India, and is able to estimate at their proper value those great deeds that won and kept the Empire. In those events and those deeds the Hyderabad Contingent played a conspicuous part. Its corps participated in the victories which crowned the British arms in the Mahratta War of 1817; they contributed largely to the pacification of the country during the ensuing forty years, when scarcely a month passed without a portion of the force being on active service in the field, and they formed a great factor in the suppression of the mutiny in Central India in 1857-58, and in the maintenance of peace in Southern India during that dangerous period. The deeds of such officers as Evan Davies, George Hampton, John Sutherland, Murtaza Yar Jang and Ahmad Bakhsh Khan, who rode forth so often through the Deccan at the head of their gallant horsemen, who made great marches and performed great acts of valour, illuminate the page of history, and lend a spirit of romance to the story of the campaign in which they bore so conspicuous a part. Our native army is justly proud of its records, and no portion of it had a greater right to such pride than the squadrons, batteries, and battalions of the Hyderabad Contingent.

During the ninety years of the existence of the Force it performed good service both within and without the confines of the Nizam's Dominions. It was entirely due to its services that a state of tranquillity was established in Hyderabad and Berar, and that a condition of profound peace has been maintained there for the past forty years. Before the regeneration of the Nizam's army by British officers the country was overrun by Pindaris and infested by predatory Naiks and Rohilla bands, who plundered the inhabitants with impunity and defied the Government, taking refuge in those strongholds which one by one fell before the irresistible assault of the Contingent troops. The story of those times abounds with glorious episodes, and is illuminated by the record of deeds of valour and devotion to duty on the part of both officers and men.

Nor was it only in the service of the Nizam that the Contingent proved its utility. Within four years of the formation of the infantry and one year of the reform of the cavalry, the whole force was employed in a great war, which, in the year 1817, involved almost the whole of India, and was characterised by several pitched battles and many sieges. At the investment and capture of the fort of Nowah, carried out by the Nizam's Contingent alone, the Cavalry and the Russell Brigade earned for themselves an imperishable name, while their casualties on this occasion exceeded those in any two of the many North-West Frontier expeditions of which we have heard so much, with the exception of the three principal ones.* When the Indian Mutiny broke out in 1857, the Hyderabad Contingent, although largely recruited from the insurgent races, not only remained true to its salt, but by its attitude and its deeds saved the situation in Southern India. And when a large portion of the force took the field in Central India they added to their great reputation by deeds that have not been surpassed by any of our Native troops. It was not in vain that Sir Hugh Rose, after they had marched a thousand miles with him and distinguished themselves in many actions, called the cavalry "the wings of the army," and they then confirmed the truth of Lord Gough's estimate of them as the finest Irregular Cavalry in the World."

When the smouldering embers of the mutiny had been stamped out, but little remained for a local Force in Southern India to do within the area it occupied. The tide of war had rolled to the north, never to return. The turbulent spirits who infested the Nizam's Dominions and plundered the inhabitants during the first half of the century had all been suppressed. The Force was, indeed, available for external service, and some of the individuals and units had taken part in campaigns in distant parts of the Empire, particularly in the last Burmese War, where two cavalry and two infantry regiments were employed. But the principal *raison d'être* of the Contingent, as set forth in the treaty of 1800 between the British and the Nizam's Government, had disappeared. In 1903 the local character of the Force was abolished, and, while its artillery was disbanded, the cavalry and infantry were incorporated with the regular army, and placed on the same footing as the remainder of our Indian forces.

APPENDIX V.

GENERAL LAKES† CAMPAIGN IN 1803.

On August 7th, 1803, General Lake marched from Cawnpore with his infantry under command of Major-General St. John. The cavalry, under Colonel St. Leger, followed next day, and on the 12th the army was concentrated in the neighbourhood of Kanauj, a city of historic interest, formerly the capital of Hindustan. It is interesting to remark the different conditions of campaigning in those days, before the British officer was limited to a kit weighing a few pounds. This was the opening of a great war, yet a contemporary writer tells us that at Kanauj "military occupations were so diversified with the scenes of social harmony and festivity, as to exhibit the confidence of tranquil satisfaction in the prospect of permanent peace, rather than the preparations for war. The heat of the day was moderate, but the nights were cold; and many officers had not only glass doors to their tents,

*In the Ambeyla Campaign, the Black Mountain Expedition, 1860, and the Tirah Campaign alone did the casualties exceed those at the siege of Nowah.

† Afterwards Lord Lake.

but chimneys of brick, by which means they were enabled to enjoy the pleasure of an English fire-side with their wives and families, who had been allowed to accompany them on this occasion. These domestic comforts were heightened by the luxuries of the table, where the finest wines of every clime, from the exhilarating Sheeraz of Persia to the ruby Carbonelle and humble Port, abounded.

"In the evenings the spacious ball-room fitted up for the purpose displayed an elegant assemblage of youth and beauty, grace and hilarity, softening the cares of life, and removing every apprehension of danger." Certainly this was campaigning in clover.

However, there were some more manly and useful amusements, for the chronicler proceeds:—"Between the enjoyments and the discharge of professional duties the intervals were filled up frequently with field sports, to which the surrounding wilds of Kanauj afforded ample scope. Here, amidst lofty grass covering the ruins of splendid edifices and the tombs of princes, lay concealed a variety of game, while beasts of prey, such as wolves, jackals, and tigers, secluded themselves in retreats which formerly resounded with the voice of gladness, and witnessed the reciprocation of human kindness. On one of these hunting excursions a tiger of large size was shot with a pistol by General Lake just as the ferocious animal was in the act of springing upon Major Nairne, by whom it had been previously speared."

At 4 A.M., on the morning of August 29th, the army marched into Mahratta territory against Perron,* the French General in Sindhia's service, who was encamped a short distance from Aligarh. The enemy, observing this approach, struck their tents, and took up a strong position with 20,000 horse, their right resting on the great fortress, and their front covered by a deep morass. The British General moved against the hostile left, and soon put the Mahrattas to flight. Perron fled towards Agra, leaving Colonel Pedron† with orders to defend the fort of Aligarh to the last.

General Lake tried to negotiate with Pedron for the surrender of the place, but that commander received from Perron the following grandiloquent instructions, and was induced to hold out:—"You will have received the answer you are to make to the propositions of General Lake. I never could have believed that for an instant you could have thought of a capitulation. Remember you are a Frenchman; and let no action of yours tarnish the character of your nation. I hope in a few days to send back the English General as fast or faster than he came. Make yourself perfectly easy on this subject. Either the Emperor's army or that of General Lake shall find a grave before the fort

* Perron was a native of Chateau du Lovie, France; came to India as a sailor under Admiral Suffrein in 1780. He entered Sindhia's service, and raised a large force of troops which were trained in the European fashion. After his surrender to General Lake he retired to his native country, where he died in 1834.

† Pedron, a Frenchman who had served many native princes since 1760.

of Aligarh. Do your duty and defend the fort while one stone remains upon another. Once more, remember your nation. The eyes of millions are fixed upon you."

On the morning of September 4th a force composed of four companies of the 76th Regiment, the 1st Battalion, 4th Regiment, Native Infantry, and four companies of the 17th Native Infantry, led by Colonel Monson, advanced to the assault, under cover of the fire of two batteries which had been erected during the night. The signal for the storming party was given by the morning gun. Arrived within a hundred yards of the gate, the assailants found a traverse mounted with three six-pounders, from which the enemy were dislodged before they had time to fire. Colonel Monson then attempted to enter the fort with two companies of the 76th, but found the guard had retired and closed the gate. At the same time Major McLeod, commanding the 76th, tried to scale the wall with his Grenadiers, but was repulsed by a formidable row of pikes. The enemy even climbed down the scaling-ladders placed against the walls, and attacked the stormers. The position appeared critical. Colonel Monson was wounded by a pike. Four Grenadier officers and the adjutant of the 76th, and an officer of the 4th Native Infantry were killed, the assailants being all this time exposed to the fire of the besieged. But no dangers could appal British soldiers, and no obstacles could preveut their advance.

Three gates were blown down in succession, the party advancing under fire from one to the other. Some delay occurred at the fourth gate, which was found too strong to force, but Major McLeod succeeded in passing through the wicket, and the place was soon in the hands of the British. The enemy had at least two thousand killed, and the surrounding ditch was choked with dead bodies, for many attempted to escape by swimming and many were drowned, whilst numbers of those who succeeded in effecting a crossing were cut up by a picquet of the 27th Dragoons. On the British side 59 were killed, including 6 British officers, while 11 British officers and 195 men were wounded. Two hundred and eighty-one guns and a large quantity of equipment and military stores were taken, as well as some tumbrils full of Spanish dollars. Pedron, who was taken prisoner, is described as an elderly man, clad in a green jacket, with gold lace and epaulettes.

The success of the operation was materially facilitated by Mr. Lucan,* a British officer who had quitted the service of Sindhia to avoid fighting against his country, and who led the storming party to the gate and pointed out the road through the fort. While these operations were in progress a large body

* Lucan, an Irishman, commended to the Governor-General by Lake for his gallant services. He was rewarded with a commission in the 74th Regiment. He commanded a body of irregular cavalry in Colonel Monson's force in 1804, where he was wounded and made prisoner by Holkar; he died a prisoner at Kotah soon afterwards.

of predatory Mahratta Horse, under Monsieur Fleury,* had entered British territory for the purpose of creating a diversion, and had attacked the Cantonment of Shekoabad on the 2nd September. The place was garrisoned by only five companies of the 1st Battalion, 11th Native Infantry, under Colonel Coningham, who withstood the attack of five thousand of the enemy's cavalry from four in the morning until two in the afternoon, when the Mahrattas were driven off with heavy loss. They, however, returned to the attack on the 4th September, the day Aligarh was taken, and eventually terms were come to between the combatants, the British Commander undertaking that his troops should abstain from further service against Sindhia during the war, and being suffered to retire with all his arms. The cantonment was then burnt and pillaged by the Mahrattas. In this action 6 British officers were wounded, and 63 sepoys killed and wounded. Other desultory actions took place during the subjection of the country, and the advance on Delhi, which was commenced on September 7th.

The great city of Delhi, towards which the British army was now directed, had been taken by many conquerors. It had been sacked by Taimur the Tartar; by Babar, the founder of the Moghal Empire which was brought to such a pitch of greatness by his grandson Akbar, but was now tottering to its fall; by Nadir Shah, the Persian invader, whose massacres gave the name to the Gate of Blood; and by the Mahrattas whose hordes were afterwards defeated at Karnal by the combined armies of the Moghal Emperor Muhammad and the Afghan Ahmad Khan. But it had not hitherto succumbed to the arms of the British, the white race from across the seas whose coming had been foretold by the Sikh Guru of old when he stood in his prison in the Imperial City, gazing with prophetic vision towards the West.

Delhi was now dominated by the Mahrattas, under whom the French adventurer Perron held in durance the wretched Shah Alam, effete descendant of the house of Taimur, who sat in squalor on the Moghal throne.

Leaving Aligarh on 7th September, the army marched towards Delhi, receiving the same day the submission of Perron, who was permitted to retire to the French settlement of Chandernagore, accompanied by some of his subordinates. On the 10th intelligence was received that Monsieur Louis Bourquien† had crossed the Jumna to attack the British, with sixteen battalions of regular infantry, six thousand cavalry, and a large train of ordnance. At 11 o'clock on the morning of the 11th September the British army encamped near the Jehna *nullah*, about six miles from Delhi. The enemy at once

*A Frenchman who, on the fall of Aligarh, was taken to Agra by his men, but escaped and joined Perron, whom he accompanied to Calcutta.

†Louis Bourquien came to Pondicheri with Admiral Suffrein, and was afterwards in a regiment of the East India Company. He was then in the Begum Sumru's service, and in 1794 entered one of de Boigne's corps. He surrendered to General Lake and is said to have subsequently retired to France with an immense fortune.

appeared in increasing strength, and General Lake, taking three regiments of cavalry, went out to reconnoitre the hostile army, which he found drawn up in order of battle on rising ground, the flanks resting on swamps, behind which the cavalry was posted, the front protected by entrenchments and defended by artillery, the whole position concealed by high grass jungle. The reconnoitring force was received with a heavy cannonade, and the British General, having seen that a frontal attack only was feasible, sent back for his artillery and cavalry. The total British force amounted to only about 4,500 men, and included the 76th Regiment, seven battalions of native infantry, the 27th Dragoons, and two regiments of native cavalry ; the opposing army numbered not less than 6,000 cavalry and 13,000 infantry. An hour elapsed before the British line arrived, during which the cavalry, exposed to a heavy fire from the enemy's guns, suffered considerably, and General Lake had a horse killed under him.

On the arrival of his troops at a convenient distance, the British General, in order by a feint to draw the enemy from their entrenchments, retired his cavalry in a regular line. The Mahrattas, thinking that this was a retreat, advanced with loud shouts, exulting in prospective victory, but their hilarity was checked when the British cavalry, opening out from the centre, disclosed the line of infantry in rear. Leading his little force in person, at the head of the 76th Regiment, General Lake now advanced straight upon the hostile position through a tremendous fire of round, grape, and chain shot, which tore through the British ranks from a hundred guns. The British troops, however, advanced steadily to within one hundred yards of the foe, without even removing their muskets from their shoulders ; the whole line then fired a volley, and, led by the Commander-in-Chief, charged with the bayonet, putting the enemy to flight in all directions. The onslaught of the infantry having been completed, they broke rapidly into columns of companies, thus allowing the cavalry with their galloper guns to charge through the intervals, and pursue the flying foe, numbers of whom were drowned in the waters of the Jumna. The whole of the enemy's stores and guns were captured, and their loss in the battle was estimated at not less than 3,000 men. On the British side 426, including 16 officers, were killed and wounded. Sixty-eight guns and 61 tumbrils laden with ammunition, besides two containing treasure, were captured.

A contemporary description of the captured ordnance is interesting. "The iron guns were of European manufacture ; but the brass guns, mortars, and howitzers were cast in India, with the exception of one Portuguese three-pounder. Some were made at Muttra, and others at Oojein, but evidently from the design and execution of an European artist. The dimensions in general were those of the French, and the workmanship highly finished. Thirteen of the four-pounders had iron cylinders, or bores, over which it would seem the metal was run in casting the piece, the adherence being so close that no chasm appeared, and nothing but the different colours of the two metals discovered the junction. The iron cylinder, or bore, was composed of four longitudinal pieces of hammered iron, remarkably close, and neatly fitted throughout the bore. The whole of the guns were furnished with well made elevating screws of the latest French improvement. To the mortars and howitzers also the same kind of elevating screws were, by a simple and ingenious adjustment, made, so as to elevate the piece to any angle, and give either of them the double capacity of mortar and howitzer."

The battle had been watched from the towers of Delhi by a crowd which afterwards greeted the victors with joyous acclamations. On the 16th September General Lake was conducted by Prince Mirza Akbar Shah, the heir-apparent, to the presence of the blind and aged Moghal Emperor who, stripped of authority and reduced to poverty, was seated under a small tattered canopy, and who was said not only to have shed tears, but, in the language of Oriental hyperbole, to have recovered his long-lost sight on the joyful occasion.

The French officers surrendered after the battle, which thus struck a final blow at French influence in Northern India. Meanwhile the armies of Wellesley and Stevenson were rapidly closing in on the Mahratta armies in the Deccan, where the sun of Assaye was about to rise.

The illustrious Governor-General, the Marquis Wellesley, whose policy had been directed towards the end now about to be accomplished, issued a stirring order to the troops after the battle of Delhi, from which the following may well be quoted :—

"In testimony of the peculiar honour acquired by the army under the command of His Excellency General Lake, the Governor-General in Council is pleased to order that honorary colours, with a device properly suited to commemorate the reduction of the fortress of Allyghur on the fourth and the victory obtained at Delhi on the eleventh of September, be presented to the corps of cavalry and infantry, European and native, respectively, employed on those glorious occasions; and that a public monument be erected at Fort William to the memory of the brave officers and men, European and native, who have fallen in the public service during the present campaign.

"In concluding his orders on this memorable occasion, the Governor-General in Council is pleased to direct that the public thanks of the Supreme Government of the British possessions in India be given to His Excellency General Lake; who, with unexampled alacrity, eminent judgment, and indefatigable courage, under extraordinary difficulties, has prepared the army of Bengal for the field; has conducted it by a rapid succession of glorious victories to the complete defeat of a powerful enemy; and has maintained the honour of the British name in India by a humane attention towards the inhabitants of the conquered provinces, and by a due respect and reverence towards the unfortunate representative of the House of Taimur."

The British Army marched from Delhi on the 24th of September, moving along the western bank of the Jumna, while the guns intended for the siege of Agra were carried down the river in boats. Next day messengers arrived from the Jat Raja of Bharatpur, offering to enter into a treaty of alliance on terms which were accepted but were subsequently broken by the Raja.

On arriving in camp before Agra on October 4th, passing before the fort of Akbarabad, the enemy saluted the army with several shot, which fell harmlessly as they were out of range. General Lake sent a summons to the fort, but received no answer, and it was seen that measures were being taken for a vigorous defence.

Seven battalions of hostile infantry, as well as a number of guns, occupied the glacis in front of the fort, the town, and the principal mosque, as well as the ravines which surrounded the south and west faces of the stronghold. The fort itself was of large size, built of hard stone from the quarries of Fatehpur. It had a ditch of great length, and a double rampart with bastions at regular intervals. Within it was a palace, as well as mosques, arsenals, and storehouses, with baths and fountains of white marble.

On the 10th October the town was attacked, and after a severe contest abandoned by the enemy, who were defeated with a loss of six hundred men and 26 guns, the casualties on the British side amounting to 228, including eight officers. These losses were largely due to a heavy fire of grape and musketry kept up from the fort during the action. Two days later the remainder of the enemy outside the fort surrendered to the number of 2,500.

The siege of the fort was now undertaken, approaches being made under cover of the ravines, and the breaching battery erected within 350 yards on the south-east side of the fort near the river. At this juncture the enemy opened negotiations for surrender through their two European officers whom they had kept in durance. The terms proposed were agreed to, and a reply

Passing by the town of Bindrabun, a contemporary gives an interesting account of the plague of sacred monkeys at that place, "whose propensity to mischief is increased by the religious respect paid to them. In consequence of this degrading superstition vast numbers of these animals, some of which are of very large size, are here supported by the voluntary contributions of pilgrims, and in such reverence are they held that no one dares to resist or ill-treat them when they commit the most flagrant acts of outrage upon casual passengers, or even in the dwellings of the inhabitants. Hence access to the town is often difficult; for should any of the apes take up an antipathy against the unlucky traveller, he is sure to be assailed by the whole community, who follow him with all the missile weapons they can collect, as pieces of bamboo, stones, and dirt, making at the same time a most hideous howling. All this, however, must be borne with perfect passive obedience; for otherwise the slightest attempt at retaliation would only provoke fresh insults from these malignant animals, and bring to their aid the interested Fakeers and infatuated devotees by whom they are so preposterously cherished. Of the danger attending a rencontre with enemies of this description a melancholy instance occurred in the year 1808, when two young cavalry officers belonging to the Bengal Army having occasion to pass this way were attacked by the apes, at whom one of the gentlemen inadvertently fired, the alarm of which drew the whole body of Fakeers and their followers out of the place with so much fury that the officers, though mounted upon elephants, were compelled to seek their safety by endeavouring to cross the Jumna, in which attempt they both perished."

was sent by a British officer, but the enemy again opened fire while negotiations were proceeding. On the 14th, General Lake, wishing to prevent further carnage, sent another messenger to the fort, but without success, for the enemy refused to negotiate.

The breaching battery was completed by the 17th, and a tremendous fire from eight eighteen-pounders and four howitzers was opened on the south-east bastion, whilst at the same time an enfilading fire was kept up from both flanks. The garrison of the fort, seeing that the breach was becoming practicable, and, with the example of Aligarh before them, not wishing to stand an assault, capitulated on the morning of the 18th October to the number of six thousand men. Twenty tumbrils laden with treasure to the value of twenty-two lakhs were found in the fort, and subsequently distributed among the troops; whilst guns, ammunition, and stores in abundance fell into the hands of the victors. Among the ordnance taken was an enormous brass gun, known as "the great gun of Agra," said to have been composed of all the precious metals. It is said that a similar gun, composed of gold and silver, is still lying in the fort of Gawilgarh in the Satpura Hills. In the case of the Agra gun there may have been some truth in the assertion, for the shroffs of the city offered a lakh of rupees for it merely to melt it down. The gun was of 23 inches calibre at the muzzle, where the metal was 11½ inches in thickness; it was 14 feet 2 inches in length, and weighed 96,600 pounds, whilst the cast iron ball weighed 1,500 pounds. Where is this great gun now? General Lake, wishing to transport it to England, had a raft made for its conveyance down the Jumna, but it was too heavy and the whole sank in the bed of the river, where a traveller in 1818 saw it buried in the sands.

The principal strongholds of the enemy being now in the hands of the British, it remained to direct attention to the Mahratta armies in the field, which were gathering to attempt the recovery of the Imperial city of Delhi.

While the operations which have been described were in progress, a force of fifteen battalions of regular infantry, subsequently reinforced by two other battalions, had been detached by Scindia from his army in the Deccan, and had taken up a strong position in rear of the British army. General Lake, with a view to the destruction of this army, marched from Agra on October 27th, moving by Karauli and Fatehpur-Sikri, where the heavy guns and baggage were left under a guard. At 11 o'clock on the night of the 31st, the British General marched with all his cavalry, and after covering twenty-five miles in six hours came up with the enemy at sunrise on November 1st. The General at once resolved to attack, but his advance was delayed by an inundation of the road which the enemy had made by cutting the embankment of a large tank. This delay enabled the Mahrattas to take up a position with their right in front of the village of Laswari, resting upon a rivulet with steep banks.

On their left was the hamlet of Mohalpur, while the entire front was concealed by high grass, and covered by seventy-two guns in line. They had 9,000 infantry and four or five thousand cavalry.

The advanced guard of the British cavalry, followed by the 1st Brigade under Colonel Vandeleur of the 8th Dragoons, at once charged the enemy's line, taking several of their guns, and penetrating into Laswari. The other brigades followed in turn, and the whole force charged several times through and through the enemy's line, their ranks meanwhile being mowed down by the incessant discharge of grape and chain shot; the fire of the hostile guns, which were concealed by the grass, being reserved until the British horsemen were within twenty yards. The gunners concealed themselves beneath their pieces until the cavalry had passed through, when, emerging from their shelter, they reloaded and fired upon their rear. Nor was their infantry idle, for drawn up behind a deep intrenchment, and covered by a laager of carts and baggage, they kept up a galling fire. At length, Colonel Vandeleur and many men having fallen, the cavalry withdrew for a time from the combat.

Meanwhile the British infantry was advancing, and arrived on the scene at noon, when arrangements were made for a renewal of the attack. The infantry was formed in two columns, one of which was to attack the village of Mohalpur, while the other threatened the front and left flank of the enemy. Marching along the bank of the rivulet, for some distance under cover of the grass which concealed their advance, the assaulting columns came under fire of the enemy's guns, which poured into them showers of grape and chain shot by which their ranks were decimated, and which for a space checked their further advance. The enemy's horse, also, had rallied at a short distance, and menaced the advancing line. The British General, therefore, ordered the 29th Dragoons to charge the hostile cavalry, which were soon swept from the scene of action, the Dragoons penetrating both lines of the enemy's infantry.

And now the British infantry pressed forward with irresistible valour, and gradually and with horrid carnage pushed back the foe, who fought to the last with stubborn heroism. General Lake's horse was shot under him, and his son * was severely wounded when in the act of offering his charger to his father.

No effort of the enemy could stem the tide of battle. Shot, bayonetted, and cut to pieces by the cavalry, the whole of their seventeen battalions were destroyed, not less than 7,000 being dead upon the field, while 2,000 surrendered themselves prisoners. Their bazaars and camp equipage were captured, together with seventy-two pieces of cannon, five thousand stand of arms,

* Major Lake was killed at the battle of Roleia in the Peninsula in 1808, six months after his father's death.

forty-four stand of colours, and sixty-four tumbrils laden with ammunition, and three containing treasure.

An officer who was present at the battle wrote :—" The setting sun, after this busy and sanguinary day, presented a spectacle to the beholder calculated to agitate his mind with a variety of emotions ; for while he could not but feel grateful at the result of the conflict, and exult in the laurels which rewarded the victors, his sympathy was awakened in contemplating the extensive plain covered with the bodies of the dead, and hearing on all sides the groans of the wounded and the dying. The terrific picture was heightened by successive explosions of powder magazines and tumbrils of ammunition, which shook the atmosphere, and obscured the horizon with tremendous clouds of sulphurous smoke. If anything could add to such a scene of woe, it was the approach of a murky night, indicating an hurricane, that came on with furious rapidity till it spread an indescribable degree of horror over the blood-stained field. "

The British also suffered severely in this contest. Fifteen officers were killed, including Major-General Ware, whose head was taken off by a cannon ball, and twenty-six were wounded ; 160 men were killed, and 630 wounded. By this battle, and the actions which had preceded it, the power of the Mahrattas in Northern India was completely broken.

In the South, as has been related, the flower of the Mahratta army had already been destroyed at the battle of Assaye on September 23rd, and the Mahratta hosts, broken alike in organisation and in spirit, had been scattered to the four winds. General Wellesley was already advancing into Berar, where the only armies that still kept the field were assembled under Sindhia and the Raja of Berar. Four weeks after the battle of Laswari these forces were to be finally defeated on the field of Argaum.

Meanwhile an army was operating under Colonel Broughton in Bundelkhand, where Kalpi and Gwalior were occupied in December, with little resistance. In Ganjam also a small force under Colonel Harcourt took possession of Jagannath, and stormed and captured Balasore, finally reducing the whole of the Province of Cuttack, which was ceded to the British under the terms of the treaty of peace concluded by Wellesley with the Raja of Berar.

APPENDIX VI.

THE PINDARIS.

Writing in February 1804, General Wellesley said :— " I think that we run a great risk from the freebooter system. It is not known to the Governor-General, and you can have no idea of the extent to which it has gone ; and it increases daily .... no inhabitant can or will remain to cultivate unless he is protected by an armed force stationed in his village."

These words referred to the Pindaris, a growing evil which at length attained such dimensions that a great army had to be assembled for their destruction in 1817. At one time the terror of India, these freebooters are now almost forgotten even in name.

The Pindaris were not a tribe, but a military system of bandits of all races and religions. They fluctuated in numbers, being augmented from time to time by military adventurers from every state, and frequently amounted to as many as 30,000 men. Captain Sydenham wrote of them :— "Every horseman who is discharged from the service of a regular government or who wants employment or subsistence, joins one of the *durras* (principal divisions) of the Pindaris ; so that no vagabond who has a horse or sword at his command can be at a loss for employment. Thus the Pindaris are continually receiving an accession of associates from the most desperate and profligate of mankind. Every villain who escapes from his creditors, who is expelled from the community for some flagrant crime, who has been discarded from employment, or who is disgusted with an honest and peaceable life, flies to Hindustan, and enrolls himself among the Pindaris."

The Pindaris * were generally armed with spears, in the use of which they were very expert ; a proportion of them were provided with matchlocks, and all were mounted. The mode of warfare adopted by these bandits, if warfare it may be called, was distinguished by the precision with which it was directed to one object—plunder ; they brought little with them and their only object was to carry as much as possible away. A party consisted of one, two, three or even four thousand. Each man provided himself with a few cakes for his subsistence, and a few feeds of grain for his horse, trusting much to the chance of plunder for the means of supplying the wants of both. They frequently marched twenty or thirty miles a day, and, in cases of extraordinary emergency, they were capable of accomplishing fifty miles in that period. To effect these extraordinary exertions, it is said they were accustomed to sustain the vigour of their horses by spices and stimulants.

The celerity of their marches was not more remarkable than their secrecy. It was scarcely possible to gain information of their movements till they had completed them. They proceeded at once to the place of their destination, and, unencumbered with tents and baggage, they soon reached it. There they divided into smaller parties, and commenced their career of plunder and devastation. Articles of the greatest value were disposed about their persons ; cattle afforded the means of their own transport. But the atrocious proper-

* This account of the Pindaris is drawn from Thornton's "History of India."

sities of these ruffians were not to be satisfied by what they could carry away. What was not removed they destroyed; and wherever they marched villages were seen in flames, with the houseless and often wounded inhabitants flying in dismay to seek a shelter which not infrequently they were unable to attain. When the ruffian visitors had laid the country completely waste, they approached a point on the frontier distant from that by which they had entered, and, uniting again into a compact body, returned home.

The horrors attending these visitations were such as could not be credited, were the evidence less complete and conclusive. Despatch being indispensable, every variety of torture was resorted to for the purpose of extracting from the unhappy victims information of the treasures they were supposed to have concealed. Red-hot irons were applied to the soles of their feet; a bag filled with hot ashes was tied over the mouth and nostrils of the victim, who was then beaten on the back, to make him inhale the ingredients; large stones were placed on the head or chest, or, the sufferer being laid on his back, a plank or beam was placed across his chest, on which two men pressed with their whole weight; oil was thrown on the clothes, which were then set on fire—these, with many other modes of torture equally frightful, were resorted to. Neither sex nor age afforded immunity. The hands of children would frequently be cut off, as the shortest way of obtaining the bracelets which adorned hem; while women were subjected to outrages compared to which torture and death were mercy. To escape these, numbers rushed upon self-destruction. It is not one of the least revolting features in the economy of these mud2rous adventurers that their women frequently accompanied their male associates in their excursions. They were mounted on small horses or camels, and are said to have exceeded the other sex in rapacity and cruelty. When the work of ruin was completed the Pindaris withdrew like wild beasts to their lairs. Then a change of scene took place; the operation of plunder was exchanged for that of huckstering. The claim of the government under which they served had first to be satisfied, or if they were pursuing their vocation independently, that of their chief; but it is not clear how far either claim extended. By some, the share of each chief has been fixed at a fourth part of the entire booty. By others, it has been alleged that the mode of apportionment was uncertain; but that elephants, palanquins, and some other articles were heriots appertaining to the highest authority recognised by the captors. After the claim of the government, or the chief, came that of the actual leader of the expedition; then the payment of advances made by merchants—for, like more civilised nations, these people occasionally contracted public debts. These preliminaries being disposed of, the scene that followed resembled a fair. Every man's share of the plunder was exposed for sale; purchasers flocked from all quarters, proximate and remote, the business of the sale being conducted by women while the men gave themselves up to amusement, of which intoxication constituted a considerable portion. This lasted until the produce of the expedition was exhausted, and it became necessary to seek in fresh outrages renewed means of gratification. Thus passed the life of the Pindari robber, in an alternation of brutal exertions and sensual abandonment.

They were, in truth, except on account of their numbers, a very contemptible set of miscreants. No redeeming feature marked the character of the Pindari: even animal courage, often the sole ennobling quality of his profession, he possessed not. The Pindari marched or rather darted upon his victims with a rapidity never equalled by any regular force; but he manifested equal or even g eater alacrity in flight. No troops in the history of the world ever displayed such a proficiency in the art of running away; and to this, their strong point, they invariably resorted, if attacked. They were mean and cowardly thieves engendered by a vicious and diseased state of society.

This atrocious confederacy received special marks of favour and encouragement from many of the native princes, who mutually employed the Pindaris against each other, to ruin and devastate their respective countries; and not infrequently remunerated their services by betraying and plundering their wretched instruments. On one occasion they made an overture to the Government of Bhopal to invade and lay waste the territories of Nagpur, with which state it was at war. Their offer was declined, upon which they made a like tender of their services to Nagpur for ravaging Bhopal. The ruler of Nagpur accepted their offer, and they executed his order so effectively that, at the distance of twenty-five years, Sir John Malcolm represents Bhopal as not then recovered from the effects of their visitation. On the return of these faithful instruments to Nagpur, the Raja very unceremoniously surrounded their camp, plundered them of all the movables of which they had plundered the unhappy inhabitants of Bhopal, and threw one of their chiefs into prison.

A noted leader amongst the Pindaris was Karim Khan, until he became powerful enough to excite the jealousy of Sindhia, by whom he was thrown into prison for four years. He purchased his freedom with six lakhs of rupees, and was joined in his subsequent outrages by another notorious chief, Chithu, who, having betrayed his friend and colleague into the hands of his enemies, set up for himself as chief leader of the Pindaris. He fixed his abode amidst the hills and forests situated between the north bank of the Narbada and the

Vindhya mountains, the practice of these miscreants being to cross the river as soon as it was fordable after the rains, generally in November, and indiscriminately plunder friends and foes.

In 1814-15-16 they raided the Madras Presidency, committing widespread depredations, and eventually spreading consternation as far as the walls of Madras itself. So great was the fear of these hordes of robbers that it is related that in 1816 "an idle rumour reached Madras of the arrival of Pindaris at the Mount; all was uproar, flight and despair, to the walls of Madras. This alarm originated in a few *dhobis* (washermen) and grass-cutters of the artillery having mounted their ponies and, in mock imitation of the Pindaris, galloping about and playing with long bamboos in their hands in the vicinity of the Mount. The effect was such, however, that many of the civil servants and inhabitants of the Mount packed up and moved to the Fort for protection."

The same writer relates that he "visited Calcutta early in 1817, when a temporary lull from the horrors and devastations committed by the Pindaris afforded a moment for reflection on the growing power of these marauders, and forcibly reminded the Supreme Government of the necessity of measures of a different temper to those heretofore adopted towards their suppression and extirpation. There was scarcely a day when some fresh rumour of barbarity or plunder by that banditti, on the Company's provinces, did not pervade and shock the public ear in Calcutta; and during this season of general alarm and disgust, the Local Government of India seemed to consider the evil passed away like the monsoon, without any effort or plan suited to arrest its fast-rising mischief. A few small detachments on the Narbada, and the Western frontier of Bengal, were the only check upon the advance of these hordes; but latterly a summary mode of treatment to such Pindaris as were taken prisoners pointed out to the whole body the serious game that was in future to be dealt to them, as all quarter ceased to be given, and they were executed on the spot."

Attempts were made to enlist the aid of the Mahratta States in the destruction of these freebooters; but, whilst they ostensibly concurred with the British Government in the desirability of this measure, they took no action, but with that duplicity which formed their national characteristic, secretly and in some places their commanders openly encouraged the Pindaris and shared their plunder. During the season of 1816-17 the ravages of the Pindaris extended over a wider expanse of territory than had ever before been attempted. Having crossed the Narbada with ten thousand horsemen, they separated into two bands; one of which proceeded due south into the country of the Nizam, and reached the banks of the Godavery. The other marched eastward, and entered the Company's territory of Ganjam, where, in the course of twelve days, they killed and wounded nearly 7,000 persons, and carried off or destroyed property to the value of £100,000. A third party crossed the Tapti at Barhanpur, and overran the dominions of the Peshwa to some distance beyond Poona.

Thus far the Pindaris had eluded the regular force stationed on the Narbada to check their inroads; yet, though they were still liable to be attacked by several detached corps that were scouring the country in different directions, they never stationed sentries or took any similar precaution against an evil to which they were always exposed. On the 25th December 1816 Major Lushington, who was at Pripatwari with the 4th Madras Cavalry, received intelligence that a party of these plunderers had entered the Peshwa's territories by the Wakli Pass, and were engaged in plundering to the south-east of Poona. The news arrived at ten o'clock at night; and three hours afterwards the regiment, with two galloper guns, moved in the direction in which the plunderers were said to be employed. The carriages of both guns broke down, and they were consequently left on the road, the regiment pursuing its way to Sogaon, where they arrived at seven o'clock on the morning of the 26th, having marched a distance of twenty-two miles. Here they learned that a large body of Pindaris had, on the preceding day, attacked the place, but being beaten off, had moved in an easterly direction.

Leaving at Sogaon the sick, recruits, heavy baggage, and camp-followers, Major Lushington, with 350 men, again marched, after a pause of only half an hour, and at noon, having performed a further distance of twenty miles, arrived at Kaim. At this place he found that the Pindaris had halted on the previous night; they had departed at daybreak, and had occupied the morning in firing and plundering several villages in the neighbourhood.

After a halt of three-quarters of an hour, Major Lushington resumed the pursuit through Pipri to Kawa, where the Pindaris were surprised by a sudden charge. They were pursued several miles, and seven or eight hundred were killed or wounded. The only casualty on the British side was Captain Darke, who was killed by a spear thrust.

In the meanwhile other parties were attacked and dispersed with heavy loss in other parts of the country; but one bold chieftain, with 260 troopers, crossed the Peninsula, swept along the Western Coast, and, ascending the Tapti river, reached his home with less than half his original number, but all of them carrying rich booty on their saddles.

Although in some few cases success attended the pursuit of the Pindaris, Lord Moira (afterwards Marquis of Hastings) when he arrived in India found that this growing evil had assumed such dimensions that a great campaign became necessary for the destruction of the bandits. In 1817 extensive measures were undertaken, and the Pindaris were practically exterminated during that and the following year.

APPENDIX VII.

THE LAST MAHRATTA WAR.

In order to understand the ultimate results of the Marquis Wellesley's policy towards the Mahrattas, and to follow the fortunes and fate of their Confederacy, it may be interesting to give a short account of the Mahratta War which broke out in the year 1817.

The wars of 1803 and 1804 resulted in a peace which could in all probability have never remained permanent. The arrangements then concluded could at best lead only to a temporary cessation of hostilities. There still remained all the elements of disorder, and the situation was fraught with danger for the future peace of the Peninsula. The fear of French aggression had, indeed, been removed by the Marquis Wellesley during his term of office as Governor-General; and had the policy of that wise statesman been continued, it is probable that much further trouble would have been averted. The Directors of the East India Company took alarm at the magnitude of the operations and designs of the Marquis Wellesley, and the fatuous policy which followed on the vigorous measures of that statesman was in itself sufficient to eliminate a great part of the results which had been attained at the cost of so much bloodshed. A policy of non-interference and inactivity soon reduced the British from the position of dominant power, a condition so necessary to the security of peace, to that of a co-equal with the neighbouring native states —a situation resulting in many years of anarchy and intrigue which was terminated only by another war.

In 1817 Baji Rao still held the Government at Poona, where he had been established in 1803 under the terms of the treaty of Bassein. He was the nominal head of the Mahratta Princes. On him devolved the leadership on those occasions when policy demanded combined action on the part of the Mahratta Confederacy. He appears to have been possessed of all the basest attributes of the nation to which he belonged, and his reign had been characterised by intrigue, cruelty, and perfidy. Already in 1814 the murder at Poona of the Gaikwar's envoy by Trimbakji, the favourite of the Peshwa, had led him to the verge of hostilities with the British, and Baji Rao had then been forced to make an assignment of territory in support of a body of horse which he was obliged to maintain under the provisions of the treaty of Bassein. Of the other Mahratta Chiefs, Mulhar Rao Holkar was a boy of 11 years of age, and the regency of his territory was in the hands of Tulsi Bai, a lady of strong though questionable character, formerly the favourite mistress of the deceased Jeswant Rao Holkar.

Appa Singh was head of the Nagpur State, having succeeded Parsaji Bhonsla, whose assassination he had compassed.

Amir Khan, in alliance with Mahdoji Sindhia, had risen to power and founded a strong military state in Malwa.

The Pindaris, of whom some account has already been given, were the primary cause of disturbance. Attempts had been made to enlist the aid of the Mahratta States in the destruction of these freebooters, but while they ostensibly concurred with the British in the desirability of this measure, they took no action ; but with that duplicity which formed their national characteristic secretly encouraged the Pindaris and shared their plunder. The Governor-General, the Marquis of Hastings, therefore undertook extensive operations to crush this growing danger.

These operations were so extensive in conception, and the force assembled so large, that it was obvious that they could not be intended merely for a campaign against these freebooters, but as measures of defence in case of hostility with the Mahratta powers.

The nature and character of native Governments rendered hostile action on their part probable, if not certain. No treaty with any such government, with whom diplomacy was merely another term for duplicity, was of more value than the paper on which it was written.

The military strength of the Native Powers at this time may be summarised as follows :—

	Horse.	Foot.	Guns.
Sindhia	15,000	16,000	140
Holkar	20,000	8,000	107
Peshwa	28,000	14,000	37
Bhonsla	16,000	18,000	85
Amir Khan	12,000	10,000	200
Pindaris	15,000	1,500	20

It will be seen that the troops at the disposal of the native powers consisted in great part of horsemen. A false glamour seems to surround the name of the Mahrattas, to whom history has lent an undeserved prestige. The Mahrattas have never been remarkable for courage. The genius of the nation has tended more in the direction of diplomacy and intrigue. They had acquired a certain military renown throughout India, but they were mere predatory hordes, and it is not easy to understand how they had risen to such power in the land. Their success must be ascribed to the acuteness and subtlety of their intelligence, and to the feeble condition of those whom they vanquished and overcame.

Their decadence appears to date from the time of the inclusion in their armies of those regular corps of infantry and artillery which were raised by de Boigne, Perron and other European adventurers. There were not wanting among the Mahrattas themselves far-seeing men who deprecated this innovation, whilst many attributed the ultimate overthrow of their power to the introduction of regular artillery and infantry. The Mahrattas originally excelled as predatory light horsemen whose mobility enabled them to assail an enemy's weak points, to reap success when it involved but little risk, and to flee from danger. Their regular infantry and artillery, composed not of Mahrattas but of mercenaries, obliged them to fight pitched battles, for which they were unfitted. They were by these establishments encumbered in their movements, and might be forced to give battle against their will.

Since the days of Assaye and Argaum they had rapidly degenerated, whilst their breed of horses, once so famous, had apparently deteriorated. Moreover, but few European officers remained in their service. Their best troops consisted of Arabs, Rajputs and Muhammadans, and it will be seen that in 1817 these alone generally offered any serious resistance. The Arabs were especially good soldiers, particularly in the defence of forts, when they displayed remarkable valour; they were at that time employed in all the Native States, and to this day some of them are in the service of the Nizam of Hyderabad. An officer who frequently fought against the Arabs wrote as follows in 1820 :—

"There are perhaps no troops in the world that will make a stouter or more determined stand to their posts than the Arabs. They were entirely unacquainted with military evolution, and undisciplined: but every Arab has a pride and a heart of his own, that never forsakes him as long as he has legs to stand on. They are naturally brave and possess the greatest coolness and quickness of sight; hardy and fierce through habit, and bred to the use of the matchlock from their boyhood, they attain a precision and a skill in the use of it that would almost exceed belief, bringing down or wounding the smallest object at a considerable distance, and not unfrequently birds with a single bullet. They are generally armed with a matchlock, a couple of swords, with three or four small daggers stuck in front of their belt, and a shield. On common occasions of attack and defence they fire but one bullet; but when hard pressed on the breach, they drop in two, three or four at a time, from their mouths, always carrying in them eight to ten bullets, which are of a small size. We may calculate upon the whole number of Arabs in the service of the Peshwa and the Berar Raja at the utmost as 6,000 men, a loose and undisciplined body, but every man of them a tough and hardy soldier. It was to the Arabs alone those Princes looked and placed their dependence on. Their own troops fled and abandoned them, seldom or ever daring to meet our smallest detachment.

"Nothing can exceed the horror and alarm with which some of our native troops view the Arabs. They will meet and fight them in the open day under their own officers ; but if attacked at night if detached from their European officers, and even under their native officers or employed in the defence of a post against a sortie or other attack, they quickly become panic-stricken, and fly in every direction."

When the campaign opened there was a subsidiary force of native troops under British officers at Poona, and another at Nagpur which had been placed there under the terms of treaties with the Peshwa and Bhonsla, respectively. The Marquis of Hastings in 1817 organised a large army which, advancing from the north and south, was to close in upon and crush the Pindaris. At first apprehensions of a rupture between the Peshwa Baji Rao and Appa Sahib Bhonsla were not entertained. Sir John Malcolm had been sent on a mission to their courts, and had reported favourably of the pacific intentions of these Princes.

For the destruction of the Pindaris it was determined to close in from every side upon their head-quarters in the fastnesses of the Narbada and Chambal rivers. And for this purpose, and to prevent their escape, as well as to provide for other possible eventualities, two armies were organised by the Governor-General—one in Northern India under his personal command, and the other in the Deccan under Sir Thomas Hyslop. The Grand Army was formed at Cawnpore in four Divisions in 1817. The four Divisions of the Army of the Deccan commenced their movement in the same month, marching separately to their several destinations. There were also a Reserve Division and a Division in Guzerat under Sir William Grant Keir. These were the largest British forces that had ever been assembled in India. In addition there were at Poona, where the Hon'ble Mountstuart Elphinstone was British Resident, a detail of native artillery and two battalions of native infantry ; and at Nagpur, as escort to Mr. Jackson, the Resident, two battalions of native infantry, a small detail of European artillery, and three troops of the 6th Bengal Cavalry.

The operations about to be undertaken were to occupy an extensive region, embracing every diversity of physical feature, and characterised by considerable varieties of climate. This area stretched across India from the river Jumna on the north to the Krishna and Tungabhadra on the south. It was crossed by ranges of rugged mountains, abounding with wild beasts, and clad with dense forests, whose solitudes were rarely disturbed by the presence of man, and culminating in tall peaks crowned by massive forts, hoary with age, and bristling with guns. There were rich alluvial plains, dotted with villages and large and populous cities, and watered by mighty rivers whose streams poured in turbid floods in the rainy season, but shrank to silver threads in the height of summer.

Within the limits of this theatre of war were many native states, and some British territories. It was inhabited by peoples of many races and many tongues. Pathans, Mahrattas, and Rajputs represented the civilisation of the Orient. Aboriginal Bhils and Gonds shared with savage beasts the fastnesses of forest and mountain. Not only the hostility of man, but the forces of nature had to be encountered and overcome. Difficult passes over the mountains, worn by mountain torrents and dark with jungle, had to be traversed by great armies with all their baggage. After heavy rainfall even the watercourses that had previously been empty were rendered temporarily impassable, and the rivers took days to shrink to their normal proportions, whilst the soil in many parts of the country became so soft as to render the progress of an army a most difficult operation. Death lurked in many shapes. Cholera followed in the track of the troops, and fever claimed numerous victims. Even the wild beasts with which the country was infested took their toll from the advancing armies.* All India was turned into a vast camp. The maintenance and movement of great armies over a wide theatre of operations called for careful organisation and masterly strategy from the commanders. The opposition of the enemy, both in the open field and in their mountain strongholds, demanded skill and valour on the part of the troops.

During October and early November the Divisions of the two Armies were disposed of as follows :—

Of the Grand Army the :—

First Division marched to the Sind.
Second Division marched to the Chambal.
Third Division was disposed north of the Eastern Narbada.

A detached force under Brigadier Hardyman was placed on the extreme left astride of the Narbada.

Reserve Division had its head-quarters at Rewari, to control Amir Khan.

By the distribution of the forces on the Sind and Chambal rivers Sindhia was enclosed and cut off from his allies, and was obliged to conclude a treaty ceding the forts of Hindia and Asirgarh to the British, and to supply a contingent of troops for employment against the Pindaris.

In the meantime the Army of the Deccan had been advancing. Although encumbered by baggage and camp followers (200,000 of the latter are said to have accompanied an army of 80,000 men), the army made rapid marches through the dense jungles on and beyond the Tapti river, and by the middle of November was disposed of as follows :—

First and Third Divisions were concentrated at Harda, and disposed to hold the fords of the Narbada.

Second Division, with head-quarters at Malkapur, watched the Berar Ghats.

*During the march of the Army of the Deccan through the dense jungles on the banks of the Tapti river many camp followers were carried off by tigers ; and a sepoy of the advanced guard was attacked and killed by one of these animals.

Fourth Division marched to Khandesh, filling the space between Poona and Berar.

Fifth Division was at Hoshangabad.

Reserve Division was between the Bhima and Krishna rivers.

In addition to these arrangements, the Madras Government established a chain of defensive forts from the most western point of the British frontier on the Tungabhadra, and along that river to its junction with the Krishna. Thence the chain extended along the latter river to Chintapili, and along the Eastern Ghats to the Chilka Lake. These posts were established at various distances in rear of the line of frontier and threw forward small parties to the passes of the rivers and hills in their front. The number of troops employed on this service amounted to six squadrons of dragoons, six squadrons of native cavalry, nine battalions of native infantry, besides 5,000 Mysore horse and foot, who continued the chain of the East. The distribution of this force along a line of 850 miles in length necessarily reduced the strength of each post to a small number. Experience, however, had shown that the Pindaris could be deterred by the smallest party of posted infantry, and that they could be beaten off by the unexpected attack of a single company.

The various events connected with his dealings with the British had fostered a sentiment of implacable hatred in Baji Rao Peshwa, who found himself reduced almost to a condition of vassalage. Moreover, in 1817, his personal relations with Mr. Elphinstone, the Resident, appear to have greatly strained.

In October of that year the Mahratta Chief assembled large bodies of troops at Poona, and adopted a threatening attitude. Early in November he demanded the withdrawal of the British troops, and on the 5th he advanced to attack the Residency and Cantonments. The fears of the Peshwa, who was distinguished by personal cowardice, had fortunately induced him to defer his attack, thus giving time for the garrison to be reinforced by the Bombay European Regiment and a battalion of native infantry. The total force now consisted of the Bombay European Regiment, a detachment of the 65th Foot, a detachment of native artillery, the two battalions 1st and 6th, and one battalion 7th Bombay Native Infantry, and Major Ford's auxiliary battalion; the whole under the command of Lieutenant-Colonel Burr. The Cantonments had been withdrawn to Kirki, and on the approach of the enemy Mr. Elphinstone abandoned the Residency and joined the troops.

Colonel Burr wished to await the Mahratta onslaught, but Mr. Elphinstone, who had ridden beside Wellesley at Assaye, well knew the value of a bold attack in dealing with this contemptible foe, and at his instance the British line moved forward with the European Regiment on the right, and the 7th Bombay Infantry on the left. The Mahratta Horse were advancing over the plain in countless numbers, levelling the hedges and standing corn as they passed over them, while the earth shook with the tramp and clatter of their hoofs. They charged down upon the British right, but swerved off on seeing the Europeans there, having a wholesome dread of the white faces, and attacked the 7th Native Infantry, who had advanced beyond the line in pursuit of a battalion of the Peshwa's infantry, under command of a Portuguese officer named Pinto. The 7th fell into some confusion, but were rallied by their officers and supported by two companies of the British regiment which were sent forward for that purpose order was thus restored, and the Mahratta Horse driven off with heavy loss. The hostile infantry, with the exception of Pinto's corps, had not arrived, and seeing the retreat of the cavalry they drew off to the city without coming into action.

This action is noteworthy, as showing the innate cowardice of the Mahrattas, their dread of European troops, and the value of the latter in saving native troops from destruction. The Mahratta army amounted to 18,000 horse, 8,000 foot, and 14 guns, whilst the British force numbered only 2,800, of whom 800 were Europeans. The loss on the British side was 19 killed and 67 wounded : the enemy lost some 500 men, including Mor Dixit, the Peshwa's Minister, who was mortally wounded by a discharge of grape-shot. The Peshwa watched the defeat of his army from the safe eminence of Parbati, where he sat like Xerxes on the rock of Salamis. The Mahrattas, during the conflict, burnt and destroyed the Residency and Cantonments, afterwards withdrawing to Poona. During this period several atrocities were committed by the enemy, including the murder of two officers who were on their way from Bombay to join their regiment.

In the meantime the 4th Division of the Deccan Army, under Brigadier-General Smith, had been advancing to the relief of the Resident and on the 13th November arrived in the vicinity of Poona, where it took up a position covering Yerowda ford across the Muta-Mula river, between the Kirki bridge (known as Holkar's bridge) and a small hill on the left bank of the stream.

The British General appears to have displayed some vacillation ; and his hesitation to attack, owing to some difficulty in getting his guns across the ford, enabled the Peshwa to escape. Thus was lost an opportunity of striking a decisive blow, which would probably have averted the necessity for the pursuit of many months which followed.

The enemy fled towards Satara under cover of a detachment of infantry, which maintained a contest with the British during the 16th November, but was at length driven off with loss. The British casualties in this action numbered 15 killed and 87 wounded. Poona was then occupied without further opposition, and some time was passed in settling affairs there before the pursuit of Baji Rao was undertaken.

It is now advisable to advert to affairs at Nagpur, where matters had assumed a threatening aspect. The news of the defection of the Peshwa had travelled with the usual rapidity of native intelligence. It was followed by that of Appa Sahib Bhonsla of Nagpur.

In October agents of Chithu, the celebrated Pindari Chief, had been secretly received by the Bhonsla ; in November a dress of honour arrived for him from the Peshwa, and was presented in open Durbar. On November 25th, Mr. Jenkins, the Resident, perceiving the evidently hostile attitude of Appa Sahib, sent a party of his force to occupy the double hill of Sitabaldi, whilst messengers were despatched for assistance to General Doveton, Commanding the 2nd Division of the Deccan Army.

The small garrison of Nagpur consisted of 3 troops 6th Bengal Cavalry, detachments of the Madras Bodyguard and Fort Artillery, the 1st Battalion 20th, and 24th Madras Native Infantry, the Resident's Escort and Major Jenkins' Battalion—a total of some 1,500 men under Lieutenant-Colonel Hopetoun Scott.

The hill of Sitabaldi consists of two eminences connected by a low and narrow ridge three hundred yards in length. Owing to the rocky nature of the ground it was impossible to entrench the summits. The suburbs of the city approached close to the base of the smaller hill, which was occupied by the 24th Madras Infantry, whilst the remainder of the infantry and the guns were posted on the large eminence, and the cavalry was in rear of the Residency. In front and on both flanks of the British position extended a village of mud huts, in which the enemy assembled with their guns.

In the evening of the 23rd November, one of the British picquets was fired upon from the village, and eventually retired to the smaller hill under a heavy discharge of matchlocks. A heavy fire was exchanged until 2 o'clock on the morning of the 27th, when there was a cessation for a time, but the attack was reopened by guns and musketry at daylight. The heaviest loss had up to now been sustained on the smaller hill. The Arabs made frequent attempts to carry it and at length, in the confusion caused by the explosion of a tumbril, they charged sword in hand, drove off the defenders, and turned the gun that had been posted there upon the larger hill, where the casualties now became very severe. Emboldened by their success, the enemy's horse and foot closed in from every direction to prepare for a general assault.

Captain Fitzgerald with three troops of the 6th Bengal Cavalry was posted in the Residency grounds. He had frequently applied in vain for permission to charge, and, seeing the impending destruction, made a last appeal. But Colonel Scott's reply was :—" Tell him to charge at his peril. " " At my peril be it !" said the gallant Fitzgerald, and immediately gave the word to advance. As soon as he was clear of the enclosures, he swept down upon the principal body of Mahratta Horse, drove them from two guns by which they were supported, pursued them for some distance, cut up a body of infantry, and returned with the captured guns. This exploit, which was witnessed with enthusiasm by the infantry on the hill, nerved the defenders to fresh efforts. At this moment an explosion of ammunition took place among the Arabs of the smaller hill; officers and men mingling together rushed forward, drove the Arabs headlong from the hill, took and spiked two of their guns, and then returned to their post. The Arabs reassembled preparatory to a fresh advance, when a troop of cavalry under Cornet Smith charged round the base of the hill, took them in flank, and dispersed them. The British now assumed the offensive, driving the hostile infantry from the huts where they were sheltered, and by noon the battle came to an end. The British lost 119 killed, including 5 European officers* and a Sergeant-Major, and 243 wounded, including 13 British officers. The loss of the enemy, who had 18,000 men and many guns, was about the same; but only some three thousand Arabs and a small body of Mahratta Horse took part in the attack. No more heroic defence is recorded in history than this gallant stand of a small force of native troops, inspired by the heroic example of their British officers and their few European comrades of the artillery. A monument stands upon the hill of Sitabaldi, the foundation stone of which was laid on the first anniversary of the battle, to commemorate the deeds of these gallant men.

The enemy appear to have been quite disheartened by this repulse. They made no further attack, and Appa Sahib made overtures to the Resident, declaring that the outbreak had occurred contrary to his wishes. The latter, however, refused to treat. Reinforcements came in from every direction, and on the 16th December General Doveton arrived with the 2nd Division of the Deccan Army.

The Bhonsla now came in and agreed to surrender all his artillery, but on the British advancing to take possession, the guns opened fire. A company of the Royal Scots had been attached to each native regiment. Line was formed, the enemy's batteries were taken by assault, and his horse was dispersed by the Cavalry and Horse Artillery, and pursued for some miles.

The garrison at Nagpur, consisting of 3,000 Arabs, still held out in the city, which was surrounded by a defensive wall having round towers at intervals. An attack made on the city was repulsed with heavy loss. The casualties in the battle of Nagpur and attack on the city amounted to 92 killed and 337 wounded, the greater number taking place during the attempts to storm the city from the 19th to the 24th December. The Arabs eventually capitulated, receiving a large sum of money, and permission to disperse in the country south of the Tapti river.

Whilst these events were taking place General Hardyman had moved down the Narbada with a view to assisting the troops at Nagpur. He advanced

* The officers killed were Captain Sadler, Lieutenants Grant and Clarke, Assistant Surgeon Niven, and Mr. Sotheby, Assistant Resident.

against Jabalpur with the 8th Bengal Cavalry, the 17th Foot, and four guns; and on the 19th December came in contact with the Mahrattas, who, with 1,000 horse, 2,000 foot, and some brass guns, were drawn up in a strong position in front of the town. The enemy were soon driven from their position with the loss of all their guns, and abandoned the town and fort, with the stores it contained, during the night.

It is now time to return to the movements of the main body of the Army of the Deccan, consisting of the First and Third Divisions, under command of Sir Thomas Hyslop, which had concentrated at Harda in the middle of November. The first measure was the dispersal of the Pindaris in Southern Malwa which was accomplished by Sir John Malcolm's Division in co-operation with the Grand Army. The Pindaris as usual did not show fight, and were dispersed in all directions with the loss of much of their baggage and some guns. A large body of them under the celebrated Chithu escaped for the time being, and eventually joined Holkar's Army on the Sipra river.

Early in December Sir Thomas Hyslop and Sir John Malcolm effected a junction of their forces at Ujjain. On the 14th of that month the army moved in the direction of Mahidpur, in the vicinity of which it arrived on the 19th, having been considerably harassed *en route* by the hostile predatory horse, who lost no opportunity of cutting off followers and baggage. The advance of the British armies and the consequent negotiations with the agents of Holkar gave rise to much dissension in the latter's camp, where there was a peace party and one favourable to war. The Regent Tulsi Bai vacillated between the two factions, and was finally seized and decapitated on the river bank by those who were in favour of opposing the British arms, whose counsels consequently prevailed. Negotiations were still carried on, but the insincerity of the Mahrattas was so apparent that they were not taken seriously by the Political Officer, Sir John Malcolm.

On the morning of December 21st the British Army advanced in the direction of Mahidpur on the Sipra river, moving through a somewhat hilly country, where the Pindaris hovered about the flanks and rear, carrying off camels and bullocks. In those days, as in our own time, our cavalry was too heavily weighted. An eye-witness of the scene says:—"We could see the Pindaris flying like the wind, at a considerable distance off, our cavalry having no chance with these fellows, even on an open plain. The Pindaris, unencumbered with accoutrements, heavy saddle, etc., will gallop round and round the most active of our troopers; and his very horse seems to partake of the master's cunning and dexterity, and to know exactly the moment for a quick and timely retreat."

A reconnaissance under Sir John Malcolm was soon pushed on to the river, where it took possession of the fort and a small village, on the right bank, driving in the enemy's light cavalry, which swarmed on the plain between the two armies. The enemy's position on the far bank of the river, about 800 yards beyond the stream, was now exposed to view. The hostile infantry, 5,000 strong, stretched across from Mahidpur to the river, where their right rested. Their front was covered by nearly a hundred guns in line. Beyond these a dense mass of 30,000 horse crowded the plain. The British Army did not number more than 5,500 men, but there were some present who had fought at Assaye fourteen years before, and knew well that British soldiers need have no fear of the issue of a conflict with any Mahratta host, however numerous. The rifle corps and a portion of the 16th Madras Infantry quickly crossed the river to drive in the enemy's matchlockmen, and were followed by the Horse Artillery. The enemy's guns immediately opened fire, and the Horse Artillery was soon overwhelmed, whilst the infantry, being badly disposed, remained in inaction for some time, exposed to a heavy fire, and suffered considerable loss. The rocket troop also attempted to discharge some missiles at the enemy, but the greater part burst or expended themselves among our own men, causing as much confusion as the hostile fire.

The situation appeared precarious when Sir Thomas Hyslop's main body arrived upon the scene with the light brigade in the centre, and the cavalry protecting the flanks. Having reached the river bank, left in front, the brigade actually countermarched under fire, in order to bring their right forward, losing heavily during this manœuvre. The European troops were at once launched against the enemy's line, followed by the native regiments, and were received with a charge of grape, chain, and round shot, which by its weight alone staggered the advancing line. But with a cheer the British soldiers charged straight at the enemy's artillery. Their onslaught was irresistible, and though the hostile artillerymen stood bravely to their guns, they could not withstand the assault and were nearly all killed, whilst the guns fell into the hands of the victors. Holkar's infantry had already fled at the commencement of the action, and the cavalry followed suit; such was the indignation of the artillerymen at this defection of their comrades, that they actually turned round their guns and fired a salvo into the ranks of their fugitive friends.

The guns being taken, the cavalry now crossed the ford, and took up the pursuit of the enemy. Young Holkar had fled in the early part of the action, but the Mysore Horse overtook and captured his regalia and jewels to the value of 70 or 80 lakhs of rupees, whilst the Mahratta camp, which had been left standing, also fell a prize to the victors. Numbers of the enemy were slain, and the country for many miles was strewn with their dead. The battle commenced at 9 o'clock in the morning, and by 11 o'clock the Mahratta hosts had melted from the field like snow from the face of the desert.

The British loss in this battle amounted to 174 killed and 612 wounded. Over 200 of the wounded died afterwards, apparently owing to unsatisfactory treatment. The enemy's loss was some 3,000 men and 76 guns. Of these latter 60 were brass, and were furnished with port-fires, elevating screws, buckets, etc., of the same pattern as our own. The battle of Mahidpur cannot be said to have been conducted with conspicuous skill. Sir John Malcolm appears to have displayed more valour than science. By a movement under cover of the far bank of the river, which afforded ample protection, the enemy's flanks might have been turned, and a frontal attack, which involved heavy loss, might have been avoided.

On the 28th December, Sir John Malcolm moved forward in pursuit of the enemy with a light detachment, and the main army marched in the direction of the Chambal river. Holkar, however, did not show fight again, but opened negotiations, which terminated in a treaty concluded on the 6th January 1818 by which the Rajput States were set free, and the Pindaris abandoned to their fate. The submission of Holkar was followed by that of Amir Khan. The Pindari freebooters were given no rest, but were pursued by the Guzerat Division, and by the various detachments of the Grand Army, until none remained but the famous Chithu with a few hundred followers. After a long pursuit these were gradually dispersed, until their unfortunate leader was left alone in the jungles on the Tapti river. There he fell a victim to a man-eating tiger, his fate being ascertained when the monster was followed to its lair, and the hapless Chithu's head discovered and recognised.

The battle of Mahidpur brought the regular warfare to a close, but a great deal still remained to be accomplished. Many forts had to be reduced; the Peshwa Baji Rao was still at large with a considerable following; and Appa Sahib of Nagpur was intriguing with that fugitive prince. The submission of Holkar was followed by two years of gureilla warfare before the country was finally pacified.

After effecting a junction with the Army of Guzerat, Sir Thomas Hyslop again turned towards the south early in February. His army was harassed by Bhils while descending the pass in the mountains north of the Narbada, but these aborigines, who were armed principally with bows and arrows, were easily driven off. The submission of several forts was received, and detachments were left in occupation, but on approaching the fort of Talner on the Tapti river, the advanced guard was fired upon. This place was to have been delivered up under the terms of the treaty with Holkar, but there appears to have been some misunderstanding with the Commandant. Negotiations for surrender followed after some little firing—but several officers who had entered the fort to receive the submission of the garrison were attacked and killed by the Arabs. Thereupon a general massacre took place, the whole garrison being put to the sword, while the Commandant was hanged from the battlements.

It is now advisable to revert to the operations of the 4th Division under Brigadier-General Smith, who, on the 21st December 1817, commenced his pursuit of the Peshwa.* The latter first fled in the direction of Satara, but turned north again from the Krishna river to Nasik on the Godavery, and thence advanced in the direction of Poona. His approach caused some alarm in that place, and the detachment at Sirur was called in to reinforce the garrison. This detachment consisted of the 2nd Battalion, Bombay Infantry, under Captain Staunton, two guns with 24 European artillerymen, and a Sergeant, under Lieutenant Chisholm, Artillery, and 250 Reformed Horse under Lieutenant Swanston.

At 1 o'clock on the 1st January 1818 the detachment reached the high ground overlooking the village of Koregaon, 27 miles from Sirur and some 16 miles from Poona. An imposing scene was presented to the little force. In the valley lay the whole of the Peshwa's army—20,000 Horse and 8,000 Foot, encamped on the right bank of the Bhima above the village of Koregaon, under the walls of which the road to Poona crossed the river by a ford.

Captain Staunton at once occupied the village, but failed to seize the most commanding portion of it, which was immediately taken by the enemy. The Peshwa launched the flower of his troops, Arabs, Guseins, and regular regiments to the attack, which was made by some 2,000 men, who were constantly reinforced during the day. The British six-pounders were disposed to cover the gateway by their fire, and the Arabs were slain in dozens by discharges of grape as they attempted to rush the entrance. Still they pressed fiercely on, and when most of the Europeans had been struck down, the guns were carried, and the remainder of their defenders slaughtered, including Lieutenant Chisholm, whose head was cut off and carried to Baji Rao.

Hearing that the guns had been taken, Lieutenant Pattinson of the 1st Bombay Infantry, who was lying mortally wounded, rose and led a charge of his grenadiers against the Arabs, re-capturing the guns, and slaying numbers of the enemy. Lieutenant Pattinson was a man of gigantic stature as well as of heroic disposition, being 6 feet 7 inches in height, and immensely powerful. He brought down five of the enemy with the butt end of a musket with which he had armed himself, and his example so excited the valour of the troops that the attackers were beaten off by night-fall. In this action not only the combatant officers, but the Assistant Surgeons Wyngate and Wyllie† led their troops to the attack again and again, and there can be no doubt the presence and example of the Europeans inspired the whole force with their remarkable

* NOTE.—In view of recent experiences with regard to mounted infantry, the following is of great interest :—" Brigadier-General Smith, during his pursuit of Baji Rao, formed one of the Bombay Native Corps into a light corps, and, mounting them on small horses, thus managed to keep always at hand with the cavalry a body of infantry, in the event of overtaking the enemy. This system might in India be much improved upon, particularly in desultory warfare, such as with the Pindaris. " "Mahratta and Pindari Campaign," by Carnaticus. Published in 1820.

† This officer was made a C.B. in 1850, and was ultimately head of the Madras Medical Department.

valour. Lieutenant Chisholm and Surgeon Wyngate were killed, and Lieutenant Pattinson died the next day. The other officers were wounded, and of the 24 European artillerymen 12 were killed and 8 wounded. Of the Natives 50 were killed and 105 wounded. The assailants lost five or six hundred men. They evacuated the village during the night, and retreated at dawn on hearing of General Smith's advance.

After this repulse Baji Rao fled towards the Carnatic, but being disappointed in his hope of assistance from Mysore, he again turned towards the north, in the direction of Sholapur, and then bent his steps towards the Tapti in order to obtain the aid of Appa Sahib of Nagpur. On one occasion General Smith came up with the retreating enemy at Ashti, with the 7th Bombay Cavalry and the 22nd Dragoons. A party of Mahrattas, headed by Gokla, a brave and famous chieftain who had been with Wellesley in 1803, charged down upon the Native Cavalry and caused some disorder; but the 22nd Dragoons galloped along the rear of the 7th and, attacking the Mahrattas, dispersed them in a few minutes with the loss of their leader, who fought bravely to the last and was killed by a dragoon. At length, after a chase lasting many months, Baji Rao with 8,000 followers was hemmed in near Asirgarh by General Doveton and Colonel Adams, where, after protracted negotiations, he surrendered to Sir John Malcolm. He was deposed from the throne of Poona, and given a pension and a place of residence at Bithur, where he resided until 1851, when he died, leaving his fortune and a legacy of undying hatred towards his conquerors to his adopted son, the infamous Nana Sahib of Cawnpore.

In the Deccan Baji Rao is still remembered. The villagers point out the places he passed during his flight, and some say that in the silent watches of the night they hear the beat of the hundred thousand hoofs of his myriad horse upon the plain.

APPENDIX VIII.

*MONSON'S RETREAT.**

Extract from a letter from General Wellesley to Colonel Wallace, dated Fort William, 12th September 1804.

"You will have heard reports of our poor Monson's reverses, but as I am on the spot, you will be glad to hear the truth from me; and as they give some

*NOTE.—Sir Robert Peel, in speaking of the Duke of Wellington, said that he considered him the most powerful writer in the English language, and that the letter upon Colonel Monson's retreat was the best military letter he had ever read, and quoted the line from Horace—

"Scribendi recte, sapere est et principium et fons."

Sir Charles Napier, after the battle of Meeanee, wrote from Hyderabad, 20th February 1843.

"The Duke's letter on the retreat of Colonel Monson decided me never to retire before an Indian army. If I have done wrong, abstractedly (for success, like charity, covers sins) the Great Master led me into it; but my own conviction is that I have done right; and that my admiration of him, and study of his words and deeds, as the great rules of war, have caused this Victory."

important military lessons to us all, I do not regard the trouble of writing them to you. When it became necessary to attack Holkar, Monson was detached from the Grand Army with 3 battalions and their guns, and a body of cavalry under Lieutenant Lucan. Holkar, who was then near Ajmeer, with an army composed only of horse (and as General Lake was at no great distance from Monson) retreated towards Malwa.

"After quitting the river Jumna, and passing through the flat countries depending on Agra, the first country going to the southward is a mountainous tract called Jeypore, governed by the Raja of that name, who had been tributary to Scindhia and Holkar previous to the late war, and who had been relieved from his tribute by the operation of the treaty of peace. Joining to the territories of Jeypore is that of the Raja of Boondy, of the same description; and joining to Boondy is the territory of the Raja of Kota. These last two Rajas had been, and are still, tributary to Scindhia; and Holkar has claims upon them which they hoped to get rid of by the British assistance, in consequence of their conduct in the war; at all events they were desirous to obtain for a time the British protection against the demands of Holkar.

"Between Boondy and Jeypore is a small territory and fort called Rampoora, which, at the commencement of the war, belonged to Holkar. This territory had formerly been part of the Jeypore territory, and had been seized by the Holkar family in some of their former contests with the Raja of Jeypore. The whole of this country between Agra and the Province of Malwa, which joins to the Kota territory, and which is entered through a pass called the Muchundra Ghat, is intersected by rivers and *nullahs*, which are either full throughout the western rains, or are filled at times by those rains, and become impassable for troops. Of these, the principal is the river Chumbal, which runs between Kota and Boondy, and the river Banas, which runs between Rampoora and Agra.

"When Holkar fled in front of the army of the Commander-in-Chief, Colonel Monson followed him successively to Boondy and Kota, the Rajas of which countries were very desirous to have the protection of the British troops against his exactions, and promised supplies and everything which Colonel Monson could want. At the same time that Colonel Monson advanced, a detachment under Colonel Don, consisting of two battalions, was sent to take Rampoora, of which place it got possession by storm; and this detachment afterwards joined and reinforced Monson's corps, which then consisted of five battalions.

"In the month of June the Commander-in-Chief withdrew his army into cantonments, leaving Monson's corps in the Kota country. Monson, towards the end of that month, passed through the Muchundra Ghat into Malwa, accompanied by the troops of the Raja of Kota, and some of Scindhia's under Bappogee Scindhia, and attacked, and took by storm, the hill fort of Hinglisghur; and after this operation, he took up a position in Malwa, recommended to him by the Raja of Kota, at some distance from the Muchundra Ghat, in which the Raja told him he was likely to get supplies, and from which Monson expected to be able to communicate with Colonel Murray, at that time on his march from Gujerat towards Ougein.

"After his retreat in front of the Commander-in-Chief, Holkar had first threatened Ougein, and afterwards had gone to Mundissor, a town belonging to Scindhia, situated to the north-west of Ougein, and on the left of the Chumbal. Between the middle and the latter end of June, he took and plundered this town; and at that time the river Chumbal was between him and Colonel Monson, who was encamped about five *coss* (10 miles) from the river on the right bank.

"Towards the beginning of July, Holkar passed the Chumbal with his army. Colonel Monson learnt that he was doing so, and intended to attack him. He moved towards the place at which he heard Holkar was, and found that the whole army had crossed the river; nearly about the same time he understood that Colonel Murray, who had made two marches towards Ougein from Gujerat, had re-crossed the Myhie; and upon the whole Monson, having only two days' provisions, thought it best to retreat. Accordingly he sent off his baggage early the following morning, the 8th July, I believe, towards the Muchundra Ghat; and he followed with the infantry about 9 in the morning, meaning to reach Muchundra that night, the distance about 17 miles. He left Lucan, with his irregular horse and Bappogee Scindhia's horse, to cover his rear, and to follow as his rear-guard. After Monson had marched a few miles, he heard that Holkar had attacked with his cavalry his rear-guard of irregular horse; and shortly afterwards he received intelligence that the rear-guard was destroyed, and Lucan taken prisoner. He arrived at Muchundra unmolested, and took up a position that covered the Ghat, but which, like all others I have seen, had many passages practicable for cavalry.

"On the next day, or next but one, Monson was attacked by the whole of Holkar's cavalry, in 3 separate bodies, who, however, could make no impression on him; and they were beat off. Towards evening he heard that the infantry had arrived at camp within 2 or 3 *coss* of the Muchundra Ghat, with their guns, 175 in number; and he determined to retreat again. He accordingly marched to Kota, the Raja of which place urged him to stay there but could not supply him with provisions; and then Monson marched on the following day, and crossed the Chumbul in boats, provided by the Raja, which he sank after he had crossed.

"The rain began about the 10th July, and became incessant, and rendered Monson's marches much more difficult than they would otherwise have been; particularly in that country, which is a black cotton ground. At last, after he had crossed the Chumbul, he was obliged to spike his guns and leave them behind, and he continued his march, getting but little provision on the road until he reached Rampoora. He was followed, but not much harassed, by a body of Holkar's Horse, which overtook him at a *nullah*, which being full, stopped him. He twice beat up the camp of this body of horse, and I believe they quitted him. On his arrival at Rampoora, Monson was joined by two battalions with their guns, and a body of Hindustani Horse, under Major Frith, which had been sent from Agra to reinforce him, and he immediately began to collect provisions at Rampoora.

" The rains, which had been so distressing to Monson, likewise impeded Holkar, some of whose guns remained to the southward of the Muchundra Ghat. His progress to the northward was likewise impeded by Monson having destroyed the Raja of Kota's boats on the Chumbal. However, at last he advanced, and towards the 20th August again approached Monson at Rampoora.

" By this time, Monson had only collected about 12 days' provisions, and the Commander-in-Chief, foreseeing the difficulty in which he might again be involved, desired him on the 20th August to retire towards Jeypore, if he should think it probable that he might be distressed for provisions.

" Monson, however, remained until Holkar approached him within 6 *coss* with his whole army, and on the 21st August, in the evening, commenced his retreat towards Agra, by Kooshalghur, leaving Jeypore on his left hand. He left 15 companies as a garrison in Rampoora. He arrived at the Banas on the 23rd, and found that it was full; on the 24th, in the morning, it fell, and became fordable and he passed over a battalion and his baggage; and between 12 and 3 o'clock, he passed over three more battalions, leaving the picquets and one battalion to support them on the southern bank.

" Holkar's troops appeared in the morning, and were seen crossing at various fords on the right and left flanks; and towards evening, Holkar's infantry and guns appeared in front. They attacked the picquets, but were repulsed; and the picquets and battalion took 8 guns; but afterwards our troops were overpowered by superior numbers, and were obliged to retreat across the river to the main body, in which operation they lost many men, being attacked on their rear, and also by the horse, who had crossed the river and moved up its bed. Monson retreated from the Banas river on the night of the 24th, leaving his baggage, and arrived at Kooshalghur, about 40 miles distant on the night of the 25th. He was followed throughout the march by Holkar's Horse, which, however, were not able to make any impression upon him. He halted on the night of the 25th and the 26th at Kooshalghur, and on the 26th, at night, marched towards Agra. Something happened on the 27th, of which I have not received any account, but on the 30th Monson and his detachment arrived at Agra.

" The Commander-in-Chief has taken the field, and it is to be hoped that he will have an early opportunity of wiping away the disgrace which we have suffered.

" It is worth while to review these transactions, in order that we may see to what these misfortunes ought to be attributed, that in future, if possible, they may be avoided. In the first place, it appears that Colonel Monson's corps was never so strong as to be able to engage Holkar's army, if that Chief should collect it; at least the Colonel was of that opinion. Secondly, it appears that it had not any stock of provisions. Thirdly; that it depended for provisions upon certain Rajas who urged its advance. Fourthly; that no measures whatever were taken by British officers to collect provisions either at Boondy or Kota, or even at Rampoora, a fort belonging to us, in which we had a British garrison. Fifthly; that the detachment was advanced to such a distance, over so many almost impassable rivers and *nullahs* without any boats collected or posts upon these rivers; and, in fact, that the detachment owes its safety to the Raja of Kota, who supplied them with his boats.

" The result of these facts is an opinion in my mind, that the detachment must have been lost, even if Holkar had not followed them with his infantry and artillery.

" In respect to the conduct of the operations, it is my opinion that Monson ought to have attacked Holkar in the first instance. If he chose to retire he ought to have supported the rear-guard with his infantry, and to have sent the irregular horse away with the baggage.

" When he began to retreat, he ought not to have stopped longer than a night at Muckundra; because he must have been certain that the same circumstances which obliged him to retire to Muckundra would also oblige him to quit that position. The difference between a good and a bad military position is nothing when the troops are starving.

" The same reasoning holds good respecting Monson's halt at Rampoora, unless he intended to fight. As he had been reinforced, he ought to have fallen back until he was certain of his supplies; and having waited until Holkar approached him, and particularly as Holkar's army was not then in great strength in infantry and guns, he ought to have vigorously attacked him before he retired. When his picquets were attacked on the Banas he ought to have supported them with his whole corps, leaving one battalion on the northern bank to take care of his baggage; and if he had done so, he probably would have gained a victory, would have saved his baggage, and regained his honour.

" We have some important lessons from this campaign. First. We should never employ a corps on a service for which it is not fully equal. Second. Against the Mahrattas in particular, but against all enemies, we should take care to be sure of plenty of provisions. Third. Experience has shown us, that British troops can never depend on Rajas, or any allies, for their supplies. Our own officers must purchase them; and if we should employ a native on such an important service, we ought to see the supplies before we venture to expose our troops in the situation in which they may want them. Fourth. When we have a fort which can support our operations, such as Rampoora, to the northward, or Admednuggur, or Chandore, in your quarter, we should immediately adopt effectual measures to fill it with provisions and stores, in case of need. Fifth. When we cross a river likely to be full in the rains, we ought to have a post and boats upon it; as I have upon all the rivers south of Poona, and as you have, I hope, upon the Beemah and the Godavery.

"In respect to the operations of a corps in the situation of Monson's, they must be decided and quick; and in all retreats it must be recollected that they are safe and easy, in proportion to the number of attacks made by the retreating corps. But attention to the foregoing observations will, I hope, prevent a British corps from retreating."

APPENDIX IX.

CASUALTIES.

The following lists of casualties, taken from Wilson's *History of the Madras Army*, are apparently the official returns of the time:—

A

Return of casualties at the action of Malavelly, 27th March 1799.

Corps.	Killed.	Wounded.	Missing.
19th Dragoons	..	8	..
1st Native Cavalry	..	2	..
3rd " "	..	1	..
25th Dragoons	..	2	..
2nd Native Cavalry	..	2	..
12th Regiment	..	..	..
74th "	5	17	..
Scotch Brigade	1	5	..
1st Battalion, 1st Madras Infantry	1	1	4
" 6th " "	..	1	..
" 12th " "	..	2	1
1st " 8th " "	..	..	..
2nd " 3rd " "	..	3	1
2nd " 12th " "	..	1	..
33rd Regiment	..	4	..
10th Bengal Infantry	..	3	..
2nd Battalion, 11th Madras Infantry	..	1	..
Total	7	53	6

Also 12 horses killed, 33 wounded, and 3 missing.

B

General return of Casualties before Seringapatam from 4th April to 4th May 1799.

Corps.	Europeans.			Natives.		
	Killed.	Wounded.	Missing.	Killed.	Wounded.	Missing.
Madras Engineers	..	1	..	..	..	..
Bombay „	..	..	..	..	..	..
Bengal Artillery	4	12	..	2	10	..
Madras „	14	21	1	9	32	3
Bombay „	4	6	..	5	4	..
His Majesty's 12th Regiment .	17	49	1	..	..	..
„ „ 33rd „ . .	6	28	12	..	..	..
„ „ 73rd „ . .	21	99	1	..	..	..
„ „ 74th „ . .	45	111	..	..	..	..
„ „ 75th „ . .	16	64	3	..	..	..
„ „ 77th „ . .	10	51	1	..	..	..
„ „ Scotch Brigade .	14	86	1	..	..	..
„ „ Regiment de Meuron	16	60	1	..	..	..
„ „ Bombay European Regiment . .	9	23	1	..	..	..
1st Battalion, 10th Bengal Infantry	..	..	..	3	3	..
2nd „ „ „ „ .	..	..	..	5	5	..
1st „ Bengal Volunteers .	..	..	..	3	3	12
2nd „ „ „ .	..	..	..	6	30	9
3rd „ „ „ .	..	..	..	2	8	5
1st „ 1st Madras Infantry .	1	..	..	3	14	..
2nd „ 2nd „ „ .	..	..	..	4	10	..
2nd „ 3rd „ „ .	1	2	..	12	47	15
Carred over .	178	613	22	54	166	44

General return of Casualties before Seringapatam, etc.—contd.

Corps.	Europeans.			Natives.		
	Killed.	Wounded.	Missing.	Killed.	Wounded.	Missing.
Brought forward .	178	613	22	54	166	44
2nd Battalion, 5th Madras Infantry	..	..	..	11	33	..
1st „ 6th „ „ .	..	..	..	..	..	..
2nd „ 7th „ „ .	..	..	..	4	16	..
1st „ 8th „ „ .	..	..	..	5	13	..
2nd „ 9th „ „ .	..	..	..	4	7	5
1st „ 11th „ „ .	..	..	..	3	11	..
2nd „ 11th „ „ .	..	..	..	1	4	..
Madras Pioneers	..	..	..	1	..	..
1st Battalion, 2nd Bengal Infantry	1	1	..	7	46	51
2nd „ 2nd „ „ .	..	2	..	8	37	..
1st „ 3rd „ „ .	..	1	..	4	10	..
2nd „ 3rd „ „ .	..	..	..	2	10	..
1st „ 4th „ „ .	..	..	..	4	15	..
1st „ 5th „ „ .	..	..	..	2	6	..
Bombay Pioneers . . .	..	..	..	3	14	..
		1	..	4	7	..
		1	..	2	25	..
Total .	179	619	22	119	420	100

The officers killed during the operations were :—*Bombay Artillery,* Captain A. Torriano, Lieutenant W. McRedie ; *Bengal Artillery,* Lieutenant-Colonel Montague ; *Madras Artillery,* Captain Jourdan, Lieutenant Cookesley ; *His Majesty's* 12*th Regiment,* Lieutenants G. Nixon and T. Falla ; *His Majesty's* 33*rd Regiment,* Lieutenant Fitzgerald ; *His Majesty's* 73*rd Regiment,* Lieutenant Lalor ; *His Majesty's* 74*th Regiment,* Lieutenants Irvine, Farquhar, Prendergast, Hill, Shaw, Mather ; *His Majesty's* 77*th Regiment,* Captain Owen ; *Scotch Brigade,* Captain Hay ; Regiment de Meuron, Lieutenant Mathey, Assistant-Surgeon Glasser ; 1st *Madras Infantry,* Major C. Campbell ; 3*rd Madras Infantry,* Lieutenant J. Fish ; *Madras Pioneers,* Lieutenant Cormick ; 2*nd Bombay Infantry,* Captain J. C. Meares ; *Staff,* Captain Cosby.

Lieutenant-Colonel Montague had his arms shattered by a cannon ball while he was in the trenches, and immediate amputation at the shoulder was necessary. In this state he insisted on being carried to the trenches, where he continued to the last to animate the troops by his presence. During 3 or 4 days he was supposed to be in a fair way to recovery, but a contusion in the chest mortified, and he died on the eighth day, May 10.

Lieutenant Falla was struck by a shot on the upper part of the thigh, which broke the bone, and passing between the fractures lodged in the fleshy part. A tourniquet was applied, but the ball was not discovered until after death, which occurred a few hours later.

Lieutenant Lalor acted as guide to the storming party crossing the Kaveri on the 4th May, and was wounded and drowned during the passage of the river.

Lieutenant Irvine was killed by grape shot on the night of the 26th April, when a party of the 73rd and 74th Regiments, occupying a post within 250 yards of the fort, suffered severely from the heavy fire to which they were exposed.

Lieutenant Farquhar commanded the European Pioneers during the assault, when, the leading officers being killed or wounded, he put himself at the head of the column and almost instantly fell. Lieutenant Hill volunteered for the forlorn hope and was killed leading the officers' party in front of the right attack commanded by Colonel Sherbrooke.

Among the wounded were Lieutenant Lawrence (father of John and Henry Lawrence of Mutiny fame), 77th Foot, who volunteered for the forlorn hope in front of the left attack commanded by Lieutenant-Colonel Dunolp, and Captain W. Browne, 2nd Bombay Infantry, who received 3 musket balls in his right arm, which had to be amputated. He had already lost the second and third fingers of his left hand by the bite of a snake in the previous war with Tipu Sultan.

C

Casualties during the Siege and Storm of Ahmednagar, 8th—11th August 1803.

Corps.	Killed.	Wounded.	Total.
19th Dragoons	..	1	1
5th Cavalry	1	..	1
Artillery	1	7	8
His Majesty's 74th Regiment	2	13	15
,, ,, ,, ,,	14	41	55
1st Battalion, 2nd Madras Infantry	..	2	2
1st ,, 3rd ,, ,,	7	12	19
1st ,, 8th ,, ,,	3	9	12
2nd ,, 12th ,, ,,	..	8	8
2nd ,, 18th ,, ,,	1	3	4
1st Pioneers	1	15	16
Total	30	111	141

Officers killed.

Captain Grant, His Majesty's 78th.
,, Humberston, ,, ,,
Lieutenant Anderson ,, ,,
,, Plenderleath, 1st Battalion, 3rd.

Officers wounded.

Lieutenant Neilson, His Majesty's 74th.
,, Larkins, His Majesty's 78th.

D

Return of Casualties at the Battle of Assaye, 23rd September 1803.

Corps.	Europeans.			Natives.		
	Killed.	Wounded.	Missing.	Killed.	Wounded.	Missing.
19th Light Dragoons . . .	17	40	..	..	..	..
4th Native Cavalry . . .	1	1	..	15	26	..
5th " " . . .	1	3	..	12	30	1
7th " " . . .	..	1	..	10	32	..
Detachment, 1st Battalion Artillery	16	17	..	3	22	2
" 2nd " " "	4	8	..	4	8	..
" Bombay Artillery .	6	6	..	2	8	..
Escort to Cavalry guns . . .	1	..	..	..	2	..
His Majesty's 74th Regiment .	124	277	..	..	..	..
" " 78th " .	24	77	4	..	..	..
1st Battalion, 2nd Madras Infantry	1	..	..	20	22	3
1st " 4th " " .	1	1	..	26	89	1
1st " 8th " " .	..	4	..	47	123	..
1st " 10th " " .	2	1	..	33	104	2
2nd " 12th " "	..	6	..	43	179	..
Pioneers	..	..	..	15	51	5
Total .	198	442	4	230	696	14

Also horses 325 killed, 111 wounded, 2 missing.

The officers killed were :—Lieutenant-Colonel Maxwell; Captains R. Boyle, H. Mackay, D. Aytone, A. Dyce, R. Macleod, and T. Maxwell; Lieutenants Steele and Fowler; Lieutenants Bonomi, Griffith, J. Campbell, J. M. Campbell, J. Grant, R. Neilson, L. Campbell, M. Morris, J. Douglas, Brown, Mavor, Perrie, and Volunteer Tew.

E

Casualties at the Battle of Argaum, 29th November 1803.

Corps.	Europeans.			Natives.		
	Killed.	Wounded.	Missing.	Killed.	Wounded.	Missing.
19th Light Dragoons	..	6	..	..	..	..
3rd Madras Cavalry	..	1	..	1	7	..
4th " "	..	..	..	1	1	..
5th " "	..	..	..	..	..	..
6th " "	..	1	..	..	4	..
7th " "	..	..	..	..	..	1
Artillery	..	11	..	2	12	..
His Majesty's 74th Regiment	4	48	..	..	..	..
" " 78th "	9	38	..	..	..	..
" " 94th "	2	37	2	..	..	..
1st Battalion, 2nd Madras Infantry	..	..	..	3	12	1
2nd " 2nd " "	..	..	..	5	15	..
1st " 3rd " "	..	1	..	5	36	..
1st " 4th " "	..	1	..	3	29	..
1st " 6th " "	..	..	..	..	1	..
2nd " 7th " "	..	..	..	..	2	..
1st " 8th " "	..	..	..	..	3	1
2nd " 9th " "	..	..	..	3	9	..
1st " 10th " "	..	..	..	4	4	..
1st " 11th " "	..	..	..	1	10	1
2nd " 11th " "	..	..	..	..	10	..
2nd " 12th " "	..	1	..	3	8	..
Total	15	145	2	31	163	5

Also 19 horses killed, 2 wounded, and 11 missing.

"WELLINGTON'S CAMPAIGNS IN INDIA"

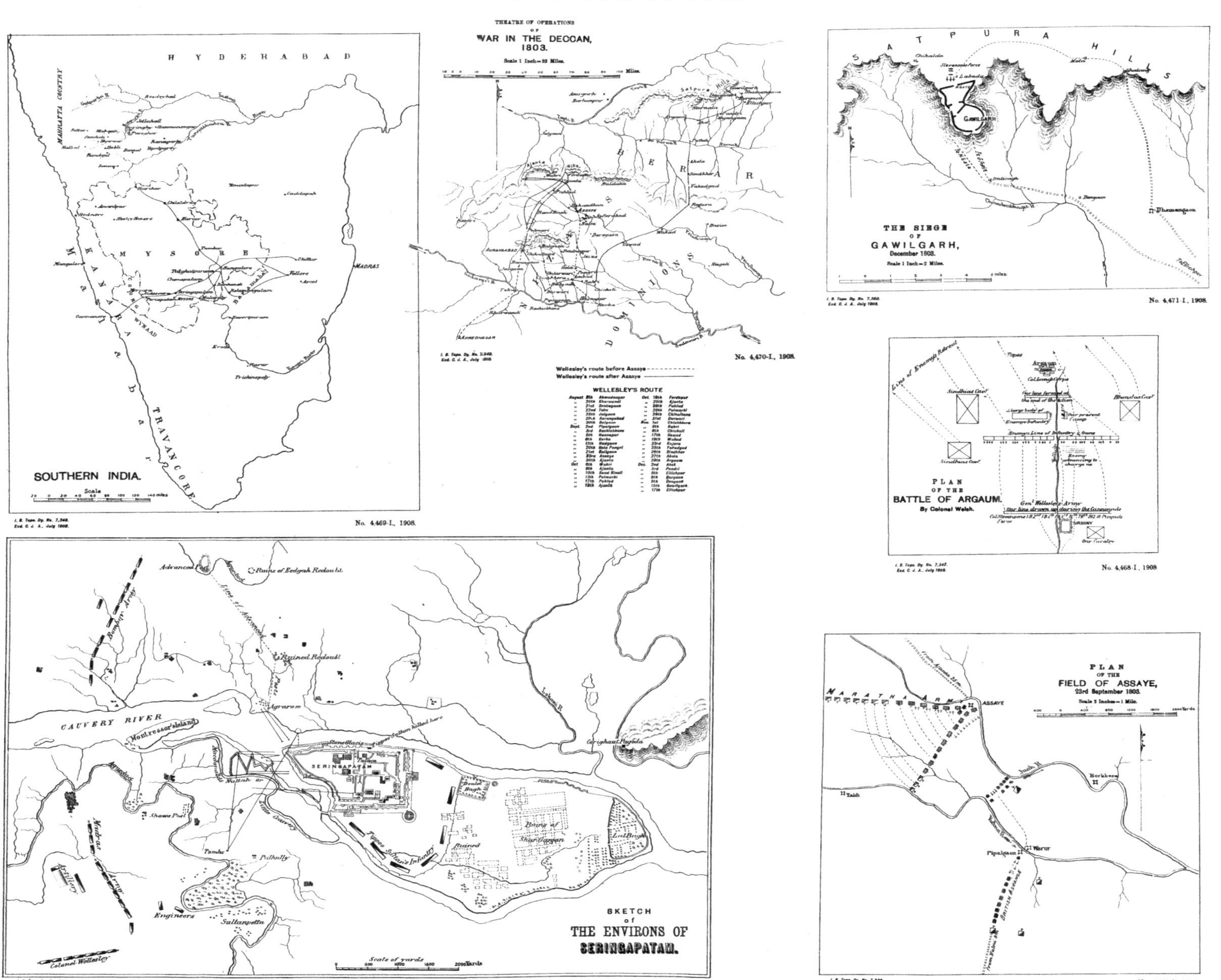

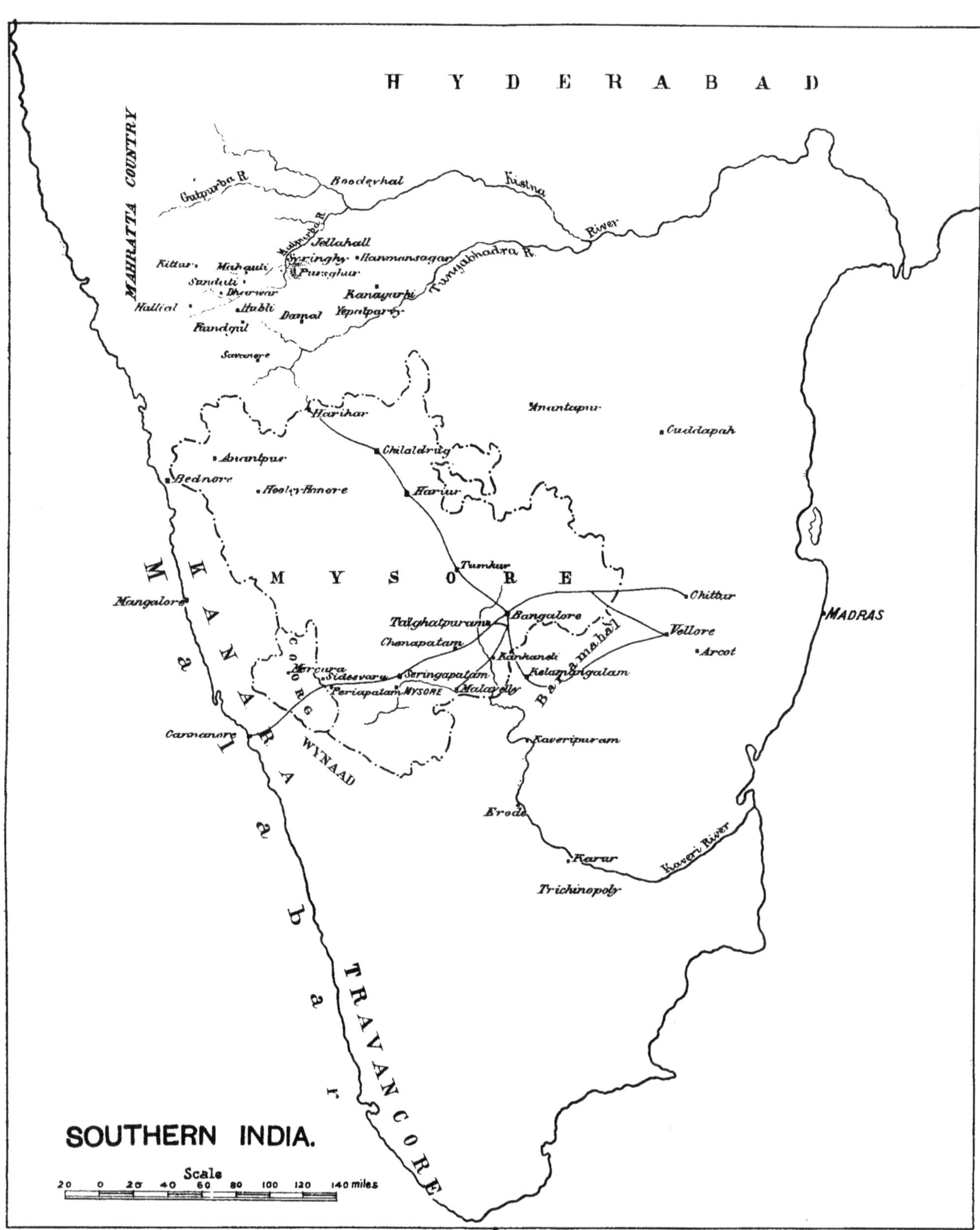

I. B. Topo. Dy. No. 7,348.
Exd. C. J. A., July 1908.

No. 4,469-I., 1908.

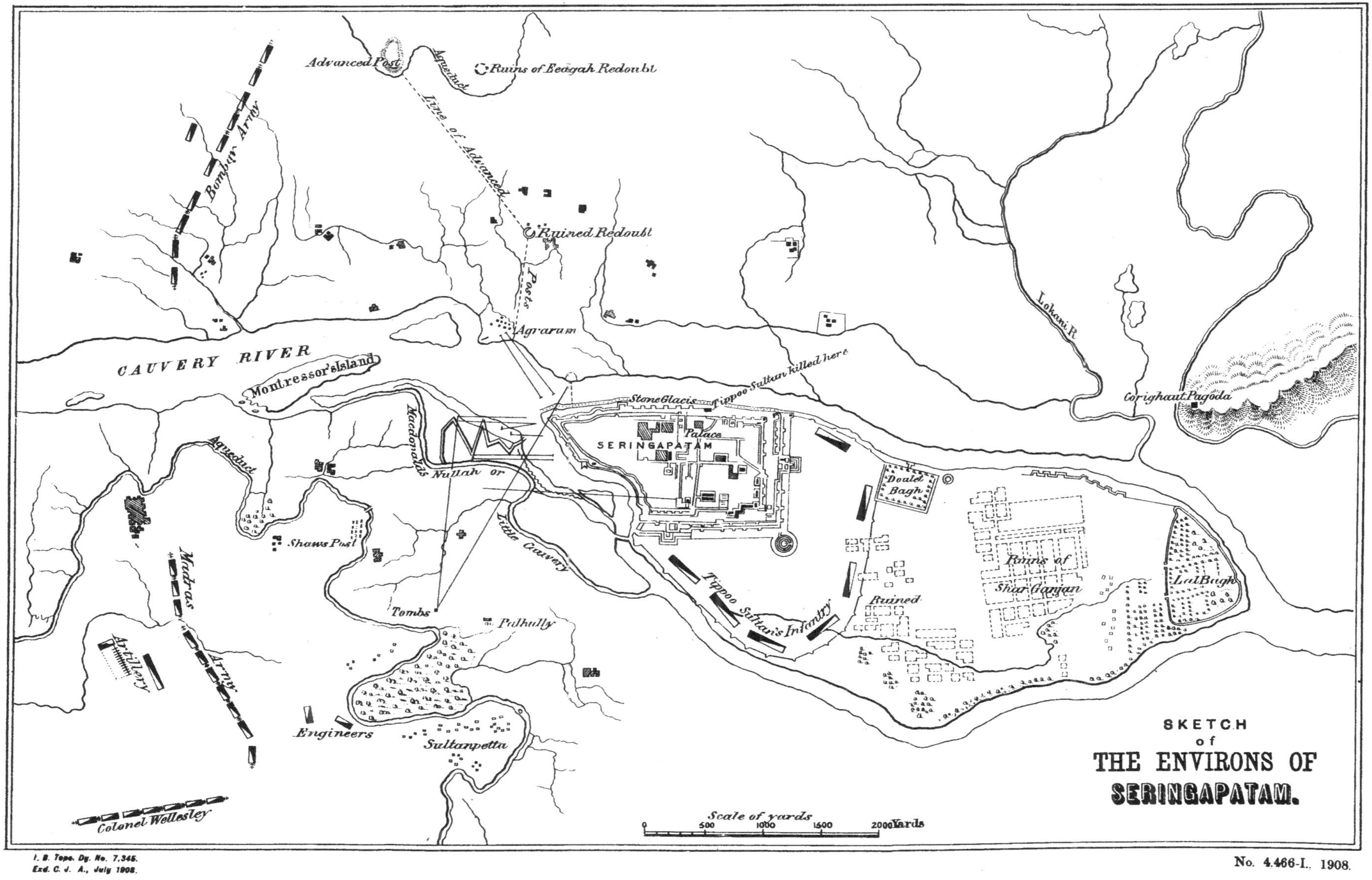
SKETCH
of
THE ENVIRONS OF
SERINGAPATAM.
Advanced Post
Aqueduct
Ruins of Eeagah Redoubt
Line of Advanced
Ruined Redoubt
Posts
Agraram
Bombay Army
CAUVERY RIVER
Montressor's Island
Stone Glacis
Tippoo Sultan killed here
SERINGAPATAM
Palace
Macdonald's Nullah or
Little Cauvery
Aqueduct
Shaws Post
Tombs
Pulhully
Madras
Army
Artillery
Engineers
Sultanpetta
Colonel Wellesley
Tippoo Sultan's Infantry
Ruined
Doulet Bagh
Ruins of Shar Gunjan
Lal Bagh
Lokani R
Corighaut Pagoda
Scale of yards
0
500
1000
1500
2000 Yards
I. B. Topo. Dy. No. 7,345.
Exd. C. J. A., July 1908.
No. 4.466-I. 1908.

THEATRE OF OPERATIONS

OF

WAR IN THE DECCAN, 1803.

Scale 1 Inch = 32 Miles.

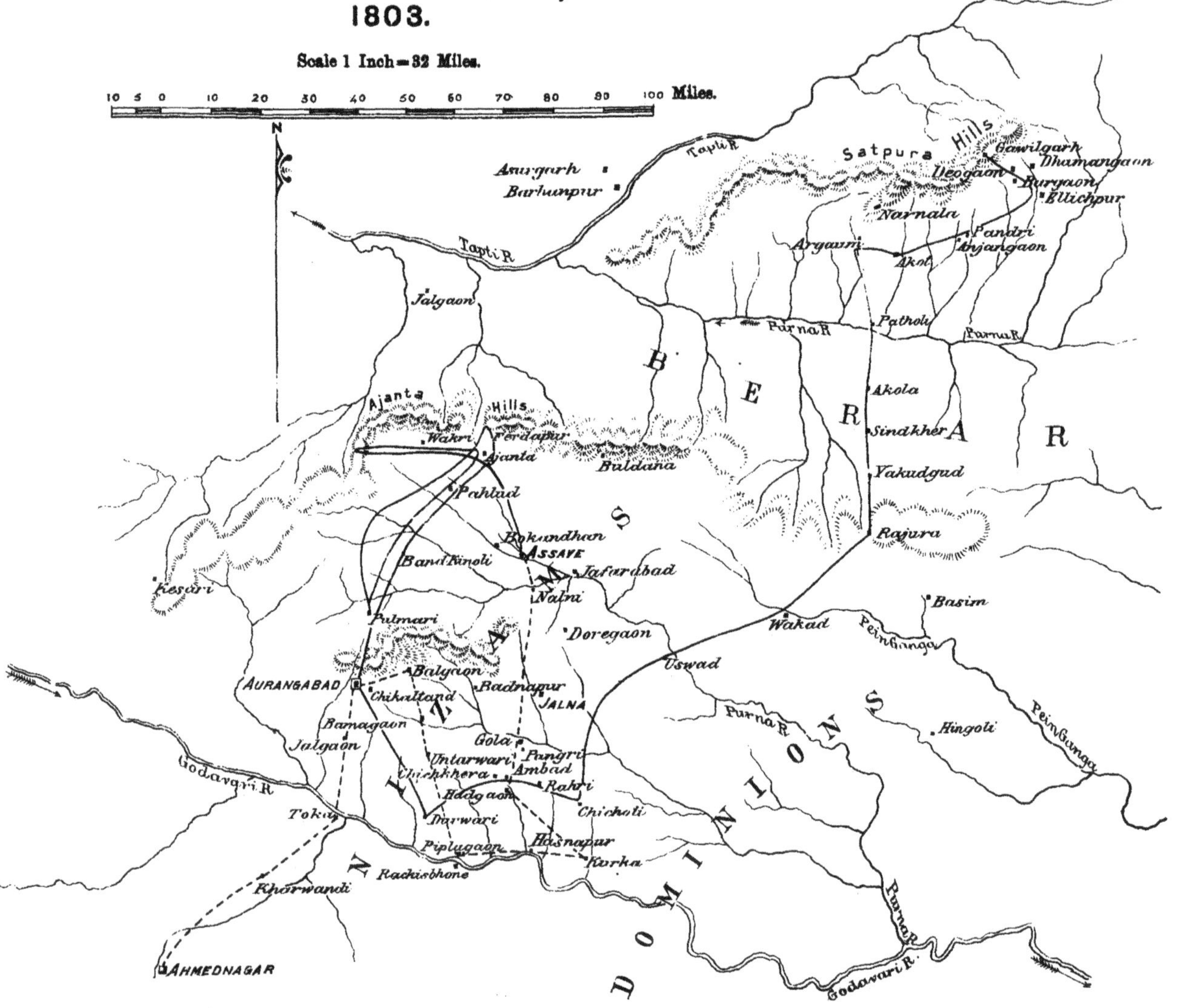

I. B. Topo. Dy. No. 7,349.
Exd. C. J. A., July 1908.

No. 4,470-I, 1908.

Wellesley's route before Assaye - - - - - - - - - - -

Wellesley's route after Assaye ————————

WELLESLEY'S ROUTE

August	8th	Ahmadnagar	Oct.	19th	Ferdapur
,,	20th	Kharwandi	,,	25th	Ajanta
,,	21st	Senbugaon	,,	26th	Pahlud
,,	22nd	Toka	,,	28th	Pulmarhi
,,	28th	Jalgaon	,,	29th	Chikaltana
,,	29th	Aurangabad	,,	31st	Durwari
,,	30th	Balgaon	Nov.	1st	Chichkhera
Sept.	2nd	Pipalgaon	,,	5th	Rahri
,,	3rd	Rackisbhone	,,	6th	Chicholi
,,	5th	Hasnapur	,,	17th	Uswad
,,	6th	Kurka	,,	19th	Wakad
,,	11th	Hadgaon	,,	23rd	Rajura
,,	20th	Gola Pangri	,,	25th	Yakudgud
,,	21st	Sailgaon	,,	26th	Sindkher
,,	23rd	Assaye	,,	27th	Akola
,,	30th	Ajanta	,,	29th	Argaum
Oct.	6th	Wakri	Dec.	2nd	Akot
,,	8th	Ajanta	,,	3rd	Pandri
,,	10th	Band Kinoli	,,	5th	Ellichpur
,,	11th	Pulmarhi	,,	8th	Bargaon
,,	17th	Pahlud	,,	9th	Deogaon
,,	18th	Ajanta	,,	15th	Gawilgarh
			,,	17th	Ellichpur

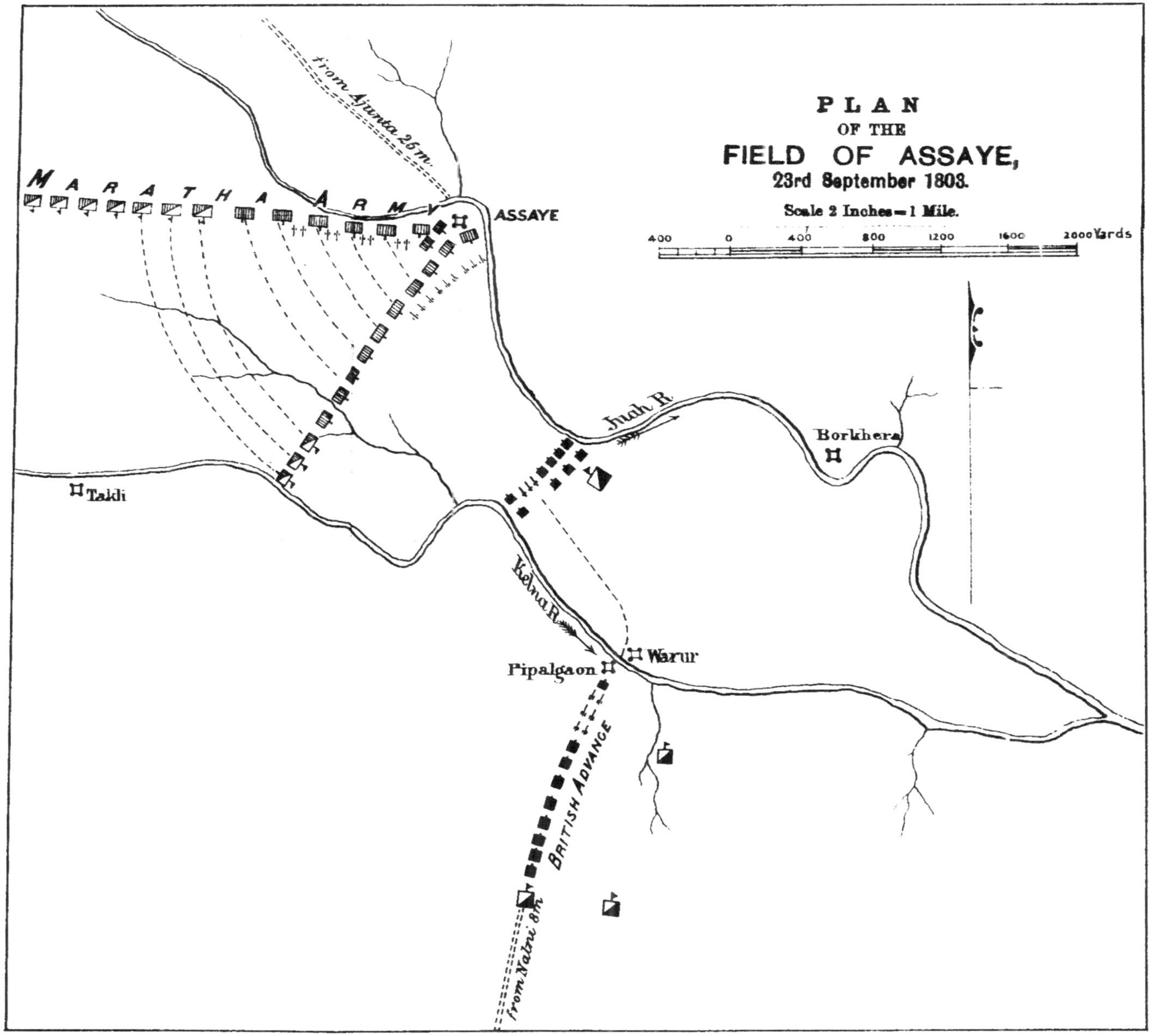

PLAN
OF THE
FIELD OF ASSAYE,
23rd September 1803.

Scale 2 Inches = 1 Mile.

400 0 400 800 1200 1600 2000 Yards

from Ajunta 26 m.

MARATHA ARMY

ASSAYE

Juah R.

Borkhera

Takli

Kelna R.

Warur

Pipalgaon

BRITISH ADVANCE

from Naini 8 m.

I. B. Topo. Dy. No. 7,346.
Exd. C. J. A., July 1908.

No. 4,467-I., 1908.

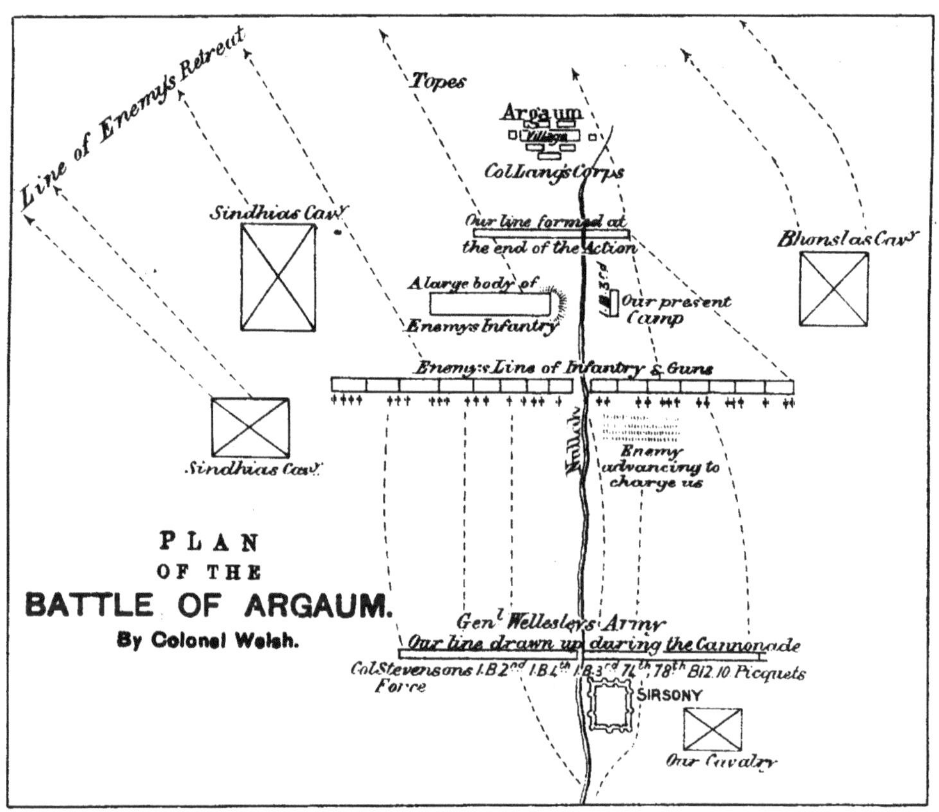

I. B. Topo. Dy. No. 7,347.
Exd. C. J. A., July 1908.

No. 4,468-I., 1908.

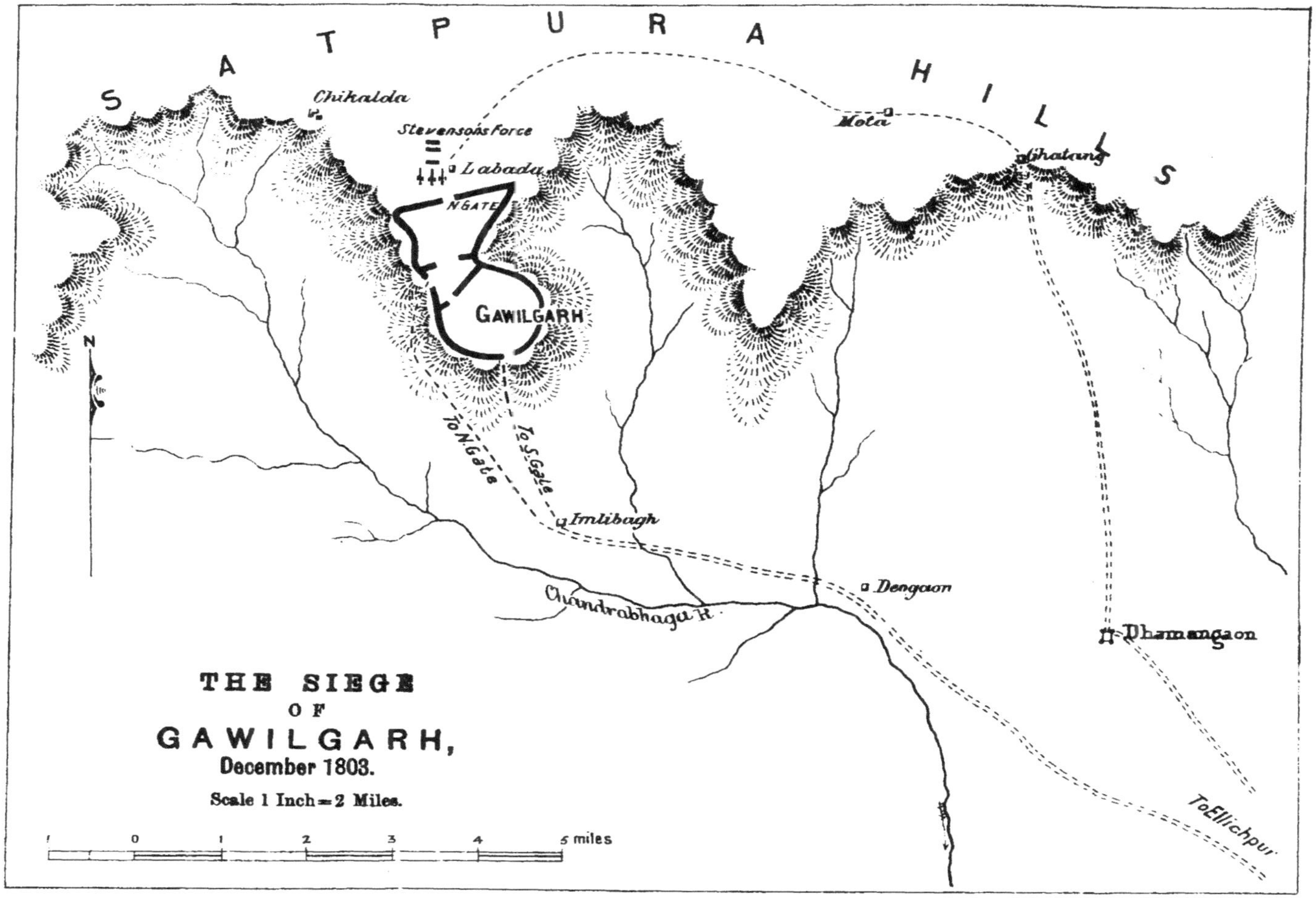

SATPURA HILLS

Chikalda

Stevenson's Force

Labada

N GATE

GAWILGARH

Mola

Jhatang

To N. Gate

To S. Gate

Imlibagh

Dengaon

Chandrabhaga R.

Dhamangaon

To Ellichpur

N

THE SIEGE OF GAWILGARH, December 1803.

Scale 1 Inch = 2 Miles.

1 0 1 2 3 4 5 miles

I. B. Topo. Dy. No. 7,350.
Exd. C. J. A.. July 1908.

No. 4,471-I., 1908.

www.ingramcontent.com/pod-product-compliance
Ingram Content Group UK Ltd.
Pitfield, Milton Keynes, MK11 3LW, UK
UKHW061831190726
13855UKWH00006B/1753